The Last Country

THE LAST COUNTRY

My years in Japan

E. W. F. TOMLIN

FABER AND FABER
3 Queen Square
London

First published in 1974
by Faber and Faber Limited
3 Queen Square London WC1
Printed in Great Britain by
W & J Mackay Limited, Chatham
All rights reserved

ISBN 0 571 08941 0

ı C

Contents

Prelude   *page*   15

  I   Feeling at Home   23

  II   Teiko-San   54

  III   In and Around Tokyo   70

  IV   Climbing Mount Fuji   92

  V   Kyoto and Nara   97

  VI   Returning to the Source: Ise and Izumo   143

  VII   Snow Country and Sado Island   177

  VIII   Shikoku and Kyushu   201

  IX   Farewell to Japan   250

Historical Outline   259

Glossary   264

Index   267

Maps

1. Japan   *page*   12

2. Tokyo   24

3. Kyoto   99

Note

The macron (e.g., ō) sometimes used in the trans-literation of Japanese words has been omitted, but the Japanese order of proper names, with surname taking precedence, has been retained (e.g., Mishima Yukio). In the Glossary, words prefixed by the honorific 'o' (e.g., *o-furo*, literally 'honourable bath') have been listed under their first letter.

I wish to thank my sister, Miss E. M. Tomlin, and Miss Judith Miller for their great help in compiling the index.

Sea of Japan

Oki Islands
Dozen
Dogo

H O N S H U

Okutango Peninsula
Kinosaki
Kasumi
Hamasaka
Iwami
Matsue
Yonago
Tottori
Toyooka
Miyazu
Maizuru
Ayabe

Lake Shinji
Taisha
Izumo
Shinji
TOTTORI
Mt. Daisen

HYOGO

Hamada

OKAYAMA
Bizen
Himeji
Kobe

Masuda
HIROSHIMA
Okayama
Kurashiki

SHIMANE
Hiroshima
Miyajima
Mihara
Osaka

Hagi
YAMAGUCHI
Takamatsu
Naruto
Wakayama

Akiyoshidai caves
Yamaguchi
Iwakuni
KAGAWA
R. Yoshino
Naruto Straits
Mt. Koya

Shimonoseki
Kitakyushu
Moji
TOKUSHIMA
Tokushima
WAKAYAMA

Yawata Kokura
Tobe
Matsuyama

Fukuoka
Inland Sea
EHIME
KOCHI
Kochi

SAGA
Dazaifu
Beppu
Oita
OITA

Arita
Saga
Otsu
ASO N.P.
SHIKOKU

MtUnzen
Mt. Aso

Nagasaki
Kumamoto

Shimabara Peninsula
KUMAMOTO

MIYAZAKI

Hyuga

KYUSHU

Oyodo R.
Miyazaki
Aoshima Island

KAGOSHIMA

Kagoshima
Sakura
Nichinan

Satsuma Peninsula
Cape Toi

Ibusuki

Miles
0 20 40 60 80 100

0   100
Kilometres

1. Japan

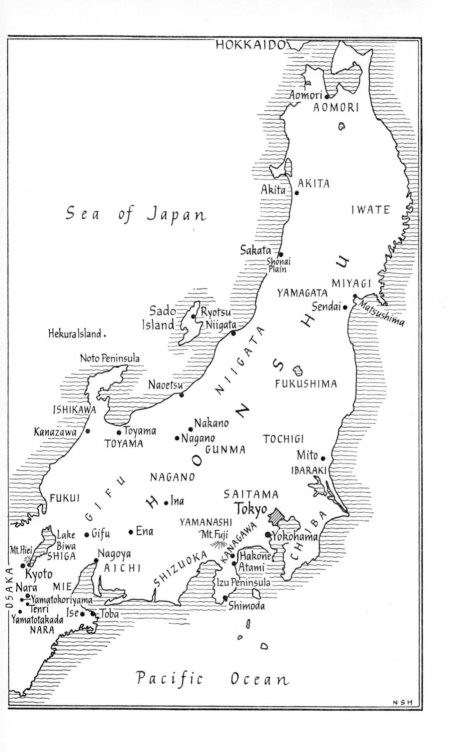

HOKKAIDO

Sea of Japan

Aomori •
AOMORI

Akita •
AKITA

IWATE

Sakata •
Shonai
Plain

MIYAGI
YAMAGATA

Sado
Island

Ryotsu •
Niigata

Sendai •
Matsushima

Hekura Island •

Noto Peninsula

Naoetsu •

NIIGATA

FUKUSHIMA

ISHIKAWA

Kanazawa •
Toyama •
TOYAMA

Nakano •
Nagano •
GUNMA

TOCHIGI

Mito •
IBARAKI

FUKUI

GIFU

NAGANO

• Ina

SAITAMA

Tokyo

Lake
Biwa
Mt.Hiei
SHIGA

• Gifu
• Ena

Nagoya
AICHI

YAMANASHI
Mt.Fuji

Yokohama •
KANAGAWA

CHIBA

OSAKA

Kyoto
Nara
Yamatokoriyama
Tenri
Yamatotakada
NARA

MIE

Ise • • Toba

SHIZUOKA

Izu Peninsula

Hakone
Atami

Shimoda •

Pacific Ocean

N S H

Prelude

I

For me she was the Last Country. The human race is not so very old, and there are societies which are much older than humanity; but until recently, human beings lived together in much the same manner. Each generation regarded it as normal to follow the way of life of its predecessor. People were organized in small self-contained units, and in due course these, added together, made up the national community. Families, though similar in the bonds which held them together, were distinguished one from another in status; and within the family itself there was a hierarchy of respect and authority. The community had its leaders and counsellors to whom due veneration was given, and the attainment of advanced age entitled a man to a special kind of veneration, since his survival in a world oppressed by mortality seemed to indicate the special favour of Providence. In the country of whom I write, however, there were those whose fame in life had been such that after death they were believed to wield power from another sphere, exercising benevolent protection over the living. And they in turn were thought to be dominated by even more remarkable beings, who had created and helped to shape the destiny of humanity and the world itself. If human gratitude were sufficient, these gods, as they were called, would permit the ancestral souls to return from time to time to the family hearth, just as they themselves could enter into certain things and lend them a special efficacy. So the gods surrounded men and watched over them, just as the ruler watched over his people, and the father watched over his family. Then there was a special watcher, the woman, who, though strong in body, and often put to great physical toil, directed part of her strength inwards for the purpose of producing the next generation, over whose welfare she watched with a special and perhaps unmatched solicitude.

This was the pattern of living seemingly laid down from the beginning, and the pattern was meticulously to be observed, and its nature was to be reflected in individual conduct. In order to discern the pattern, however, the heart or soul needed to be purified and lent vision, and so there was brought into being a whole system of liturgy and worship, ritual, lustration, oblation and annual observance, geared to the cyclical movement of nature itself. For while the object of life was to attain prosperity, above all for one's family, this prosperity itself depended upon due reverence for the gods and for the ancestors who had themselves become gods. If prosperity were a sign of divine favour in this world, the true end of existence was to experience the joy of living under divine tutelage.

Here I pause to ask myself a question. Was this really what I found in Japan during my years there? Did the people seem like Sun Children engaged in the perpetual worship of nature? Was the country a potential earthly paradise? What about the dull streets of Osaka under a smoke pall, the dismal and sulphurous industrial belts, the squalid streets of many provincial towns, the inferno of the Tokyo underground, the 'dead' rivers, the desecration of the countryside, the struggle for subsistence? What is all this about beauty and purity and grace, and living according to nature's precepts?

True. All these ugly things exist and are proliferating in Japan. But beneath the surface the pattern is still there, and the lives of the ordinary Japanese, however humdrum, conform to it. In Japan, you still feel, though dimly, that you are living in a community which obeys the rules not merely of politics and economics but of the cosmic order. You feel nearer to the essence of things and to the beginning of things. You feel that there *is* a natural life and a natural order, which, perpetually renewed and sanctioned, are the fount and condition of human happiness. No other land that I have known retains precisely this quality, though I think that ours did until recently. That is why I have called Japan the Last Country.

The man who first 'interpreted' Japan to the West was Lafcadio Hearn, of whose life in Matsue and Kumamoto I shall speak. Hearn's 'interpretation' is now much frowned upon, even though his memory is still greatly revered in the country of his adoption. Perhaps the most balanced view of him was that expressed by a Japanese writer, Nohara Komakichi. This is what he wrote back in the Thirties, and his words are perhaps truer of conditions today, and they provide a warning to the foreign observer: 'Lafcadio Hearn, although the best writer on things Japanese, has been the greatest obstacle to the dissemination of accurate ideas about Japan.... Every word in Hearn's books is true, but the truth is only part of reality: what he describes is only one aspect of Japan. There is another side: the vulgar, the teeming, the iridescent, the feverish, and often not quite so dignified and hallowed. No, unfortunately, we are not so noble, so restrained, so knightly, nor endowed with so much true emotion, as Hearn represents us as being.'[1]

True again. No one is. But Hearn was right, as Nohara says, up to a point, and in one respect; and this aspect still counts, having survived much that might have swept it away. Without it, Japan would lose her identity altogether; and her identity is the one thing that Japan has somehow managed to keep inviolate.

That much of what I say will forfeit the approval of others, even of friends and colleagues with whom I shared some of the experiences retailed, I fully realize. There will also be those who, having spent longer in Japan than I did, will regard my interpretation as wholly mistaken. They will declare that I have sentimentalized Japan; that I have 'found' a traditional country that has long ceased to exist; and that I have consequently misled my readers from start to finish. There will also be Japanese who, however well-disposed, may not recognize their country in the picture I have painted of it, and who will even deplore my search for the traditional Japan beneath the surface, because this is something which they themselves repudiate or wish to disown. A Japanese who, having lived some years in the United Kingdom, were to write a book eulogizing Old England or even Merrie England, would certainly receive short shrift from most British critics, especially the younger ones. All this I know. For that reason, I have deliberately given my book the sub-title 'My years in Japan': first, as an explanation of the title itself, and secondly as evidence that my reactions and conclusions are unashamedly my own. A foreigner can record only what he sees and feels; and his *reportage* will be of interest, and possibly of value, only if he is faithful to

[1] *The True Face of Japan: A Japanese upon Japan* (1931), p. 13.

his vision and insight.[1] If I have on occasions gone in search of the Old Japan, it was because I was very conscious of the New Japan, and because I wanted to find an explanation of certain aspects of this New Japan which made her different—often vastly and fascinatingly different—from other 'new' countries. In reality, I do not believe that there are two Japans, an Old and a New; I believe that there is a country which, following unprecedented disasters of which the last nearly proved fatal, has succeeded in regenerating herself in a special and remarkable way. That is what lends the country and the people such interest for the observer. That is what may justify a personal account such as the present.

II

In retrospect, I consider that I arrived in Japan at a crucial moment. My experience of that country both before and after the Olympic Games of 1964 enables me further to justify my title. The Games proved a landmark in the history of Japan. That memorable event signified for many Japanese the restoration of their country to self-respect and to the comity of nations. Apart from the psychological factor, the Games transformed Tokyo. Consequently, those whose knowledge of the capital is confined to the period following 1964 will have missed an experience which I found invaluable.

In fact, my stay in Japan occupied some crucial years in a decisive decade. Between 1960 and 1970, the whole of East Asia underwent profound changes. Writing of this period, William P. Bundy observed: 'I believe that the change has been vast in degree, almost wholly unpredicted in many of its salient aspects at the outset of the decade, surprising and yet not without reassurance, the end of much, the beginning of other things.'[2]

It was a significant moment to live in the Orient.

Soon enough it will become apparent that I differ from many foreigners in my views on the Japanese character. It is better to record these views for what they are worth and without apology. A visitor, even

[1] Even so, I have omitted my extensive travels in the northernmost island, Hokkaido, to which I hope to devote a separate volume.
[2] 'East Asia Turns the Page', *Asian Affairs*, October 1971, p. 260.

one who stayed as long as I did, can of course go hopelessly wrong in his judgement and I am not so arrogant as to assume that I have not gone astray on certain issues. On the other hand, my work took me to all parts of the country. Sometimes the people I encountered were meeting an Englishman for the first time. I lived day in and day out with Japanese, and one cannot do so without assimilating something of their attitude to life. In Chapter II, I shall give a particular account of such prolonged contact. Finally, I believe that my stay was long enough to temper first impressions which proved misleading, and not too long to risk losing the capacity to absorb what was unusual. Of one thing I have become convinced in consequence of living in a variety of countries, namely that those who have spent longest in a particular place are not necessarily those who may be counted the experts. Everything depends upon the capacity to keep an open mind.

Let me begin *in medias res* and take up a particularly controversial point, which nevertheless has a bearing on what I have just said. It is repeatedly maintained that the Japanese have no sense of sin. Here I join issue with some observers. That human nature is basically the same the world over seems to me evident; and I would go back in time and say that it has always been so; but certain features will necessarily differ in their manifestations, depending upon local conditions. Granted, the Japanese sense of sin differs from the Christian one; but to say that this difference has nothing to do with morality is surely to take a very narrow view of ethical values.[1] A people which lays such stress upon purification and inner cleanliness must possess an acute sense of moral health. Almost it might be said that the Japanese emphasize certain aspects of sin more than we do. They certainly possess a sense of guilt. This has manifested itself more than once on the political plane. Part of the trauma resulting from the 'unthinkable' defeat of 1945 was due no doubt to extreme humiliation; but it also generated a sense of guilt and the need for expiation. The Japanese Government still speaks of its 'blood debt' to the countries which it occupied, and in some cases devastated, during the last war. I recall a photograph in one of the national dailies depicting a group of weeping women in a cemetery. The caption beneath was: 'Burmese women weeping over the graves of their menfolk killed as the result of the

[1] Cf. *East Asia: The Great Tradition*, by E. O. Reischauer and J. K. Fairbank (1962), pp. 472–3.

atrocities of our troops.' What other country would be capable of such a frank avowal? And what does this attitude signify save an admission of moral responsibility? The number of new religions to have arisen in Japan since the war must signify a profound sense of spiritual disquiet and inadequacy, even though some of these faiths place undue emphasis upon material happiness. What in particular distinguishes the Japanese mentality from that of the West is, it would seem, *a refusal to draw a distinction between the sacred and the secular*. All life is sacred, or all life is secular. It makes no difference. Life is one. The flower-arrangement in the privy, to us so incongruous, harmonizes with the Shinto conception that there are few inherently unworthy things or functions. Indeed, there is a god of the *benjo* or water-closet. Needless to say, there are marked exceptions to this attitude. References to death are taboo. There is at least one outcast people, the Eta. But then many Japanese, including an increasing number of the young, are ashamed of the traditional attitude to these unfortunate people. It does not befit those born in the Christian tradition to condemn members of other faiths for inconsistency or hypocrisy.

The Olympic Games, or rather their successful organization, caused many Japanese to feel that they had to some extent 'worked off their karma', at least as regards the last war. The other form of expiation had already been forced on them by the dropping of the two atom bombs. Much has been written about the effect of this horror on the Japanese mentality. No doubt it is still too early to analyze the full psychological impact. If challenged, many Japanese will admit that if they had possessed the bomb they would unhesitatingly have used it. This seems most probable. Others take the view that, given the misery they admittedly caused to prisoners and occupied people, the Japanese only got what they deserved. But the real horror of the bomb, to most Japanese, was that it released a new form of 'uncleanness', in the form of radioactivity. This touched the quick of the communal psyche even more than the appalling death-roll and devastation. No comparable feeling was generated by the fire-raids on Tokyo. If the Westerner visits the atom bomb museums in Hiroshima and Nagasaki, he tends to miss this point. The photographs and exhibits are somehow less horrific than he had imagined, unless it be that we have grown accustomed to horror pictures. (Some of the comments by foreigners in the visitors' book at Hiroshima show an obtuseness or obliquity which take the breath away. On 3 May 1965 one visitor described the exhibition complacently as 'very fine'.) The 'truth' of the disaster is not explicit. It can be better discerned in the two hospitals themselves. Of this I shall say more in the account of my visit to these towns (see pp. 212 ff. and pp. 233 ff.). A similar and understandable outburst of national revulsion occurred when some Japanese fishermen died as the result of exposure to radioactivity following the nuclear test at Bikini atoll.

Though I have taken 1964 as a landmark, it is not with a view to suggesting that thereafter Japan identified herself with a world dominated by Western values. In many respects, the reverse may have proved true. Between 1945 and 1964, there was a tendency, not for the first time, towards the renunciation of tradition and the wholesale adoption of Western ways. For Japan's conquest by the West, and above all by the United States, appeared to demonstrate the superiority of the alien, if suspect, way of life. A similar attitude had been displayed after Commodore Perry's arrival in 1853 and his demand for the opening up of Japan; but at that time, the politicians were anxious to adopt Western technology as a means of defence. And following the Meiji Restoration of 1868, there was another wave of pro-Western sentiment. After 1964, I believe there came over Japan the feeling that, having been accepted once more as a 'civilized' nation, she could go in search once more of her national *ethos*. This feeling may not have been manifest on the surface, though we may underestimate the degree to which nations display sensitivity regarding their image in the world. There never was a time, surely, when such image-consciousness was more acute: hence the importance attached to 'cultural relations'. Although I witnessed not a few changes in Japan, especially in the behaviour of young people, I observed also a subtle return to tradition; and in the case of so complex a people, the two movements, forward and back, could proceed concurrently. To take a minor but significant example, the *newest* hotels in Tokyo (which are among the most up-to-date in the world) contain Tea Ceremony rooms, in contrast to hotels built a few years earlier; and of my own residences in Tokyo, the one to possess a proper Tea Ceremony room was the latest to be built.

The claim that the Old Japan is dead is therefore repeatedly being refuted. Basil Hall Chamberlain writes in his *Things Japanese* (1905), 'Yes, we repeat Old Japan is dead and gone and Young Japan reigns in its

stead'; but within a few lines of this incisive pronouncement, so typical of
the author, he is writing: 'It is abundantly clear to those who have dived
beneath the surface of the modern Japanese upheaval that more of the
past has been retained than has been let go. It is not merely that the revolution itself was an extremely slow growth, a gradual movement taking
a century and a half to mature. It is that the national character persists
intact, manifesting no change in essentials.' This is still the case.

The real danger behind Japan's adoption of Western technology is
that it may involve the risk of contamination by a crude 'materialist'
philosophy. This danger did not become really acute until after the last
war. Such a philosophy is capable of eroding the delicate structure of the
Japanese psyche; I believe that it may already have done a good deal
of harm.

In what follows I am going to make the minimum allusion to my
official duties in the British Council. These were at times heavy, but they
were a source of inexhaustible interest. I worked with congenial colleagues, and with the ever ready support of London. I could not have had
better guidance than from Leah Kitchingham, Director of our Far East
Department and my debt to Sir Paul Sinker, then Director-General, was
overwhelming. Both visited Japan when I was there; both came away, I
believe, with something of my admiration and affection for the country.
Nor was I less fortunate in my Ambassador, whose Cultural Attaché I
was: Sir Francis (Tony) Rundall. I owed him a debt, then and later,
which I cannot repay. In my six years, I attended innumerable official
functions and ceremonies. I digested a great many official meals, at table
or on the floor. I made speeches, composed messages, opened exhibitions,
called on and received a variety of officials, lectured up and down the
country, struggled with the language, and bent over my desk or my
dictaphone for hours. It was by far the busiest time of my life. There was
not a day that could have been called idle, and there were many days that
could have been called frenetic. But I would not have missed the experience. Both in degree and in kind it was different from any other. I
realized that in Japan I had found something for which I had always been
looking: a new kind of life which enriched my own life in a manner
which I shall seek to define, and a balance between work and leisure so
well adjusted as to enhance the value of both. Indeed, Japan was more
than an experience: it was a revelation.

CHAPTER I

Feeling at Home

I

Tokyo, when I first saw it from the air on 26 November 1961, consisted of a vast rash of lights, like the inverted night sky. It was on the whole an ugly city, though possessed with extraordinary dynamism. After the devastation of the war, many buildings were run up at haphazard, but the rate of construction was slow. It is calculated that at least 770,000 houses were destroyed by enemy action, many of them being consumed in a few minutes owing to the huge conflagration and the fact that they were made of wood;[1] but between 1945 and 1964, no more than 132,764 houses were built and, even more surprisingly, the target for the decade of the 1960s was only 9,000 to 10,000 annually. Even although the population had fallen at the end of the war from 7 million to about half that number, increasing by 300,000 to 400,000 annually (with a drop from 1968), this rate of construction was wholly inadequate. Consequently, a large number of people, perhaps as many as 45 per cent, still lived in what were called 'non-dwellings', that is to say, outbuildings, warehouses or shelters, much as they had to do after the bombings. Rents climbed to fantastic heights; and since more than 71 per cent of accommodation was rented, the economic burden on the working-class and middle-class families was crushing. Furthermore, the price of land had risen more steeply than other costs; it was 2,500 times that of the pre-war level, whereas other wholesale prices had increased about 380 times. This put land values at ten times those of New York or London. The only

---

[1] At least 130,000 people died in the fire-raids on Tokyo. Curtis LeMay, the American general, described this holocaust as 'a dream come true'.

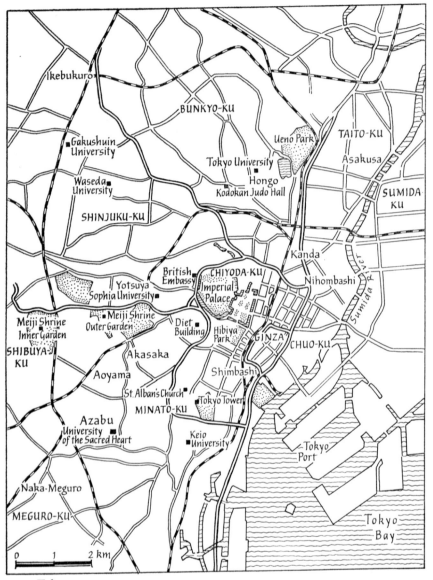

Ikebukuro

BUNKYO-KU

Gakushuin
University

Tokyo University

Ueno Park

TAITO-KU

Asakusa

Waseda
University

Hongo
Kodokan Judo Hall

SUMIDA-
KU

SHINJUKU-KU

Kanda

Nihombashi

British
Embassy

Yotsuya

CHIYODA-KU

Sophia University

Imperial
Palace

Meiji Shrine
Inner Garden

Meiji Shrine
Outer Garden

Diet
Building

Hibiya
Park

GINZA

CHUO-KU

SHIBUYA-
KU

Akasaka

Aoyama

Shimbashi

St. Alban's Church

Tokyo Tower

MINATO-KU

Azabu
University
of the Sacred Heart

Keio
University

Tokyo
Port

Naka-Meguro

MEGURO-KU

0   1   2 km

Tokyo
Bay

Sumida River

2. Tokyo

compensation was that building costs were a great deal lower than in Western countries.

Under foreign occupation, the city, despite unparalleled disruption, resumed work with surprising speed. For the initial alarm felt by the population, due to wartime propaganda representing the enemy as ruthless savages, soon gave place to a satisfactory relationship, and the task of reconciliation and rehabilitation began in earnest. As America and the Americans have recently come in for a good deal of abuse, and as their various *maladresses* tend to receive wide publicity, not least in the United States, it is as well to bear in mind that their conduct of the Occupation of Japan was on the whole beneficent, even though 'incidents' involving American troops never received mention in the press. The task of getting the country on its feet again was nevertheless a long and arduous business; and even by my time this task was far from complete. Notwithstanding the glamour proverbially associated with the Ginza, the centre of Tokyo continued to look unplanned, unfinished and a little scruffy, especially by day. Indeed, according to reports issued by the Tokyo Metropolitan Government, and to those drawn up by Professor William Robson, who during my stay visited Japan at the Tokyo Municipal Government's invitation,[1] the standard of public service and amenity was far below expectation. Only one-third of the centrally developed part of the city enjoyed proper sewerage facilities, while about 600,000 people lacked piped water-supply. Given the enormous number of shops, hotels, offices and not least bars, in the area, this is hard to believe. Less hard to believe, from the reports of at least one sense-organ, was the fact that the rivers, because of the inadequate drainage, were nothing but huge sewers themselves. Despite the literature which they have inspired, the city's rivers remain mournful, turbid strips of water; and no town-planner, if Tokyo can be said ever to have had such a person, has thought of endowing them with the grace and charm possessed by the Seine or the Thames.

For despite the new luxury hotels, enormous department stores, concert halls, sports palaces, etc., the city remained without general

[1] Some of the facts I have cited are derived from the T.M.G.'s two White Papers *Sizing up Tokyo*, which Professor Robson, the distinguished political scientist, regards as the most comprehensive report ever made on a big city, and *The Civil Minimal Plan*, together with his own papers, *Report on the Tokyo Metropolitan Government* and *Second Report on the Tokyo Metropolitan Government*, published in 1967 and 1969 respectively, following his visit to Japan.

design. On the whole, the environment was both dull and tasteless, save
for a park or two. This troubled the Japanese less than might have been
supposed: for, unlike cities of the West, those of Japan have never known
a tradition of civic architecture. There are few dignified squares, vistas,
esplanades, or splendid avenues.

In Tokyo, only the Marunouchi area, with its redbrick Western-style
buildings, banks, etc., possesses the character associated with a particular
'quarter'. Happily, this area survived the war more or less unscathed; and
the same was true of the Emperor's Palace, though it suffered damage,
and also of the rail network, which the Americans had deliberately
refrained from bombing. The rest suffered appallingly, though not for
the first time in its history.

To these sombre features I allude at the outset, because, in what I say
hereafter, I do not wish to appear oblivious of that 'other' Japan of which
I have spoken—the squalid and seething community of which the foreign
visitor remains all too often unaware. Nor do I wish to ignore still other,
and increasingly unpleasant, features of life in the world's largest city.
The traffic problem, especially before 1964, was the worst I have encountered, not excluding Paris. There were hold-ups which, if one were
in a hurry to fulfil an engagement, could sorely rack the nerves and make
one appear ludicrously dilatory and incompetent. The discharge from
cars, as from factory chimneys, had reached dangerous limits in my time:
it grew much worse, until in the summer of 1970 a cocoon of white mist
enveloped Tokyo, due to the sun's rays playing upon petrol fumes.
Suddenly the fact of lethal pollution struck home.

It was, as I say, bad enough in my time. To fly into the capital from a
provincial town, especially one in the North, was to encounter, almost at
the moment of touching down, the reeking smell of gas. (In Osaka, the
pollution was as bad, and the smoke-pall overhanging that city was in
some ways more dense.) Consequently, I never felt really well in Tokyo.
Most of my colleagues shared this slightly dazed and sometimes depressed
feeling. It was no fun realizing that one was slowly being poisoned.

The horror of pollution took hold once again of the Japanese, and
perhaps they will be the first to deal effectively with this menace. Everywhere there is a great deal of talk: there are signs that the Japanese propose
to act. They were certainly the pioneers in measuring the amount of
carbon monoxide in the atmosphere above their cities; and, at the time of

writing, they are coping with this newest menace, often at some inconvenience to the Tokyo commuters. (These number at present 1½ million,
but they are likely to amount to nearly 3 million by 1985, if indeed the
transport system does not break down under the strain.)

Many people have speculated on the future of Tokyo; for the city is
reaching such proportions as none other on earth can parallel. Something
needs to be done to accommodate the huge population which, however
much decentralization may take place, will doubtless remain in the
urban area. If no planner has yet been put to work to sort things out, plans
have certainly been drawn up; and one of the most interesting is that of
Tange Kenzo, the architect of world stature whose acquaintance I enjoyed. Tange's idea, like many others which are practical, is basically a
simple one; and like some other Japanese projects, it would make use of
the sea. What Tange would like to do would be to project Tokyo into the
most convenient sea-area available, namely Tokyo Bay. Here he would
construct enormous concrete platforms on stilts for the accommodation
of groups of about 20,000 people. In other words, he would depart from
the traditional concept of the city, which implies a nucleus with concentric circles of expansion. This he regards as the result of the exclusively
hierarchical structure of society; and it is the measure of his originality
and daring that, though himself passionately attached to Japanese tradition, he is prepared to think in radically different terms when it comes to
solving Tokyo's immediate problems. In point of fact, the hierarchical
structure of Japanese society has been reflected less in Tokyo than elsewhere, at least since the Meiji Restoration. In modern conditions, instead
of the nucleus, it would appear more logical to have a 'spine', with
branches growing out of it.

Whether Tange's project will be realized is another matter. When I
heard him expound his views at International House on Monday, 5 November 1962 he seemed more than doubtful on this point. But events have
moved on since then. During the last ten years, the problem has become
far more acute. It needs to be tackled on a big scale. It will cost an immense
sum of money. One day, the Tokyo Metropolitan Government may
turn to Tange for help. Already he has beautified the city with the
Catholic Cathedral and the Olympic Sports Pavilions at Yoyogi. Finally,
if any people is prepared to undertake this enormous task, it is the
Japanese. They are already pioneers in the cultivation of the sea. Perhaps

they will be the first to thrust out a new city over the waves adjoining their capital. And if Tange is given his head, he will combine beauty and utility in such a way as to make the two appear indistinguishable.

II

This was the city in which I was to make my home for the longest period I had worked abroad. I have said that I did not feel particularly well in it, but was I on the whole happy? This leads me to wider considerations. In many ways, there were obstacles to happiness. Apart from man-made afflictions, the life of Tokyo was not enhanced by the climate. Unless I happened to strike a bad patch, the weather proved a great deal more trying than that of London. Throughout the winter months there was much rain. The summer was often appallingly humid. Spring was brief, if idyllic. Of the seasons of the year, autumn was in my experience the most congenial. Then the sky would clear, the smoke-pall would partially roll back, and there was a keen, invigorating influx of pure air. But even this delightful season was ephemeral, lasting scarcely more than a month. For me, Tokyo is associated with grey skies, torrents of rain, and weeks of enervating heat, both by day and by night. Indeed, the humidity was sometimes so great as to draw pools of perspiration from one's fingers splayed on the desk, and made it necessary, when writing a letter, to place a towel over the lower half of the notepaper to prevent it from acquiring a greasy transparency.

Even so, I experienced, upon arriving in Japan, a sense of what I can only call, for want of a better expression, psychological security. I shall try to account for this. I am aware that the experience was not shared by all foreign residents, and as a rule less by women than by men. It is a state difficult to describe with accuracy; but it made living in Japan not merely tolerable but even exciting. In my own mind, I have no doubt that it was produced partly by something in the character of the Japanese people: not just the fact that they were physically clean and wholesome, but the fact that this wholesomeness went deeper. Everyone knows that it is easier to work and live with certain people, taken in groups, than with others; and few would deny that this is a feeling generated at the *psychic* level. I also think that such feelings are capable of being trained, and that they are themselves the result of training. This brings me to the twin points of hierarchy and veneration for the past. In Japan, the outward hierarchy of status and class is merely a secondary manifestation of a psychological scale of values, just as the ceremonies associated with ancestor-worship are the outward expression of forms of communal memory little studied save by psychologists such as C. G. Jung. The fact that Japanese people, especially the young, move about in groups, apparently without a leader, like a colony of amoebae, is often explained in purely mechanistic terms, as if they were so many externally related units. In my view, the centripetal force operates at a more profound level, and derives from deep-seated instincts and memories, assisted by training from generation to generation.

The paradox is, if it be a paradox, that this communal solidarity, this slightly introverted form of society, does not alienate the foreigner but attracts him, and lends him a sense of 'belonging', even though he can never really participate.

There must, indeed, be few peoples today who have undergone the kind of collective training to which the Japanese have been submitted. This training was not simply the result of propaganda, though the Japanese know what submission to such pressure can be. In most totalitarian regimes, the official political ideology is so preposterous as inevitably to impose a strain upon the people, even though it may be nominally accepted. The mind, in order to cope, is obliged to switch off; and if it cannot switch off completely, it resorts to deliberate forms of self-deception. In the case of Japan, the training had its markedly idealistic side; it was something real and capable of being grasped, even though it involved the pursuit of ideals beyond the normal range. The popular schools of *Terakoya*, which catered for the non-samurai classes[1] towards the end of the eighteenth century during the Tokugawa Shogunate, concentrated mainly on the teaching of writing, a hard enough discipline in the case of Japanese; but we have only to look at the *Terakoya* precepts concerning the art of calligraphy to perceive the high ethical principles which were kept before the students. I cite a few injunctions.[2] 'To be born human and not to be able to write is to be less than human. . . . Goodness

---

[1] These classes comprise the peasants, the artisans and the merchants.
[2] These are drawn from Ronald Dore's *Education in Tokugawa Japan* (1965), Appendix II.

and badness depend on the company you keep. . . . Co-operate with each other to behave yourselves as you should, check in yourselves any tendencies to be attracted to evil ways, and put all your heart into your brush-work. . . . One who treats his brushes or his paper without due respect will never progress. The boy who uses carefully even the oldest, most worn-out brush is the one who will succeed. . . . Torn and dirty clothes look bad. Even more they are a sign of a torn and dirty spirit. . . . Ill-natured pupils can never learn to write a good hand. Honour your parents, revere your teacher, respect your elders and be kind to your juniors, *for this is the heart and origin of the Way of Man*' (my italics). And so on, precept after precept, based largely on the ethics of Confucius, and combining the practical with the idealistic.

Although the direct influence of Confucius waned after the Meiji Restoration, its indirect influence is still very great, and should not be underestimated. It can be detected in a document issued in my time by the Ministry of Education, namely a report published in 1965 by the Central Council of Education, an advisory body of the Ministry, on the 'Image of the Ideal Japanese'. The contents of the report provoked a great deal of controversy, which is still going on. On the surface, much of the 'definition' appears to be in harmony with advanced contemporary thought. It enjoins the student to think in a rational manner, and to arrive at independent conclusions. But it also enjoins love of the Emperor, as the symbol of national unity, and by implication a reverence for the traditional virtues. Not unexpectedly, it was this part of the report which provoked the most heated debate. The chief criticism came from the extreme left-wing students' organizations. Such criticism was to be expected from Marxist and radical circles; but despite the enormous publicity given to student troubles, which were seething during my stay in Japan and became even more bitter thereafter, the gist of the report would appear to represent or reflect the views of the majority of Japanese. This suggests a line of continuity with the principles of the popular schools of the Tokugawa period; for the report is concerned above all to provide a moral basis for the state system of high school education. Much thought went into its composition, and those concerned with the original draft included men distinguished in different fields. Among them were Professor Okouchi, who was President of Tokyo University for a period and a good friend of mine, the famous industrialists, Idemitsu Sukezo and

Matsushita Konosuke, and the novelist Osaragi Jiro, author of one of Japan's most famous post-war books, *Homecoming*.

It was on the first appearance of this report that the truth was brought home to me that Japan was 'the last country', in the sense that here was a progressive, developed nation which was determined to mould the future on the lines of its past. The past was the source of values, and the future would be propitious only if these values continued to be honoured as the basis of a stable and contented community. The idea of *repudiating* the past, or of winnowing it away in favour of 'progressive' ideas, was entirely foreign to the Japanese mentality.

I do not say for a moment that this lofty social ideal is everywhere lived up to, or that the Japanese people are morally superior to their neighbours; but I believe that they possess certain qualities which are partly the result of their educational *ethos*, and that the 'wholesomeness' which they communicate is one of these qualities, and that it is something of great value, which may be disappearing in countries less traditionally minded.

The extent to which students, and teachers too, can entertain radical views and yet contribute to the stability of the country is remarkable. After the war, the confusion and poverty were enough to encourage a certain radicalism; and when the Occupation was over, political acrimony intensified. But prolonged contact with students in Japan led me to believe that the majority, though familiar with Marxist jargon, had little idea of what it meant and how the theory could be applied; and when they left the university, they forgot all about it and sought congenial and stable employment. Even those who became student leaders, or professional agitators, occupied the position for the sake of the steady job it provided rather than from a sense of dedication to a secular gospel. In any case, the economic progress of Japan has by now lent such radicalism a somewhat old-fashioned air. It continues to flourish because, at a student level, there are so few other gospels to take its place.

The University of Tokyo has traditionally been the centre from which the Japanese élite has been recruited; but in 1968 most of the Faculties went 'on strike' so that for the first time the entrance examinations could not be held. In organizing this and later stoppages, the militant radicals' aim was to cut off the supply of reinforcements for what they described as the 'monopoly-capitalist' ruling classes; but in fact the process of democratic education was interrupted for the sons not merely of the rich but of the poor. As the entrance examination is extremely stiff, only the intelligent can hope to gain admission. The outcome, if the strikes had been allowed to get out of hand, would have been to deprive the country of able men from all parts of society. In March 1969 one of the first student-police encounters took place at the University of Kyoto, the academic centre second in importance to Tokyo. It was of extraordinary violence. Armoured cars, tear gas, and water-cannon were used to dislodge about 1,500 radical students. After a pitched battle, the police confiscated, among other weapons, 300 incendiary bombs and ten lorries of stones. In due course, the agitation spread to several hundred universities and there was something like a total academic shut-down. In fact the police, provided with search-warrants, had entered the Kyoto campus originally to investigate clashes between rival groups of militants. For the radical movement no longer preserved the monolithic character it had assumed immediately after the war; it was split between pro-Soviet and pro-Chinese factions. One might visit a campus on which the two groups were organizing rival demonstrations (as I witnessed at Waseda, the great private university in Tokyo, where the issue was the familiar one of Vietnam), both of which were illegal. Nevertheless, the violence engendered at this level proved in the end self-defeating: first, because it damaged the cause of social justice itself, and secondly because such ruthless militancy could not be sustained indefinitely. Today, as elsewhere, it has lost its impetus.

III

Apart from such examples of group-hysteria, it is natural that the self-control exhibited by so many Japanese should break down from time to time. The conduct of Japanese troops during the last war was inferior to that in the Russo-Japanese war; and the recent student agitation was more violent than at any other period, though university radicalism has a long history in Japan. On the other hand, anger and frustration would appear usually to be directed inwards, especially in the case of women.

At the same time, I feel that too much stress has been placed on the 'indirect' approach of the Japanese, whether in official negotiations or in the course of everyday life. Given the opportunity, or if their opinions were deliberately sought, they could be very blunt; and this applied as much to the women as to the men. Nor did I find it necessary, in discussing an important project, to spend an inordinate amount of time 'leading up' to the point at issue. In this respect, I fancy there has been a change in national habits, because my own reading and instruction before going to Japan dwelt much upon the need for temporizing and for devious approaches; and admittedly the language is so constructed as to make vagueness into a fine art. The more experience I acquired, however, the greater was my conviction that our own manner of negotiating was not very different from theirs. In Japan, there were the usual friendly exchanges, and then if all seemed clear, the point at issue was forthwith, if delicately, introduced; for the very constitution of the Japanese language makes precision, at some point, obligatory. It was the duty of those subordinate in the hierarchy to ensure that their chief knew exactly what needed to be discussed. Consequently, whenever I paid a visit to an official of importance, or whenever a delegation came to discuss something with me, I noticed that the subject for negotiation had been summarized in a few lines and was kept in evidence throughout the meeting. Partly because of problems of copying, and partly because of the infrequent use of the typewriter, the elaborate writing of memoranda, *aides-mémoires*, and the composition of minutes by several hands, was kept to a minimum; and although decisions were sometimes delayed, this delay was due not so much to the cumbersome workings of bureaucracy as to the prolonged discussions that went on behind the scenes. The more delay there was, the more obvious it became that a favourable decision was unlikely to be forthcoming; and no amount of further contact made any difference. As a general rule, if a project were going through successfully, some intimation would be given at the first, or at least an early, meeting. But it took me some little time to grasp this simple fact. Meanwhile, I used on occasions to nourish hopes, on the basis of a series of calls or meetings, for which there were no longer any grounds. Thus although the British 'diplomatic' method was not much different, as I thought, from the Japanese, the *modalités* differed to a marked degree. This, and many other national characteristics, had to be learnt at first hand. For that reason alone, I was grateful that my stay in Japan extended over six years.

My Japanese staff worked as a team more successfully than any other office staff I have known, and I had a great feeling of ease and security in working with them, as I did in living with the Japanese in general; but I must not give the impression that our relations were close, or that we were on terms of friendship, as usually understood. This was not so at all. At first I used to worry about this apparent 'failure of communication', but gradually I came to accept it. The distance between us was to some extent understandable. True, some members of the staff had been to England, and their grasp of foreign psychology was invaluable. There was Mr. Takahashi Koretake, son of the famous Liberal statesman, who had gone to Queen's College, Oxford. He was at the stage of life which entitled him to the status of *Genro*, that is to say, a man of experience and reputation, whose advice was sought on every subject,[1] and whose loyalty and integrity belonged much to the Old Japan as to the New. He had one of the nicest natures of any man I have known, and, what is more, he possessed a keen sense of humour. Then there was Miss Eguchi Shizuko, who had been born in England and had spent some years at Hornsey High School, where she had taken her General Schools Certificate with exemption from Matriculation. Her English, both written and spoken, was perfect; and as she had occupied in her time most of the posts on the staff, from accountant to confidential secretary, her experience was unrivalled. Her extreme accuracy, her devotion to the work, and her tenacity of character, rendered her of the greatest assistance to me; and I appreciated her support all the more in that she had to do battle for much of her time against ill-health. If I do not refer to the other members of the local staff, save in passing, it is not because I did not appreciate their services or their loyalty; and the same applies, naturally, to my British colleagues.

It was not easy for a Japanese, sometimes very young, to join an office run by foreigners, whose ways were strange and whose characters were so different. As for the language, I was frequently amazed at the swiftness with which English was picked up; and talking of English, I cannot praise too highly the standard of written work maintained by my secretarial staff. Girls in their early twenties would do shorthand and typing not merely with accuracy, but with a pride in the layout and neatness

[1] Originally the *Genro* were the elder statesmen of the Meiji period who chose the prime minister.

which I have scarcely seen rivalled. When the great differences between Japanese and English were taken into consideration, and the fact that point after point needed to be verified and checked, the rapidity and efficiency with which the work was done never ceased to fill me with admiration.

The paradox was, and it runs like many other paradoxes throughout Japanese life, that although so great a distance prevailed between us, it was a distance combined with a measure of strong personal attachment. The Japanese like to work with a particular individual. The 'pool' system of secretaries, which is becoming so common in British and American offices, is ill suited to the Japanese character, which thrives on loyalty to a master. The enormous popularity of stories such as that of the forty-seven *Ronin*, the retainers who out of loyalty planned secretly to avenge their master's death (they are buried in the Sengakuji temple at Takanawa in Tokyo, which has become a place of pilgrimage), can be attributed to admiration, sometimes reaching the point of fanaticism, for such loyalty. The same applied to contacts with the Japanese administration. The art of securing co-operation and expediting decisions was to cultivate the personal regard of key-officials. This did not involve securing extra favours in any corrupt sense. The integrity of the Japanese civil service is very high. (Charges of corruption, of which much is heard, rarely apply at this level.) It merely rendered day-to-day conduct that much smoother, because one could enter with confidence into direct communication with one's habitual acquaintance.

These acquaintanceships were further cemented by the social contacts which play so important a part in Japanese life. Although the salaries of public officials and university personnel were far from high, even taking into account the scale of bonuses received, especially at the New Year, men above a certain rank had access to fairly generous expense accounts. This meant that throughout the year there was a good deal of official entertaining. Some of these occasions proved of great value in the conduct of business; all were thoroughly enjoyable. The visit of an official from abroad would provide the occasion for a Japanese meal at one of Tokyo's choicest restaurants, or, if at a university, at the special entertainment centre on the campus. At such times, even the most remote or deadpan-faced officials would relax, as the *sake* was generously poured out. From the official point of view, the advantage of such functions lay not so much in the opportunity of having detailed discussions on points of business as in the reduction of tension and the establishment or re-affirmation of personal bonds. If the occasion demanded a degree of sumptuousness, the meal would include extra entertainment, often by geisha. Needless to say, some of the best occasions of this kind were those organized by the *Gaimusho*, or Foreign Office.

There were no more relaxing occasions than those provided by well-organized parties of this kind. The restaurant would be entered usually through a narrow, shaded yard; and upon entry the guest would be greeted by kneeling hostesses, usually in exquisite kimonos. Before mounting two steps of polished wood he would be required to take off his shoes, which would be deposited in a rack at the side. At first I used to wonder how, on departure, there was rarely any confusion about these shoes, until I realized that ours were easily identifiable on account of their disproportionate size. Moving over the smooth wood floor, warm to the touch, the guest would be led along corridor after corridor, until, the *shoji* or sliding-doors of a particular room being quietly drawn back, he would step on to the *tatami*, or straw matting.[1] The habit of never touch-ing the *tatami* with anything but the stockinged or bare feet had to be acquired rapidly, as the very idea of desecrating it with footwear was abhorrent to the Japanese. On entering the room, the guest would be greeted by the sight of a low table, usually of lacquered persimmon, along which cushions were disposed. The position to be occupied by the chief guest was always with his back to the *tokonoma*, a recess in the wall, decorated with a scroll or *kakemono*, and often with a vase with a simple flower-arrangement. This *tokonoma*, was equivalent to the 'altar' of the room. The *kakemono*, which usually bore a simple brush-drawing with a text, might be of great value. The host would sit opposite his guests, and his colleagues would be placed on either side in order of seniority. To my mind, one of the most pleasant Japanese customs was that of including, even in quite select gatherings, those of junior rank, who thus remained identified with their organization, and who partook of its pleasures as well as of its duties. In many cases, however, those subordinate officers would remain anonymous, for they were never introduced. They did a good deal of quiet organizing on the side. Every-one having taken his place, the serving of the meal would begin rapidly

[1] This is made in standardized portions of six by three feet.

and efficiently, the more delicate dishes arriving first; it is no longer true that all the dishes are brought in at once. Then, at a special moment, the *sake* would arrive in small, heated bottles. *Sake* had to be poured either by the host or by a waitress who would sit beside the guest; and this pouring of *sake* continued non-stop throughout the meal. For those who did not fancy *sake*, there was always beer, or, for the total abstainers, fruit juice, pronounced by the waitresses rather attractively as 'jerse'. As *sake* tends to be thirst-creating, I enjoyed it best accompanied by beer, especially the admirable brands of Asahi or Kirin. The oldest beer in Japan, Sapporo, being rather heavier, did not go so well with *sake*; but it was a drink admirably adapted to the winter months.

To sit for any length of time in the true Japanese fashion was tiring. This graceful posture entailed resting on one's heels, and crossing the feet at the back, an irresistible target for frivolous geisha. As a rule, women were a good deal better at it than men, and some of our British girls excelled the Japanese of the younger generation, especially the males who tended to despise this along with other traditional habits. I could manage tolerably well the 'lotus seat' in a modified form. More often, assisted by a back rest, and sometimes an arm rest too, I was lazy enough to stretch out my legs under the table, though in my case indolence was not the only reason. Fortunately, the Japanese are extremely tolerant of those who, with the best will in the world, are unable to conform to their customs. It might even be said that they do not necessarily approve too great or too literal a conformity to the Japanese way of life, save in special cases. The young, ardent Japanophile, bent on strict conformity, may excite discreet mirth and on occasion a vague suspicion.

A Japanese meal, well-served, generates a mood of good fellowship. This, combined with the relaxation it affords, possesses genuine therapeutic value. If the occasion warrants it, there are toasts and speeches; but these are neither so lengthy nor so numerous as in some other countries, unless a wedding is being celebrated. *Sake* can go gently to the head; and the result is that, when geisha entertainment is provided, the guests need but little encouragement to join in some of the dances. At such moments, status and rank cease to count. The atmosphere resembles that of a somewhat sophisticated nursery. The childlike quality of the Japanese, which is far from being childish, comes out on such occasions. Enjoying the fun as much as anyone present, the geisha are expert at putting the guests through their paces, and can manage without offence to give a push here or a pull there to great lumbering Western bodies, so that the dance, performed to the music of the *koto*, does not break down in disorder, though a little chaos adds to the general amusement. The *koto* players and singers are usually recruited from older geisha; it must not be thought that these women are regarded as past their prime as entertainers.

When the rice is served, followed nowadays sometimes by fruit, the sign has been given that the meal is at an end. As Japanese meals begin early, they end early too; and to me, this was one of their supreme merits. The evening did not have its back broken, as happens so often elsewhere. Owing to the lightness and delicacy of Japanese food, and the simple drinks, both stomach and head were not as a rule overloaded. This was another difference from the usual run of Western entertainment. Our food seems to be getting increasingly heavy, as the habit of interesting conversation falls into desuetude. Not that drinking *sake* to excess was uncommon, and then the party would sometimes continue in the form of visits to bars and clubs. This tended to happen more frequently in the provinces, where the guest had scarcity value. But, as a rule, the official functions were brief enough to permit even the fulfilment of a Western dinner-engagement afterwards, if one's programme made such a gastronomic marathon necessary.

Despite the advantages of Japanese entertainment, it did not always result in a more *open* relationship between the guest and the hosts, which is supposed to follow from the equivalent Western functions. At least, not on the surface. The next contact with officialdom would be as formal as before. One learnt to accept this repeated reimposition of the 'barrier', especially as it took place as much among the Japanese themselves as between foreigners and the Japanese. Nevertheless, the personal bond was somehow subtly strengthened and confidence was placed upon a firmer foundation. The very formality of the relationship, having been pleasantly interrupted, was made more tolerable. And the sense of 'security' was reinforced.

I experienced a similar reaction in the case of the parties I gave for my local staff. These were occasions to which I always looked forward, as I think most of them did too. Among such functions, the Christmas party was usually the most successful. It took place, if not at the time of the festival itself, then during or soon after the New Year holiday, when

Japan 'shuts down' for about ten days. The guests would arrive in car-loads, sometimes accompanied by wives or husbands, and very occasion-ally by fiancés. The girls were always beautifully dressed, often in their choicest kimonos. Indeed, I was immensely proud of them at all times, not least when I took them in a body to the Embassy for the Queen's Birthday Party. Then, as at other functions, there was always a word of praise for the British Council secretaries, who were said to have been chosen for their beauty and their intelligence, in that order. In fact, all were chosen primarily for their competence; and if they should happen to be pretty too, that was no disqualification. At the celebrations at my house, we used to have a good meal first, and then the room would be cleared for games. The staff often arranged these themselves. They were familiar with Western games, especially the 'round' games at which their quick wits were shown to advantage. The young Japanese are also fully conversant with Western music, songs and even Christmas carols; and, besides having pleasant singing voices, they are adept at picking up new tunes. When I introduced Scottish dancing, the music and the steps made an immediate appeal to them; and their lightness of foot, together with their sense of rhythm and order, made them admirable exponents of this most enjoyable of popular dance forms.

As usual, the next occasion on which we met, when everybody was back hard at work, the relationship had returned to its former one of distance. Naturally, there would be references to the party and generous words of thanks; but the barriers remained, and I learnt to understand that this would always be so. Nor do I now think that the situation was to be deplored. At least, the tensions of office life and the inevitable personal animosities were reduced to a minimum. As for the 'matey' office atmosphere which we try to generate in our Western world, with sub-ordinates behaving with familiarity to their superiors, this often has to be paid for by explosions or emotional scenes; and the result may be that colleagues fall out with one another and harbour prolonged resentments. I do not mean that in Japan there were never any difficult or painful moments; but I knew always that because of the hierarchical structure of our little society, which reflected the social structure outside, equilibrium would in the end be restored. And so it was. Japanese pride would never allow ugly scenes to take place in the presence of foreigners; and the same pride was partly responsible for the high standard of work maintained.

IV

What I have said above about psychological distance applies primarily to the *collective* behaviour of the Japanese. It is a distance which can be crossed in individual cases. This happened several times in the course of my stay. Two of my secretaries took British husbands, and of this I was glad. The modern Japanese girl, like her forebears, has all the qualities required of a good wife. She possesses a will of her own, combined with a deference which is not the same as submissiveness; and she manages somehow to convey the impression of lack of inhibitions with a dignity and ladylikeness which inspires respect. In cases where these traditional characteristics have been broken down, the result is not becoming, though a Japanese woman who has travelled abroad can sometimes prove more open, relaxed and receptive of outside influences than her husband, while still remaining very Japanese. Possibly the Japanese woman has a stronger sense of humour than the male. At the same time, I have noticed that the more thoroughly emancipated a Japanese girl, the less she seems to attract the foreigner. For this there are obvious reasons. The rush of G.I.-Japanese marriages after the war was not so very surprising, though unfortunately many of them came to grief when the girl was taken back home.

Since the quality of a nation's culture depends to a great extent upon its womenfolk, I will dwell for a moment upon this subject, for it is closely related to my present theme.

What made me convinced that the Japanese girl is free from the inhibitions of so many Western women (whose occasional aggressiveness is due either to the inhibitions themselves or to a violent attempt to discard them) was the serene and tender look of Japanese married women, especially in middle- or old-age. To this I have seen no parallel in any country. Such an expression may be due partly to the satin-soft skin which the women, in contrast to the men, possess, and which they retain far longer than their Western sisters of however fine a complexion. But partly, I am convinced, it is due to deep sexual fulfilment. The Western woman is always being reminded of the lack of sexual satisfaction and of the danger that this entails, so brow-beaten is she with articles and books on the subject, to say nothing of films which set a standard of sexual encounter far beyond the capacity (though unfortunately not the dreams) of the average person. Consequently, she tends to remain in a state of perpetual anxiety. Like every other trend in the West, this one has recently been taken up in the Japanese magazine and film world; and the result may prove disturbing, especially to adolescent girls. Naturally, the generation of which I speak is largely uninfluenced by such tendencies; and because its expectations were not excessive, or influenced towards excess, it accepted sexual experience as a normal episode at a certain stage of life, i.e. marriage, and therefore probably enjoyed it in a more natural manner. For through the tangle of diagnosis, *reportage*, and sociological jargon, the truth is leaking through that sexual satisfaction-cum-enjoyment among the ordinary run of persons in the West is less common than the torrent of propaganda might suggest; that it is rendered more unlikely by the undue emphasis upon the physical act and its performance; and that for most people, above all the average woman, it is the romantic prelude to intimacy, and the excitement of setting up a home with a congenial partner, that are among the keener and more enduring pleasures of the man-woman relationship. No wonder the popularity of the Western romantic novel, recently the subject of an interesting piece of academic research, remains undimmed, even in respect of its artificial vocabulary. This romantic tradition survives still in Japan. No doubt it partly accounts for the continuing popularity of Kabuki plays, which outdo in romantic sentiment almost anything produced in our world. These plays appeal chiefly to the middle-aged, as the average audience in the great Kabukiza theatre in Tokyo demonstrates. A romantic aura about the suicide of frustrated lovers still lingers, though such episodes are rarer than they were even a few years ago. For suicide is chiefly a romantic act. Above the Kegon Falls near Chuzenji, the summer resort not far from Nikko, there is a plaque commemorating the 'brave' act of a young man who, frustrated in love, threw himself down from that great height.

My purpose in raising this subject here is to point to another reason why, despite distance, the experience of living in Japan can be so pleasurable and satisfying. For, as I have said, a country must always owe much of its stability to the presence of a contented womanhood: a womanhood largely free from neurotic troubles and not deluded by a minority of advocates of women's rights into believing itself oppressed. Notwithstanding the influence of American propaganda, especially by Women's

Lib., Japan still possesses a womanhood of this order; and it will be a sad day when she throws away this priceless heritage. It is conceivable that the revulsion which some European and American women feel in Japan may be due, when not caused by identifiable distresses, to a half-conscious envy of the basic happiness of Japanese women. That Japan is a man's country is true; and I can feel no more idiosyncrasy in this situation than to object to an army on account of its being 'led'. But there is a sense, not to be underestimated, in which she is a women's country. The longer I lived in Japan, and the more I tried to observe the actual conditions of life there, the greater was my impression of the power of Japanese women. This was largely a behind-the-scenes power; and it has yet to be demonstrated whether female authority, save in exceptional cases, can be satisfactorily exercised in any other way.[1]

Owing to out-of-date *Madame Butterfly* images on the one hand, and highly coloured accounts of the Floating World on the other,[2] the foreign image of the Japanese woman tends to ignore the new middle-class housewife, especially one whose husband is a salaried employee of a large firm or a civic organization. This gap in knowledge is understandable, because the middle class is of comparatively recent formation. The obvious advantage of dependence on salaried employment is its stability; and the emergence of this new element in Japanese life, after the deprivations of the war and post-war period, is no doubt another reason why, with all the turbulence of the students and the intrigues of factions and the operations of gangsters, Japan gives an impression far more stable and balanced than many European countries, and certainly than parts of the United States. Even so, to live in a household in which expenditure can be regulated and controlled, does not mean that the housewife is able to sit back and to enjoy a life free from worry. One reason for Japan's great economic advance, especially over the last decade, is that her educational system is far superior to any other in Asia. Indeed, her traditions of literacy go back, as indicated, a long way before the Meiji Restoration. This high standard of education demands of each generation, and from

---

[1] The heroine of the novel *Yuki*, by Ronald Kirkbride, seems to me to be a travesty of Japanese womanhood, and the actress's voice, during the serial B.B.C. broadcast in the winter of 1971, was as unlike any in Japan that ever I heard.

[2] The Floating World, or *Ukiyo* (hence *ukiyo-e*, the coloured prints depicting it) refers to the fleeting life of actors, courtesans, etc. during the Edo period of the seventeenth century onwards.

each family, an effort which would be beyond the capacity of many other peoples. And it is upon the mother that the chief weight of responsibility for this effort rests.

Success in life in Japan depends both for boys and for girls upon the school and university attended. With rare exceptions, no institution of higher education, and few of the lower, can be entered without passing a pretty stiff examination. This applies even at the kindergarten stage. Surprising as it may seem, many Japanese begin working for examinations as early as four or five. Entrance examinations surpass in importance 'exit' examinations. Merely to enter a good school or university is, in many cases, to be assured of a satisfactory position in life; and as almost no one ever fails to graduate, the inducement to study during the years at university is not so very great.

As the child must be set upon the right course at so early an age, it rests with the mother to ensure that her offspring receives adequate preparation. In all families which cannot afford to employ tutors—even students who wish to earn a little extra money—the mother has to apply herself to teaching. In most Western countries, the mother does something towards the child's nursery education, as well as towards instilling some moral or perhaps religious instruction; but except in rare cases, her pedagogic activities end there. Certainly, her efforts do not approach those with which the Japanese mother finds herself saddled. If her child is not to fall behind, and thus to injure his or her chances in later life, she must instil into him the habit of unremitting work, and she herself must master the subjects in which the examination is being held. Such prolonged contact between mother and child creates a bond which is stronger than that forged in countries where the mother's work is confined to 'bringing up'.[1] Nor is the Japanese mother's work confined to the home. In Japan, parent-teachers' organizations are becoming increasingly powerful, and a mother who absents herself from the meetings (which can prove something of an ordeal) may lose face in the neighbourhood.

Thus the 'examination hell', as it is popularly called, imposes a continuous strain on both child and parent. Even so, I was often surprised that there were not more breakdowns. It soon became clear to me that only a

[1] Cf. *Mother and Son, a Japanese correspondence*, by Isoko and Ichiro Hatano (English translation 1962), which covers the war years and the post-war period. This is a most moving book.

people with centuries of moral and civic discipline behind it could have sustained such an effort. The increasingly bitter student outbreaks may constitute a natural rebellion; but this is not the whole truth, as the phenomenon is world-wide. And if, as is the case, a number of students have breakdowns when they study abroad, this may be due to finding themselves for the first time 'on their own'. (It is also due, I am convinced, to their failure to come to terms with the *mœurs* of the foreign country, especially one which wears an air of permissiveness.) More remarkable, to my mind, is the fact that more *mothers* do not have breakdowns. Here are women who, unless they belong to the affluent class, are obliged to be experts on domestic economy, mistresses, mothers and teachers. They have little diversion; they have few close friends; and they are sometimes saddled with in-laws or grandparents, or both. Here are women who, on the rare occasions when they appear in public, must take second place to their menfolk, and who have few spokesmen.[1] And yet . . . Well, I used to be invited annually to the meeting of the Japanese Academy, presided over by the Emperor, at which prizes were awarded to those distinguished in the arts and sciences. Behind the prize-winners, grave in morning dress, sat members of their families. A majority of these were, so far as I could tell, wives and mothers. What a touching sight they presented! Taking the accustomed 'back seat', they remained immobile and unobtrusive in their dull-coloured kimonos and duller *obis*; but upon their faces were looks of tenderness, peace and serenity, mirroring not merely pride but, as it seemed, a deep inner satisfaction. Admittedly, these women belonged mostly to the older generation; but they had been through a devastating war, followed by a painful process of readjustment, sometimes (in the case of those from academic families) involving pinching and scraping to a humiliating degree, so that their brave, silent dignity was all the more admirable. As for their daughters, they have known a happier world; but my impression was that many a Japanese girl, however emancipated, inherits certain sterling qualities from her mother which the Japanese boy tends to lack. I recall a young college girl, who was taking part in one of the numerous English speech-contests of which I was invited to act as judge, making an impassioned oration in favour of a return to the old virtues, and asking her sisters whether they put out their

[1] There is, however, a powerful Housewives' League (*Shufuren*), with many thousands of members.

father's bed in the evening, as a dutiful daughter should. When another 'dutiful daughter', Simone de Beauvoir,[1] came to Japan in 1964 and made what seemed to me to be a wearisome appeal for female emancipation, observing that true womanhood had hitherto been crushed and must now express itself freely, she was listened to in stony silence by the audience of primarily young people. This may have been due to hostility on the part of the male section of the audience; but partly I believe it was due to an uneasy feeling, among both sexes, that this doctrine did not quite hit the mark in the case of Japanese womanhood. It is interesting that one of the most popular books in Japan today is an attack upon sexual 'liberation' by a novelist who graduated at the Sacred Heart University in Tokyo.[2]

The truth is that, however 'inferior' their status, Japanese women command enormous respect among their menfolk. This is something which the foreigner comes to realize only after a fairly prolonged stay. One of the Japanese whom I came to know well, and who was not unresponsive to the charms of the other sex (to put it mildly), used to speak of his wife with a kind of mystical awe, and even adoration. Although this was perhaps an extreme case, I found ample corroboration of his general attitude elsewhere. I did a good deal of travelling by train in provincial Japan; first, because I wanted to see as much as I could of the country, and secondly, because this mode of travel had less of the tedium it presents elsewhere. What lifted my spirits was the frequent sight of family couples genuinely enjoying each other's company. In almost all cases, it was the animated, smiling wife who radiated happiness. Often with no claim to beauty or prettiness, these women were the product of training from an early age in the art of being agreeable, so that it had become a settled habit. This capacity to be agreeable and helpful was reflected in many stray encounters during my journeys. Whenever I sought information about directions, or in the not few cases when I was lost, it was usually the woman who volunteered assistance. This was attributable sometimes to superior linguistic ability; but more often, I suspect, it was due to an innate sense that a woman ought to make herself useful, especially to the man in need.

In the 1965 report defining the 'Ideal Japanese', there is a section of

[1] Cf. *Memoirs of a Dutiful Daughter* (*Mémoires d'une jeune fille rangée*).
[2] Sono Hyako (Mrs. Miura Shumon), author of *Love for Whom?*

great interest concerning the home.[1] It is sub-titled 'What is expected of a Japanese'. Every home, says the report, should be a place of love. Secondly, it should be a place of rest. Thirdly, and this may seem somewhat contradictory of the former, it should be a place of education. Fourthly, it should not be a 'closed society', but a group open to other social groups and finally to the entire Japanese community.

It is clear that the second provision refers to the man of the family, and the third to the children. This indeed is proved by references, in the second provision, to the importance of increasing social and national productivity, and in the case of the third provision, by references to home-education in contrast to school-education, the first being described as 'natural' and the second as 'planned'. In both cases, the wife is saddled with the chief burden. In another section, there is an injunction to reverence the 'origins of our life'. This embraces parents, race and mankind in general: for, says the text, 'such reverence for the origin of life is a real and true religious sentiment and constitutes the firm basis for the attainment of real happiness.' So far as I can judge, this is the only direct reference in the report to religion; but in fact the whole of it is animated with a spirit of such lofty idealism as to make it a religious charter. Furthermore, it is a manifesto which, apart from its remarks upon the advance of the natural sciences and upon the importance of understanding true democracy, might have been written at any time during the last two centuries, or even earlier. It enjoins that piety towards the past which dates from the beginnings of recorded Japanese history.

In the spring of 1969 the Liberal Democratic Party, which had been in power for many years, began to think of revising the secondary school textbooks, with a view to placing greater emphasis upon traditional myths. Not unexpectedly, this proposal provoked further bitter opposition from the radical groups. It had something to do with the university disturbances and there were those who saw it as a throw-back to pre-war fascism; but the prime minister, Mr. Sato Eisaku, a man of caution, would hardly have sanctioned this move unless he had been reasonably sure that he could carry moderate opinion with him. The inference was that, despite the rapid modernization of Japan and the youthful turbulence, the country had been feeling its way back to its psychological centre of gravity.

[1] Chapter II of Part II.

V

Thus, the nation most rapid in its advance towards modernity has put out feelers towards its past, and somehow re-established that continuity which helps to lend meaning to common existence. It would seem that a community needs to be inspired either by a numinous past or a numinous future. The totalitarian states hold out prospects of a future of golden prosperity, following an interim period of laborious striving and loss of freedom ('the dictation of the proletariat,' etc.). Without this, they would be unable to extract from the people the effort needed to provide them with a modest standard of living, let alone to overtake the lead of the capitalist countries which, despite the use of an eschatological vocabulary, seems to be their ultimate aim. The alternative is to achieve the sense of community not with the unborn but with the dead. Whatever the superstitions of Shinto, there is a beauty about ancestor-worship compared with which a 'veneration of the future' holds out little attraction.[1] Granted, some of our sociologists would dismiss both views as a kind of dream fulfilment, with slightly greater opprobrium for the backward-looking one. As for the Japanese people, they have shown that they do not wish to repudiate the 'sacred view of life'. Not only have they never really abandoned their traditional forms of worship, but they have shown tolerance of, and embraced in their thousands, new religions which place emphasis upon the sacred in however naive a form. Moreover, the older 'new faiths', such as Tenrikyo,[2] have shown a vitality not merely in the homeland but overseas.

Here I tread upon dangerous ground, because my views may commend themselves neither to foreign experts nor to some members of the Japanese intelligentsia. Also, Japan is a country so rich in culture as to permit the visitor to find his 'own' Japan, and to live in it quite comfortably, while remaining indifferent to the rest. Those who have sought an erotic Japan have found it. Those who have sought a materialistic Japan have found it, within a few minutes of arriving at Haneda airport, Tokyo. I claim to have found a religious Japan; but to me this was not so

[1] Ancestor-worship was probably grafted on to Shinto at a fairly late stage, no doubt on account of the influence of Confucianism.
[2] See Chapter V, Section X, p. 139.

much a belated discovery as a realization which formed part of my sense, on arrival, of psychological security.

Writing in 1910, in her *Journal from Japan: a Daily Record of Life as Seen by a Scientist*, Marie Stopes made the following observations:

'I once asked an "atheist" scientific professor what he would do if a woman whom he loved should die. He told me that he would engrave her name on a tablet in his shrine, before which a prayer would be made every day. The religious instinct is a far greater thing than any formulated religion, and though missionaries may continue to tell the world that the Japanese are naturally irreligious, that will not prevent the Japanese from being deeply religious—until they have assimilated the western attitude to religion, as they are doing towards other things. Perhaps one reason why the missionary finds the Japanese irreligious is that they take religion so happily, and make of it so much a part of their daily life, laughing in the temples, playing around the temple grounds, lighting the light in their little shrines in their homes when their household lamps are lit. One of the commonest sights in Japan is a band of peasant pilgrims on their way to some shrine, and it is the ambition of innumerable poor folk, who can never afford ordinary travel and holidays, to visit every temple of importance in the country. How many English commonfolk since the days of the Canterbury Pilgrims would travel on foot a hundred miles to lay a wisp of straw on a shrine? Because the Japanese are not (and I think will never be in our sense of the word) Christians, there is no excuse for our concluding that they are not religious.'

Written fifty years ago, I find myself agreeing with almost every word of that. (In passing, I may point out that the missionary view to which the author refers was not shared by one of the greatest of all, St. Francis Xavier, who pronounced the Japanese to be *animae naturaliter Christianae*.)[1] And I can cap her story of the atheist scientist with some experiences of my own. I was once in Kyoto for the *Setsubun* or bean-throwing ceremony, accompanied by a colleague and a Japanese friend. In discussing the festival, which symbolizes the expulsion of evil spirits, we asked our friend to what extent the people, who were gathered in

---

[1] See Chapter VIII.

large numbers, 'believed' in the ceremony and the religious ideas behind it. He replied that, while he personally entertained no belief whatever, many of the people still clung to the traditional faith, and would never miss this particular festival. Just as we were about to go home, our Japanese friend disappeared. On his catching up with us again, we ventured to ask him what he had been doing. Without a touch of embarrassment, he told us that he had just purchased a candle, and had deposited it in the appropriate place in the shrine.

Again, I was once talking with a Japanese anthropologist who had spent so many years abroad that he had become to some extent *déraciné*. The subject moved to the history of religious beliefs, and finally to the more personal question of religious experience. He confessed to me that, though he had for many years forsaken the Buddhist faith, a recent death in the family had so affected him that he found himself impelled to buy a little statue of Kannon[1] and send it to the bereaved relative. He would not say that his motive was more than the wish to provide comfort; but he added that his own acute sense of loss had turned his mind back to his Buddhist past and that he had begun to consider taking up his devotions again.

These are but two of a number of examples I could give. Even so, the case for the other side is very powerful. I shall mention examples of Buddhist priests who had 'demythologized' their faith to the point at which it was indistinguishable from Western humanism (see p. 193). As opposed to this somewhat prissy secularism, however, the vast bulk of the Japanese people remain, I am convinced, profoundly religious at heart. This may manifest itself under the guise of aestheticism; it is sometimes maintained that art is the true religion of Japan. Perhaps this is so. But if we examine the Japanese attitude to art (by which I mean their instinctive or natural attitude, and not their fascination with the latest experiments of the West), we may find that it is based upon that profound sense of the sacred, especially in nature, which fuses it with the religious vision. Nor do I have in mind a vague attitude of impressionism. The basis of Japanese art is calligraphy; and the rendering of the characters is much more than 'writing' in our sense. The whole approach, even now, is bound up with a discipline which enlists both the traditional virtues and an ancient symbolism. To write the characters carelessly, if indeed this

[1] The Goddess of Mercy.

were possible, would be to commit a kind of *moral* lapse, as the principles of the *Terakoya* schools made clear.

I come back therefore to the question of discipline, purification and reverence. The deeper I familiarized myself with Japanese life, the more I found that behind the common activities, as well as behind the more specialized ones, the sense of the sacred was present. The purpose of the Japanese bath, for instance, is not simply hygiene in the secular sense, but purification. You can take a bath only if you are physically clean: that is to say, the body is cleaned *outside* the bath, and this cleaning is a vigorous operation, undertaken until every spot of dirt has been removed. Then only are you fit to enter the bath itself, where the truly *cleansing* process begins, involving a form of relaxation which is certainly more than physical. After becoming accustomed to the Japanese *o-furo* (literally 'honourable bath'), it is not easy to reconcile oneself to the Western bath, where cleaning and cleansing are supposed to be carried out simultaneously, though in fact you end up by washing in dirty water. Again, the form of wrestling called *Sumo* is hedged about with an elaborate ritual, which reflects it as sacred in origin. And the same applies to the Tea Ceremony, to Flower-Arrangement, and to the Noh plays, which are unintelligible without an understanding of certain forms of Buddhism. Granted, all these activities can be pursued in the secular dimension; and for many Japanese, and for most foreigners, their sacred character is ignored, though the careful attention paid them indicates that they are not to be viewed lightly or to be practised casually. The young man who professes to have no philosophy of life, and little reverence for the past, will think twice before marrying a girl who has failed to qualify in Tea Ceremony, which entails the possession of a certificate indicating several years of training. For this reason, 'preparation for marriage' for the girl is a serious business, sometimes involving resignation from a well-paid job. When one of my staff came to me to explain that she was obliged to quit in order to undergo such preparation, I assumed that she was about to announce her engagement, and I murmured a few appropriate words; but her purpose was simply to acquire better qualifications for the married state, and so far as I know she is still acquiring them. The more practical arts, such as cooking, are not ignored; but whereas a few cookery lessons will suffice for the Western girl's 'preparation' for marriage, at least on the practical side, the Japanese girl needs a thorough grounding in arts having behind them centuries of tradition. Without such qualifications, her chances of finding a good husband are considerably reduced. Like the arranged marriage, such training is more common in modern Japan than is realized.

Perhaps another reason why I felt at ease in Japan was that despite the hierarchical structure of society, there was a force operating in the reverse direction. The desire for status was balanced by a drive towards equality. This is to understand equality not as a universal levelling process, but as equivalence in *respect*. In the report on the 'Ideal Japanese', it is laid down that all professions are equal in respectability and esteem. Partly for reasons to be given in the next chapter, I became convinced that this principle was not merely offered as an ideal but was largely accepted as a reality. Granted, it had not always been so. Up to the Meiji Restoration, class distinctions were so rigid as to render the idea of equality out of the question. There were also the Eta, or outcasts, whose occupation put a stigma on leather-work, which still clings to it. (I found that some Japanese were a trifle bewildered when, in a lecture on Shakespeare, I referred to the probability that Shakespeare's father was both a glover and a dealer in hides and skins.) Nor are the Japanese any more free from snobbery than other peoples. Yet the fact that every Japanese, no matter what his station in life, is now addressed in the same manner, with the attractive syllable -San being placed after the name, reflects and guarantees a certain measure of respect. In Japanese, very subtle forms of address have been developed, conveying the status of the speaker and putting the person addressed very much in his place. Of these nuances, many are altogether beyond the comprehension of the foreigner. And the Japanese spoken by women is both more elaborate and more laden with honorifics than that spoken by men. Nevertheless, opposing this pressure towards inequality of status is the feeling, expressed in the common form of address, that all people are equally honourable. The fact that, in the course of ordinary life, you address your servant in the same way as you address your superiors, helps to create an atmosphere which is genuinely democratic; and it is difficult to appreciate what this entails unless you have seen it in operation. For the verbal address carries much greater weight than is sometimes supposed; and I would go so far as to say that, given such mutual respect, the more subtle variations in status lose their offensiveness.

The Japanese therefore enjoy what I would call hierarchical equality; for their new affluence has helped to shore up this egalitarian tendency. Politics and economics have worked in harmony; but we should not underestimate the part played by traditional codes of conduct—loyalty to the group, striving for national prosperity, respect for those older and presumably wiser—in preventing labour-management relations from becoming soured to the point of rancour. Although there may be several classes in Japan, the important thing is the virtual absence of two nations, in Disraeli's sense of the rich and the poor. Ten years after the end of the war, a Japanese diplomat, Kawasaki Ichiro, wrote of his country that 'misery and poverty surround us on every side.' By the time I arrived, all that had changed; his statement did not seem remotely relevant. I encountered something like an affluent society. A sense of energy and purpose could be detected everywhere. I could almost *feel* the country moving ahead, propelled by the efforts of millions of workers.[1]

And now to a final point. In other major industrial countries, the upsurge of prosperity has been accompanied by a disproportionate emphasis on the rights of youth. This is a trifle puzzling, because the longevity of mankind in economically developed countries has greatly increased, and consequently there are more elderly people in the world than ever before. Every attempt is made, however, to conceal the scandal of age. In Japan, despite the growth of industries producing substitute human appendages, including objects still much in demand (such as false hymens), the attempt to camouflage age has not been pursued to the same degree. On the contrary, age is respected; and the older you are, the more respect you acquire. Truer in the country than in the towns, this tendency is still very strong. One of the most enjoyable experiences I had was meeting in my last year a group of old people in Nagano prefecture. They gathered in a temple, and a more vivacious concourse it would have been difficult to find. As they felt they were 'wanted', their hold on life was stronger. From another point of view, Japan is a land of youth. Both town and country swarm with school-children and students.[2] But,

---

[1] Speaking to a London Conference in February 1969 on Japan's commercial development, Sir John Figgess observed: 'Leaving aside a small minority who through sickness or other misfortune or sheer bad luck have missed the bus, the entire people may be said to share to the full the national prosperity—something quite unthinkable in pre-war Japan.'

[2] In 1967 the majority of inhabitants of Tokyo were under twenty-five.

despite this, there is as yet no extravagant youth cult. It is precisely this balance between the age-groups which may contribute to the stability which distinguishes Japan from her neighbours, and also from some countries in the West. Japan is a country without a human scrap-heap, without Boweries or Skid Rows. Consequently, it is a country which extends a welcome, however shy and hesitant, to the visitor who is prepared to take the trouble to sympathize and to understand.

The respect accorded to age means that there is a conservative back-bone supporting the frame of the country. It is remarkable how many men of advanced age remain, by virtue of their experience, in command of large business enterprises and national organizations. One of the great men of modern Japan was undoubtedly Yoshida Shigeru, the post-war prime minister. This is what he had to say about diplomacy:

'In the early days of our diplomacy, it was for a while the practice to send former lords such as Hashisuka and Date as ambassadors and ministers to foreign countries. Being *daimyo*, they naturally did not depend upon salaries from the government to carry out their duties abroad. Perhaps there has been a progressive decline in the quality of our diplomacy as our diplomats come to depend more and more on their salaries. The *daimyo* spirit is perhaps not compatible with the psychology of paid officials. But some such combination is still necessary in diplomacy.'[1]

I believe the secret of Japan's vitality and stability lies to a great extent in the combination of traditional principles with the judicious encourage-ment of youth. I believe I found Japan so stimulating because of this respect for the past and investment in the future. No other country that I know strikes precisely this balance. When I read old books about Japan, I am repeatedly struck by their authors' conviction that Japan's sole wish is to renounce the past. I cannot see it. Moreover, I did not see it. I hope I shall not live to see it.

[1] 'The Art of Diplomacy', from *This is Japan*, anniversary special issue, 1963 (*Asahi Shimbun*). A *daimyo* was a feudal lord.

CHAPTER II

Teiko-San

I

I well recall my first meeting with Teiko-San. It was at the entrance to the ground-floor flat in the Azabu district of Tokyo where, on arrival, I took up temporary residence while my colleague, Cyril Eland, was on leave. She was not alone. There, shoulder to shoulder—or shoulder slightly beneath shoulder—stood the two servants who, having worked for my predecessors, Ronald and Margot Bottrall, were now to pass into my employment. Soma-San, the cook, was of short, stocky build, with a large head. He was in the late sixties, looking very grave and a trifle apprehensive, as if to ask: 'Whom have these British people sent us now?' Beside him, very neat and precise, her mouth gathered in the *moue* with which I was to become so familiar, but soon breaking into a smile, was Teiko-San, now promoted from under-maid to maid-housekeeper, in view of my single status and the need to reduce the staff.

I had been careful to enquire in advance how I should greet my servants, knowing that in Japan these matters counted for so much; and I had been told, at this first meeting, it might be appropriate for me to shake hands with them. This would be the one occasion, save perhaps that of departure, when such a gesture would be both understood and appreciated. Naturally, both of them had begun to bow almost on my first appearance, Teiko-San bending much lower than Soma-San; but after this traditional greeting, they shook hands quite unaffectedly, Soma-San doing so first, as befitted the custom of the Last Country. Forthwith, they began to busy themselves with my luggage. I was from the beginning struck by their imperturbability and apparent lack of curiosity, for I had been used in other countries to a very different reception; but I was to learn soon enough that the Japanese possessed a remarkable gift of sizing up a person without his perceiving it. Call it intuition or telepathy, or *kan*, it does not matter under what name the gift is known: the Japanese possess it to a degree which I have not seen equalled. Certainly, Teiko-San possessed it in large measure. It was one aspect of her extraordinary intelligence.

If I say little about Soma-San, here or elsewhere, it is not because I regarded him with less respect than I did Teiko-San. He was a man of the utmost loyalty and integrity. Throughout all the days he remained with me, which was until the day of my departure, he travelled from his farm two hours' journey away, and never once arrived late. He would also do most of the shopping before he left his village, thereby saving me a fair amount of money. He was absolutely reliable. His cooking in Western, Chinese and Japanese style was just as I liked it, and he had a great, if slightly concealed, sense of humour. But his home was naturally the kitchen, and also the garden, where he spent all his hours not occupied at the stove. By contrast, Teiko-San had to be everywhere—sometimes, when we had big parties, virtually everywhere at once; she was on permanent duty and a model of vigilance. So it is of Teiko-San that I shall chiefly speak, because in the natural course of our lives we came to know each other very well.

At that time in her late twenties, Teiko-San was a robust, healthy-looking girl, not beautiful in the conventional sense. She had a rather flat face, very 'Japanese' as I then thought, but one which was full of kindness, serenity, and expressiveness. This serene expression could break out into ripples of good humour, and indeed there were times when she would bubble over with laughter. She possessed a tremendous sense of fun; I have known no one who kept up her spirits, and consequently mine, so consistently as she did. During the whole of our acquaintance, I never once saw a cross look even so much as flit over her face. Admittedly, she could occasionally look troubled, usually when she felt she might have misunderstood something I had said or done; and indeed her sensitivity to my moods was so acute that, in the absence of other means, I used her as a barometer of my own temperamental climate. But, whatever the problem, her equanimity was soon restored; and as time went on, I came to regard her not merely as the guardian but almost, to use Patmore's epithet, as the 'angel in the house', because she lent both peace and comfort to the place.

Before my arrival, I had read of the formal Japanese smile as more often than not the superficial cover for oriental duplicity and deceit. In some cases it may be so. But so far as most of my own acquaintances were concerned, I felt that they revealed, by their smiles, a genuine sincerity. I am speaking here of Teiko-San, the individual; for in due course I came to forget that she was Japanese and that I was English, with an enormous 'cultural gap' between us, and regarded her as a person who understood me, and whom I understood, better than many who were far closer by race and tradition.

That was the remarkable thing about Teiko-San. Like all Japanese, she had learnt a certain amount of English at school; but during the war years, when she was a child, the standard of spoken English was very low and she had acquired her knowledge chiefly from serving in British households. Her proficiency, in the circumstances, was remarkable. It consisted of much more than kitchen English, with certain dining-room and drawing-room extensions. Whether through listening to fairly sophisticated conversation in the course of her work, or possibly through reading (because she was a great reader), she had at her command a vocabulary, including a number of abstract terms, which she could bring out with the most telling effect; and naturally she understood a great deal more than she spoke. Consequently, it proved possible, as I very soon discovered, to hold prolonged and deep conversations with her on a variety of subjects, and to discuss quite intricate matters with her, helped out admittedly by some Japanese on my side, and, when we were stumped, by the admirable *Kenkyusha Dictionary*, with its pleasingly flexible green leather cover, which she kept in the kitchen drawer. Sometimes I would wonder, after these talks, how we managed to conduct such a prolonged exchange of ideas; and then I would conclude that much of what I said must have been grasped intuitively. For it was clear from her subsequent actions that she often understood matters which, though I had casually alluded to them, I had assumed to be beyond her. She was no less good at interpreting instructions, often hurriedly given, over the telephone (a very good test of linguistic ability); and she was constantly consulted by my colleagues and others when there was some domestic matter to resolve. 'Ring Teiko-San' became a habitual recommendation. I do not imagine that this mutual understanding, this example of *solvitur inter-loquendo*, would have obtained with everyone. Few others, I gathered, had comparable experiences with their domestics. I am sure it was due partly to some basic sympathy between us, and partly to the sheer native intelligence of which I have spoken.

I had an example of this latter quality soon after I had taken up my duties. I had to deliver at short notice a lecture on T. S. Eliot, and I needed urgently the *Collected Poems*. I rang Teiko-San. It was one of my first calls to her. I explained that I was sending the chauffeur down for a book, which I then began to describe in some detail: colour, size, and whereabouts. She listened intently, and then, satisfied that I had completed my description, said to the point as always: 'Name, master?' whereupon I began slowly and rather sceptically to spell out the T and the S and the E - l - i - o - t. 'Oh, you mean T. S. Eliot,' she said after the briefest pause, and promised to go in search of it. The book was ready for the chauffeur as soon as he arrived. This identification was all the more remarkable because my books were at that time in some disorder. It did not therefore come as such a surprise when, after my installation later at the house in Naka-Meguro, I returned home one day to find all my books arranged not merely roughly according to subjects, but with books by the same author together.

Indeed, I never ceased to marvel how, on this as on many other matters, Teiko-San was so well informed. Not merely could she read English, but she could write it with perfect intelligibility, and many were the messages she left for me, usually of telephone calls, but sometimes in the form of little notes pinned to my door. I shall never forget one of the first of these, written on 24 December, when I had come home late. It ran: 'Merry Christmas. What time bath?' Nor did foreign names defeat her as they normally did many of her people. She possessed an excellent ear, though the sound of certain names afforded her enormous amusement, and she would come to me practising them repeatedly and trying them out, in the expectation that I would share her enjoyment, which, because they were often slightly mispronounced, I usually did. I noticed, too, that she had a remarkable capacity, unless it were my fancy, of pro-nouncing the name, or as near as she could get to it, in such a way as to convey something of the personality of its owner. She was good at discriminating between the nationalities of those who telephoned; and in the case of those whom she knew (and her acquaintanceship was very wide), she would utter the name in a manner indicative of her opinion of the bearer or what she presumed mine to be.

Teiko-San had some of the best manners I have known in anyone. She was exquisitely polite, and a superb mistress of ceremonies. When we had guests, she put on a kimono in strict conformity with the importance of the occasion, and she had a considerable range from which to choose. To be received at the door by Teiko-San was to be given a sense of importance. Few Japanese women bowed so gracefully and so low as she did. I never learnt to follow the many polite expressions which she would murmur on those occasions, save that I knew they were adapted carefully to the visitor, and, if addressed to a lady, possessed, as coming from a member of her sex, a special elaborateness.

The Japanese servant, at least of the traditional sort, is very much a member of the household. In return for devotion, she (or he) feels entitled to a good measure of confidence; to the right to express her views on household matters, including visitors; and to the luxury of a good down-to-earth discussion once the function is over. I have alluded to the sense of equality of the Japanese, which balances their sense of status and hierarchy. When Teiko-San came to know a visitor, there ensued not so much familiarity as a slightly increased warmth of greeting, and some polite conversation often mixed with affectionate *badinage*. On her better acquaintance, they were entitled to something like honorary membership of the household. In this as in so many other matters, I found myself quite naturally deferring to Teiko-San's judgement, including the character of guests ('character' was one of the words she could use to great effect); and as the years passed, and our confidence in each other increased, I felt that Teiko-San and Soma-San and I composed a family of our own. She in particular looked after my welfare, was careful of my reputation, and could be very firm with importunate strangers. As was natural, she applied Japanese standards of etiquette, but she was always anxious to conform to British. If there were some matter that I thought should be changed, and she could perceive that I was in earnest about it, she would look at me intently and with some little anxiety, and, in a voice lower than usual, say 'Bad manners?' and thereafter the thing was rectified.

Fortunately for the smooth running of our household, Teiko-San could be firm not merely with others—including the waiters hired for large parties, who would sometimes tease her—but with me. Not infrequently did I return from the office a trifle overwrought with business and perhaps later than I intended, and express apprehension lest the arrangements for some party would not be completed in time. How she managed to smooth me down on such occasions I do not know, but she always did so. When I look back and realize what a strain such functions must have imposed upon her, with eight or so men to keep in order (I include myself), and a mixed concourse of guests to help receive, I admire her that much more. Never once did she neglect her duty on the plea of tiredness, nor was she ever late in the morning, however heavy the work of the previous day. Nor did I know her but twice admit to feeling unwell.

It was through Teiko-San, as much as through my female staff at the office, that I came to appreciate something of the strength of character of Japanese women. Here again, I found that I had been largely misinformed on this subject. I had read of fragile, giggling little creatures, subservient to the male, lacking in personality, of no great mental acumen, and often casual in morals. I had to unlearn all this, and I did it first in my own household. Teiko-San was far from fragile, and could laugh heartily; she deferred to men and to myself in a manner the reverse of servile; she was (as I have said) possessed of acute intelligence; and she seemed to me the model of rectitude. No doubt this self-control was the result of a traditional upbringing. I do not suggest that she lacked the usual weaknesses or failings. But among all the people I have known she was one of the most successful at concealing them. Of dishonesty, as opposed to the mild dissimulation which must go with so much everyday conduct, I believe her to have been incapable. She shared this quality, priceless in a servant, with most of the Japanese I came to know. The samurai tradition ordained a contempt for money. I had read of feudal lords and their retainers who regarded finance as a business fit only for the lower orders. But Teiko-San, so far as I could tell, was of good, sound peasant stock; and although I would not suggest that she shared the samurai code, she, like Soma-San, lacked altogether that grasping, nervously-careful attitude to money which characterizes so many from their walk of life in other countries. Every time I paid her wages, she would thank me as if I were doing her some special honour and favour. While Soma-San neatly wrote out his household accounts in an exercise book which I inspected weekly, never once finding a mistake, Teiko-San would organize the payment of the services: electricity, gas and water. She did this with meticulous efficiency, commenting on any marked increase, seeming to take pride in ensuring that I was not being overcharged, and if necessary suggesting ways of economy. I used to keep all the little bills she wrote out, as well as the official ones, destroying them annually in conformity with the old Japanese custom of making a bonfire of the old year's débris and starting afresh; and I was able by this means to observe how accurate she was in her arithmetic.

By the time I arrived in Japan, the number of beggars was much reduced. After the war, there were a great many of them. In the neighbourhood of certain places, such as temples and shrines, mutilated ex-servicemen presented a pathetic sight. Their plight was the more miserable in that they excited contempt rather than pity, since it was more glorious to die for the Emperor than to survive maimed in his service. Although few beggars called on us, we had regular collectors on behalf of the local shrines, and annually for the neighbourhood festival. In the case of the shrines, I deferred entirely to Teiko-San's judgement, as I had no idea which places were most deserving of support. After studying the document which would as a rule be presented on such occasions, Teiko-San always seemed to know what I, as the Dana-San or master, should do, and how much I should contribute, if the cause were a worthy one. These papers, often much worn, were written in a highly stylized Japanese, and her brows would knit for a while as she digested it. Then, enlightenment suddenly dawning upon her, she would turn to me, screw up her eyes in a confidential smile and, if her conclusion were positive, deliver a series of rapid nods. On such occasions no words were exchanged. I just produced a few notes, from which she selected the appropriate sum, continuing her reassuring gesture. From time to time, a paper in English, prepared specially for *gaijin* or foreigners, was submitted. This was usually a much thumbed photostat on livid blue paper, into which the type-written appeal had all but merged. This made little difference, because the rendering, even if decipherable, was to me well-nigh unintelligible, and quite beyond Teiko-San's linguistic capacity. Such appeals Teiko-San would view with a certain suspicion. She had lived long enough with foreigners to be aware that on occasions they were 'put upon', though less in Japan, if she but knew it, than in many other countries. These direct attempts to by-pass her as comptroller of the household usually failed of their purpose; and this no doubt accounted for their rarity, even though we exchanged districts three times.

I recall two occasions only when letters arrived through the post which disturbed Teiko-San's equilibrium. Both were in English, at least of a sort. One, pouring out a lengthy grievance, threatened the burning down of my house if I did not at once forward to the sender a substantial donation. The writer, whom the police later identified as a prolific correspondent on this theme, was clearly a mild lunatic. The other, which I still possess, was one of those chain-letters which threaten disaster and ill luck if the recipient fails to send it on. The visitation was due to be swift. I shall never forget how worried Teiko-San was on my account (not her own), and how she anxiously enquired how I felt when she brought me my breakfast next morning. Otherwise, I think she was virtually without superstition. Even now, as I write, I realize that I never asked Teiko-San about her religion, though I am sure she was attached to some faith, if only through her family: for most Japanese are nominally attached to a temple, as a matter of convenience, identity, and location as a Japanese citizen. I learnt little of Teiko-San's attitude to Shinto, or to Buddhism for that matter, whereas Soma-San was a marked traditionalist. On the death of his wife, he would pay the prescribed visits to the temple at regular intervals, as if they were obligations impossible to ignore. But Teiko-San knew something about Christianity and the Church, first because of her long association with Western families, and secondly, because I believe she had a sister who had been baptized. But her religion, as regards the practice of a faith, was somehow inside her. There was something 'clean' about her nature which, though I am hard put to define it, was apparent to anyone who lived, as I did, in close contact with her. She somehow gave the impression of being a creature of innocence, as if born—how shall I describe it?—without original sin. Unfortunately, as we know, the Japanese have frequently shown a very different side to their nature, nor am I going to commit myself to the view that such lapses were exceptional. I simply believe that, like some other peoples with a marked sense of solidarity, they are capable of acts in concert which they would shrink from committing as individuals. And I am speaking for the moment of one individual. Teiko-San showed me, by repeated acts, that she had a tender, almost childlike nature.

Many have remarked that the Japanese are unkind or at least indifferent to animals. To our minds, this accusation has some basis, though a public conscience is being aroused at some of the cruel vivisection experiments carried out in Japan, not least in famous university laboratories. We had two dogs in our household, of whom I became very fond. The first was found by the wife of one of my predecessors wandering disconsolately outside Shinjuku Station. She had called to him in English, and he ran up to her. It seemed likely that he had been left behind on the departure of his foreign owner. She took him home, called him Luke, and he became one of the family. Luke was one of the most affectionate dogs I have known; and it was Teiko-San's task to look after him, which she did with great solicitude. We were constantly anxious lest he should run away, especially at the likely periods. Many times have I seen Teiko-San's buxom form (for she put on a good deal of weight in my service) dashing after him, her slightly bandy legs kicking sideways as she did so. One evening, during a cocktail party when she could not keep as close an eye on him as she was accustomed, Luke got away. We were dejected, all of us, even Soma-San, who liked the dog even though he did not dote on him. Fortunately, Luke had a collar with our address, and after three or four days, we received a telephone call from a girl who, spotting him wandering about obviously lost, had noticed the collar and made contact with us. We were jubilant, and none so much as Teiko-San, as, armed with a strong lead and a bottle of whisky as a gift, she sallied out cheerfully to fetch him. When I returned from the office, there he was again, but very chastened and obviously bewildered. All through that evening he sat by my desk while I worked—something he rarely did, as Teiko-San usually kept him with her downstairs. For hours on end he trembled and twitched, I do not know as a result of what horrible experiences.

More than a year later, Luke disappeared again. This time, alas, he was never found. I put an advertisement in the papers; Teiko-San went to the Dog Pound where stray animals were rounded up; we scoured the district, but all to no avail. Sometimes when I was driving about Tokyo, I thought I had caught sight of him, but it always proved a mistake. By that time I had become so fond of him and so accustomed to his presence, and not least to his invariable following Teiko-San round the house, which he did with absolute fidelity, that I was for some time tormented with the idea of his wandering too far and trying in vain to find the way home, and to his gradually starving, or being ill-treated. Both Soma-San and Teiko-San could see how unhappy I was. One evening, when I was again sitting in my study in the large house in Akasaka, Teiko-San came in with an air of suppressed mystery and glee. Looking round, I saw that she carried in her arms a small black animal, which she stroked in a reassuring way, as it blinked up at her and then at me uncomprehendingly. 'Soma-San found Shinjuku Station,' she explained. Yes, indeed. He had come across the little creature at the usual rendezvous, thought I might like him, and brought him home. At first I was not sure whether he was a dog at all. 'Like bear', commented Teiko-San in her usual way, for indefinite and definite articles and prepositions presented great difficulties even for Japanese who had specialized in English. She was right. But I took to him instantly; and, feeling a special interest in him since he had been found in the manner of his predecessor, we called him Luke, and so he joined the household.

The second Luke preserved his cub-like aspect for a long time. He was a wild little animal. At first, he led Teiko-San something of a dance. He would snap at her nose playfully, often leaving a scratch, and he several times tore her dress, though fortunately never one of her fine kimonos. He left me unscathed, but he was a demon for gnawing the covers of my books. Paperbacks he despised; only good, thick handsome bindings and covers were worthy of his attention. Some of my most precious volumes bear the marks of his teeth. Fortunately, he gradually grew out of this habit, and at most times he was docile and lovable, as well as being a good housedog.

Luke II took a little time to become house-trained. On one occasion, he disgraced himself in the hall of the very modern house at Shoto-cho, near Shibuya. Soma-San took him by the neck and gave him a beating. Teiko-San suffered at this, batting her eyelids nervously as if scarcely able to endure the sight. If sometimes people tell me of the Japanese callousness towards animals, I remember Teiko-San, just as I remember the young girl who had gone to the trouble of restoring the lost Luke to us. Indeed, the Japanese have a sentimental side towards animals. Outside Shibuya Station, in a very crowded area where political meetings are sometimes held, there is a statue of a dog who was accustomed to await his master at that spot, and who, for some time after the man's death, continued to take up his position there. It is one of the sights of that busy part of Tokyo.

Luke II grew into a big strong dog, gradually losing his bear-like features. But, alas, his fate was the same as that of his predecessor. One evening during a large cocktail party after my departure, he escaped and was never seen again. I have wondered sometimes whether there was another dog wandering round the precincts of Shinjuku Station awaiting adoption.

II

One of Teiko-San's most endearing characteristics was that she was invariably 'game'. She loved to share a joke, and to participate in an entertainment. As a conjuror of modest attainment, I found Teiko-San the ideal confederate. When we had a staff party, I would perform one or two tricks in which her ready and intelligent co-operation was a necessity; and it was most satisfying to see how she entered into the spirit of the thing. Again, it was at such times that I observed the Japanese capacity for accepting people as equals. Like Soma-San, Teiko-San had a sense of service worthy of one of the old retainers. She was proud of her position. The idea that there was anything inferior in being 'in service' would never have entered her mind, though it must be admitted that this attitude is disappearing. Furthermore, my staff, many of whom were from 'good' families, seemed never to treat her as an inferior. As she discharged her task well in her own sphere, she was, so far as they were concerned, an equal, and they regarded her with as much respect as she regarded them. In a country such as Japan with 'hierarchical equality', this was perfectly natural; and this is perhaps the most satisfactory way in which human beings, with all their inherent differences and in-equalities, can be organized in community. When the guests left, Teiko-San was the servant *par excellence* again. She gave each person the bow to which she felt him or her entitled, observing gradations quite outside the comprehension of a foreigner. The result was that she always appeared socially at ease.

Although the various 'functions' at my house involved a great deal of preparatory work, Teiko-San always seemed to enjoy them. She became known in Tokyo for the grace of her manners not merely among Western guests but among Japanese of the old school, who were specialists in formality. This grace of carriage and manner was an essential part of her; and although it was enhanced by the wearing of the kimono, it was not cast off at other times. Every morning, when I left for the office, she and Soma-San would come outside the door to bow, and Soma-San was always summoned from the kitchen for this little ceremony. They made an excellent pair, and were good at teasing each other, though Teiko-San observed always a degree of circumspection in token of Soma-San's years and his being a man. At the point of departure, however, all *badinage* was dropped, bodies were bent, and I left in solemn state.

For everyday work, Teiko-San wore Western clothes; and, with a few exceptions, she always went out in them. On such occasions as her weekly holiday (for which she would invariably make a request, in order to ensure that it was convenient for me), she looked very smart. But for all formal occasions Teiko-San would wear a kimono, and there can be few Japanese women whose charms a kimono does not enhance. As it is a complicated garment to put on, all hurry is to be avoided. We used to give our girls at least two hours off in order to enable them to get into their kimonos and to have their hair done properly, for the appropriate hair-do is essential. In a household without a hostess such as mine, we would usually be in something of a flap on party evenings, as I would return home from the office with little time to spare. As running about and seeing to arrangements was difficult in formal dress, Teiko-San would defer putting on her kimono until the last minute; but, despite the complications involved, especially with the fixing of the *obi* at the back (the kimono has neither buttons nor fasteners), she always managed to be ready in time to answer the door. I do not know how she did it.

As we became better acquainted, Teiko-San would show that she was open to consultation on any matter. Although I never discussed official problems with her, I would sometimes come home worried about some particular point. She was quick to observe my disquiet. Occasionally I would mention the problem in the most general or devious manner, as whether to act this way or that. At such times, she showed extraordinary insight into my perplexity. After reflection, she would come out with 'Master must say no,' or something equally forthright, and I often felt that her judgement was sound. After years of her society, I came to regard her as a fund of good sense, who would know the answer to any general matter I might have put to her, or merely suggest in a roundabout way.

If I have had loyal foreign servants, I never had one so staunch or so shrewd as Teiko-San.

This growing habituation made me forget the language barrier altogether. I would talk to her in Japanese when I could; but anything complicated had to be in English, as was the case at somewhat higher levels. When I began learning *Kanji*, she was a great help to me. I found this work difficult, especially as I had to prepare for my lessons after a hard day's work. My teacher was Mr. Nakasato, who was an Embassy instructor of great ability, and he taught me as much I was capable of learning, given my late start and my manifold duties. From Teiko-San's competence, I perceived how thorough was the basis of Japanese school instruction, and what an enormous advantage to a country was a grounding in genuine literacy. I often wondered how many foreigners could rely on their servants to give an accurate account of their own language. She wrote the characters with exquisite neatness. She was likewise indispensable when it came to giving directions to taxi-drivers and others. A note would be written in a few seconds, sometimes accompanied by a sketch-map, and as a result I knew that I should reach my destination. In finding one's way about Tokyo, it was a question not so much of language as of geography. When I first arrived at the end of 1961, most streets had no names; and the numbering system of houses, though based upon a logic of its own, defeated most taxi-drivers.

Apart from her forebodings over the two strange letters I received, Teiko-San had a holy fear of doctors. Fortunately, this fear was rarely put to the test. She enjoyed excellent health, whereas Soma-San, who was over seventy, showed signs of ill-health, and had one bad attack of angina when he was with me. Once Teiko-San, to my surprise, said she was feeling 'a bit sick'; but, equally to my surprise, she was all smiles again an hour or so after. In my last year, however, she suffered acutely for a period from some form of fibrositis, which affected her legs. Could I get her to go to the doctor? No, I could not. Half-scared and half-amused, she would tell me that she could not endure the thought. On the other hand, like many other Japanese, she had great faith in medicines. And to my relief as much as to hers, the medicine—or perhaps just time—worked: Teiko-San was convinced it was the medicine.

I came to the conclusion that one of the reasons for Teiko-San's general equanimity, with these minor exceptions, was that she expected little from life. Her tastes were simple. She was accustomed to spend long hours by herself. She was never idle. Apart from the housework, there was mending to do, newspapers and magazines to read, and often a special task which required great concentration. Thus one day, shyly and proudly, she produced a beautiful doll which she had 'dressed' in the traditional costume. She must have spent hours on it. But dolls mean a great deal to the Japanese, and the making and dressing of them is not a juvenile occupation. So the time would be whiled away without her seeming to get bored, though during my vacations in England she often had no company but the dog. Once she went to her home near Sendai, but during my later leaves she insisted on staying in Tokyo. On her days 'off', she would usually go to an aunt who lived not far out of the city. She also had a brother who was training to be a doctor, and she would sometimes hear from him. But in the world's largest city, with all its amusements and distractions, she lived a calm, measured life, and she never seemed to fret or to crave variety. I think she was happiest in our house in Naka-Meguro, which was one of the quieter suburbs, though we suffered from the noise of a children's playground nearby—or at least I did; so that when my colleague John Mitchell left, I moved into the British Council house in Akasaka. This had the advantage of being within walking distance of the office; but the absolute quietness of the former house at night was exchanged for the noise, continuing up to the small hours, of guests issuing from nightclubs and from the geisha-houses which were just round the corner.

There were other disturbances. One day, while I was writing in my first-floor study in the Naka-Meguro house, Teiko-San came running up (a thing she rarely did), and confiding the word 'Fire!' in my ear, without panic but with great urgency, set about filling pails of water from every tap available. The nearby Meguro Primary School was ablaze, and the wind, veering in our direction, had borne aloft a shower of sparks and deposited them on our roof. A few more gusts and we should have been in as great a danger as the school, for both structures were of wood. Teiko-San, who, being Japanese, knew all about fire, resolutely tackled the flames, while Soma-San and I gathered all the containers we could. And then a remarkable thing happened. Almost as if from nowhere, a band of young neighbours none of whom I had ever seen before, gathered from all directions, with vessels of water. They scaled the walls, and, aided by Teiko-San from within, extinguished the flames in a matter of minutes. Then, just as swiftly, they disappeared. I never saw them again. What I had witnessed was an example of spontaneous mutual aid, or instinctive communal discipline.[1] From the *Yomiuri* newspaper the next day, 19 February 1963, I discovered that the fire had been the second largest in Tokyo since the war, and that forty-five fire-engines and seven ambulances had been on the scene. We had had a narrow escape. Other houses had been set ablaze, and their inhabitants had been obliged to evacuate them, rescuing such belongings as they could. Not long after, Teiko-San brought me a printed card, issued by the school, apologizing for the inconvenience caused me. She herself had regarded the incident as simply 'one of those things' that happen in Japan, like typhoons and earthquakes.

Indeed, we had our quota of typhoons and earthquakes, though the latter happened usually when I was at the office. The worst typhoon I recall started up on 24 September 1966. I was awakened at 3 a.m. by the sound of roaring wind and the crashing of metal. All the lights in the district were out. On my tiny transistor I listened, as if it were our only connection with the outside world, to the Far East network (the American Forces Radio) issuing regular bulletins. Soon Teiko-San appeared, perfectly calm as usual and armed with a torch, and quietly got out my mountaineering clothes. She had good reason to take precautions. The winds round about Fuji were reported to be 200 m.p.h., and we later ascertained that the typhoon had been the most violent since 1959. Gradually it subsided, until in the afternoon it was moaning vaguely and heaving great sighs in the distance, as if unsure which way to go. Whatever happened, I knew that Teiko-San would be equal to it. And her first thoughts were always for me.

It has been my happy lot, then, to live in the company, and under the care, of an 'oriental' for a period of six years, though interrupted by months in England and on tour in South-East Asia. For me it was a remarkable experience. I felt at the end that Teiko-San was one of the most congenial of my acquaintances, even though I did not claim to understand her as deeply as she, I sometimes felt, understood me. What her innermost thoughts were, I did not pretend to know. Some of my

[1] In fact, these young men were probably members of the local Fire Association, which provides training for just such emergencies.

friends told me that the Japanese 'secret' was that there was no secret at all. In other words, there were no 'innermost thoughts' to penetrate. To use one of Teiko-San's own favourite expressions—'I don't believe it.' I think Teiko-San, like her sister Japanese, had a very active and subtle brain indeed. On the other hand, I think her feelings were uncomplicated and therefore serene.

III

During my last year in Tokyo, my diary refers repeatedly to the sadness that began to overtake me as the breakup of our happy household approached. Its impending dissolution haunted me. I realized then, as I realize still more now, that without the 'home' that Teiko-San and Soma-San created for me, I could not have sustained the burden of my official duties. Whenever I left the office or some function, it was with a light heart that I turned my steps back to the house they kept so faithfully for me. Awaiting me, I knew there would be smiles and laughter and all the comforts I needed. Naturally, this regular routine of quiet contentment had its moments of different tempo; for, quite apart from the crises and a great deal of entertainment, we duly kept all the festivals, especially Christmas, which is now firmly entrenched in Japanese tradition. Then there would be present-giving, and decorations, always including a Christmas tree; and of all the gifts, those I received from my servants remain among the most precious to me. I still have the card accompanying one such gift, which was signed 'Soma, Teiko and Luke (dog)'. How they shared my excitement as I opened the elaborate parcel, entering into my enjoyment as much as they exclaimed in return over my own gifts to them! As for Teiko-San, she had a way of 'keening' her appreciation, in a manner quite her own. It would go on for minutes at a time.

When finally I told Teiko-San that I had to leave for good, she looked bewildered for a moment, and then said that perhaps 'the British Government' would change its mind. Some days later she came to me to say that she had decided to give up service after I had gone, and to leave for home. Soma-San also thought he would probably retire. Within a few months of my leaving Japan, he was dead. My departure from the house at Shoto was fortunately swift and businesslike. From that time to this, I have never heard from Teiko-San. Somehow that, too, was part of the understanding between us.

CHAPTER III

In and Around Tokyo

I

Once my heavy luggage had arrived, and I had established myself in good accommodation, I decided to explore Tokyo. This I did by using transport from Azabu to the office, by going for walks with Luke, and by venturing farther afield as when I went to the Kodokan for judo classes. In the No. 7 tram which I took to Yotsuya san-chome, I enjoyed examining the variety of Japanese and Western costumes, though the latter predominated. I was curious to understand the 'running commentary' of the conductor, as he prepared us for a particular bend or lurch; and gradually I came to piece together what he was saying. Nothing is quite so elaborate or amusing as these street-travelogues which, in country districts, can include the rendering of local songs. I grew accustomed to the 'vertical' character of much Japanese life: the neon signs that ran up and down instead of horizontally; the sub-titles of foreign films that trickled down the sides of the screen; the predominance of poles and staffs, shooting aloft, and the balloons from which advertisements were suspended. All this involved a new adjustment of the eye. The hand, too, had to adjust itself. Knobs and handles placed nearer the edge of the doors than in Europe or America took the skin off my fist during the first few weeks; and low wooden beams supporting the ceiling in Japanese-style rooms would be the cause of unexpected blows of stunning effect.

Luke used to tug so vigorously at the leash that I was obliged to go at twice my normal pace; but the best exercise I took was at the Kodokan, which I first visited in the company of my friend John Hanson-Lowe, holder of a black-belt. He was a retired officer of Shell and had knocked about the world a good deal before settling in Japan. He seemed to have known everyone, from Teilhard de Chardin to the latest Japanese novelist. The Kodokan, founded by Kano Jigoro in 1882, whose statue stands outside, was a large building in which classes in judo at every level were held, with a small section for foreign aspirants. After the exhausting formalities of diplomatic entertainment, it was invigorating to change into the stout but loose off-white garments, or *judoji*, and to practise the standard 'throws' on the mat.

After the first exercises, I was stiffer than if I had climbed a high mountain at speed. My difficulty was to find time for regular practice, as the journey from the office proved such a long one, and rush-hour at that pre-Olympic period was a nightmare. Without regular and unremitting practice, there was no hope of winning the black-belt to which I at one time aspired. Occasionally I would find an odd man out similar in standard to myself and we would spend a useful evening perfecting various movements. At other times I would have to be content with watching the experts. On 14 January 1962, I attended my first *Kagami-biraki*, a kind of New Year inauguration, though not confined to the world of judo. A large audience gathered in the main hall, most of them sitting in the traditional fashion. After an opening address, a series of demonstrations took place. I was impressed above all by the performance of the older men. Their bodies had been trained over the years to move with the resilience of lynxes. One particular demonstration consisted in going through the most complicated throws and falls without a single bodily contact. Never had I seen such a 'ballet' performed by men of advanced age. Then followed a demonstration of women's judo, which was as graceful in its way as women's Japanese. Finally, there came a demonstration of 'utilitarian' judo, in which men were rapidly disarmed of guns and knives, even when approaching from behind. One of the most able foreign judoists, Don Draeger, whom I met in Hanson-Lowe's company, took part in this display. He must be among the few non-Japanese practitioners to understand judo as a 'way of life', which is how, like all the Japanese martial arts, it should properly be regarded.

I wondered often how much damage would be done if the judo technique were used in a 'real life' emergency. The impact of a fall on the *tatami* was always cushioned by a well-timed thump with the wrist and palms, whereas a similar fall on a pavement could be crippling. Of recent years, judo clubs have sprung up over all the world, particularly in Britain, so that its mysteries have been somewhat diminished. Even so, the background to the 'art' may tend to be forgotten. The *Kagami-biraki* ceremony ended with a huge meal of rice, Japan's sacred food. *Kagami* means 'mirror', which the large round cakes, eaten first, are thought to resemble. This symbolized the fact that judo, like the other arts, was part of Japan's sacred heritage. For this reason, the failure of Japan to gain the world championship of judo proved no little shock to the nation. It was as if, at some international drama competition, the prize for the best Noh play were to go to a European country.

As regular practice at the Kodokan proved difficult, I decided to put myself under a private teacher instead; and it was through Hanson-Lowe that I was introduced in March 1962 to the famous Dr. Takamura. He had a judo studio attached to his medical consulting room, and there I used to go for my lessons. He put me thoroughly through my paces. His criticism of my technique was that I tended to be too violent, especially when he allowed me to 'throw' him; I soon came to see that the essence of good judo was a rhythmic lightness of action which came only through patient repetition of the simpler movements. Muscular force was not enough. Dr. Takamura was an admirable and sympathetic teacher, and I was grateful to him for instructing me, often at short notice and between the calls of his profession. Much to my regret, however, I found that official duties became so pressing that I was unable to see him regularly, and finally I had to abandon the lessons altogether, though I tried to continue practising on my own. I regretted this abandonment very much, because I realized that I was missing a useful means of keeping in touch with an important aspect of Japanese life, and of following one of the famous disciplines.

About this time I used to walk a great deal, partly for exercise, and partly in order to acquire the 'feel' of Tokyo. Sometimes these walks were hazardous. Many streets lacked proper pavements, or the latter had disintegrated, whereas the volume of traffic had increased. With the Olympic Games in mind the Metropolitan Government realized that a new road system was necessary and soon works on a gigantic scale were initiated, which made the pedestrian's lot even more uncomfortable. One consequence of this huge upheaval was the difficulty of knowing one's precise location. In desperation, I would resort to a taxi. In those days, taxis were both numerous and cheap; and difficulties of communication, which could be exasperating at times of hurry, were compensated for by the extreme politeness of most of the drivers. At the beginning of a journey, a box of matches would be presented to the passenger, and at the end any change would be handed back on a decorated plate. The refusal to take tips was most satisfying. Not long before, the Taxi Association had passed a resolution condemning the practice of tipping as undignified. The same applied in many other walks of life. Thus one of the curses of the Western world was almost entirely unknown in Japan.

II

Picking one's way through piles of masonry and rubble, or diving under scaffolding, or avoiding puddles, could become wearisome, though, for some reason, Tokyo 'pavements' never seemed so hard as those of London or New York. If I were in the Ginza district, the so-called Piccadilly of Tokyo, once the centre of the guild of silversmiths (*gin* means silver), I would drop in one of the cafés which featured classical music. These institutions possessed great charm. They consisted usually of two storeys, plus a gallery; and with their well-upholstered seats, they were most comfortable and soothing to the spirit. The lighting was subdued, though as a rule good enough to read by, and the music was moderate in pitch. There were numerous petite waitresses. The clients were for the most part young. Undoubtedly this was the kind of place where friendships were initiated not merely among customers, but between customers and the staff. In the latter case, a proper ritual had to be observed, involving an intermediary through whom an assignation would be fixed. The girls had a talent for standing demurely in parts of the café where they could best be observed, without appearing to attract attention. They nearly all had good figures, and their small stature was compensated for by high-piled hair and chignons. (The modern Japanese girl has a more robust physique than her pre-war sister, but the larger ones were rarely to be found here.) What struck me most about these congenial places was the decorous behaviour of the young people. Hardly out of the boy and girl stage, couples would sit down quietly together, order simple refreshments, and then 'commune' with each other not by speech but through the music. Hands would be held, or sometimes the girl would rest her head on the boy's shoulder, but there was little overt flirting. Meanwhile, they both listened as if intoxicated.

At the beginning of my stay in Tokyo, I spent much time in such cafés. The one I favoured most was the 'Ambre', just off the Ginza. I rarely took anyone there; it suited me to be alone, as I could rest or think more easily. There were other single people, often girls, who, like me, would spend the time reading. The Japanese seem to read books in public more than others; I noticed on my daily tram-ride that a book was often preferred to a newspaper. Not all the frequenters of the café were young by any means. Never shall I forget an elderly man who would sit invariably in the same place, with a score on the table in front of him, conducting with immense vigour the piece being rendered. Like the young people around him, he was lost in his concentration on the music and he would smile with great satisfaction when a favourite passage arrived. Despite his liberal gestures, he interfered with no one, and he must have spent hours of happiness in this regular occupation. How he obtained his supply of scores, I have no idea. I do not suppose he consumed more than a single cup of coffee during any particular session. That was another advantage of the café life of Japan. The client was not badgered to have more than he wanted. In any case, most students could afford only a very small outlay.

When I emerged from the 'Ambre', the Ginza lights were usually coming on; and as darkness fell, the rather nondescript streets assumed a totally different character. A surge of life seemed to roll through the district. The number of bars in the Ginza alone must run into hundreds, and new ones are continually being opened. There are streets which seem to contain nothing but bars, each one with its neon sign, often richly coloured, and its exotic name. The other great bar centres are Ueno, Shinjuku, Akasaka and Shibuya. All these districts I visited, especially in my early years.

Many books on Japan go into great detail about the life of bar-girls. This is understandable, because the bar world of Japan differs from that of any other. Nowhere else is entertainment organized on such a scale. Like everything in Japan, however, it had undergone great changes, at least on the surface, especially since the Olympic Games; and, judging from what I had read, it had changed a good deal in the years prior to my arrival. Granted, I may have seen only certain aspects of a rather complicated system; but it was certainly not my impression that the majority of bar-girls were disguised prostitutes, as is often suggested. That some of them made assignations or went on the streets after closing-time, I do not doubt; but, if so, they must have been pretty discreet, as the anti-prostitution laws were strictly enforced, at least in Tokyo. Yet I heard that most bar-girls would agree, if the subject were raised with discretion, to sell their favours. On the other hand, I am sure that many of them had their patrons. The 'system' would otherwise have been unworkable.

My impression is that the average Japanese girl of the entertainment world is an industrious, agreeable creature who, when her work is over, desires nothing more than to have a good rest. This observation is based on my pre-Olympic experience, when I wandered round the town more than in the period after 1964. In those early days, many bars would stay open as long as the clients wished to continue drinking. True, the door might be closed, but life would go on just the same inside. At the time of the Olympic Games there was a general tightening-up of regulations and few bars were permitted to remain open after 11 o'clock. Night life was thereafter confined to little 'pockets', especially in the sprawling district of Shinjuku, and the expensive night-club and geisha-house area of Akasaka; and so it has remained.

Some bars are reserved for 'Japanese only'. If so, the foreigner is soon made aware of the fact. I committed the mistake of entering such places only once or twice, but in each case I was turned away with extreme politeness. I do not know what distinguishes a 'Japanese only' bar from another; but I never felt any particular sense of discrimination. Nor can I see why the inhabitants of a country should not be allowed to meet freely among themselves if they wish to, though in some countries the practice would be condemned as 'racist'. In all other places, the welcome was open and friendly. Some of my most pleasant hours were spent practising Japanese with bar-girls, though I had to fit in these visits at week-ends, and in my last years I was so busy that such moments were very rare. Once or twice in my first year, when my circle of friends was limited, the cost of living reasonable, and my energy abundant, I would make a night of it. One such occasion, I recall, was during the first hot, enervating summer. Feeling that sleep would have been impossible in any case, I sat drinking beer with an agreeable companion in a bar overlooking a canal. This sounds a trifle vague, but to this day I do not know where it was.

Judging from the time it took me to get home by taxi in the early hours, I fancy I had landed up in Asakusa, the old Yoshiwara or 'pleasure' district, now on the whole respectable. A benevolent Mama-San stood behind the counter, and we all communicated in a mixture of English and Japanese. The sound of laughter nearby showed that we were not alone in our conviviality, though the enormous stretch of Tokyo was subdued, as if dazed by the extreme humidity. One by one the clients left, freeing other girls, who moved in to attend the unusual guest. At such times, the custom is for all the girls to be treated. Happily, these were content with a fruit-juice, whereas in cabarets—places I quickly learnt to avoid—the bill would have run up sharply. We chatted on, and perhaps we dozed a little; I remember that Mama-San had no wish to see me leave, so long as I was content to stay, and an unfinished bottle remained on the table. At one point, when I glanced up, I noticed a strange alteration in the view framed by the windows. The darkness had fallen away, as if a curtain had dropped. What had happened? Was it one of Tokyo's fires? No, it was the dawn. When I got up to go, we kissed all round in the unaffected way which was customary on such occasions, for we were by now old friends. *Mata dozo* ('Come back again') was repeated almost with emotion. Stepping out, I remember feeling both exhilarated and refreshed. I had never encountered people quite so entertaining, so different from the rapacious harpies that await the visitor in American bars and burlesque shows. At such moments I felt again that the Japanese were somehow a race apart.

It must not be thought that the entertainment world of Japan is run by a group of philanthropists, aided by hundreds of delightful creatures who radiate goodwill and affection alike upon the tired Japanese male and the wistful foreigner. Behind the façade, there is often gangsterism, protection-rackets, extortion, and certainly vice; but it is difficult to know how far these evils have acquired a grip on the industry as a whole. With regard to vice, I used to hear a great many lurid details, often from foreign women, who had been 'told' about the things that 'went on', not only in bars but in geisha and bath-houses. Although I have no doubt that some of these reports were true, I considered that many of them were exaggerated; but the obsession with them tended to confirm my view, expounded in the first chapter, that some foreign women felt a morbid envy of a way of life in which extreme femininity and a remarkable degree of power were combined. If much of the entertainment world in Japan is controlled by gangsters, it is done with considerable finesse; I certainly felt safer wandering about Tokyo than about some American cities. An exception should perhaps be made of certain parts of Shinjuku; but in all my years on my own in Tokyo and other cities I never ran into any unpleasantness, racketeering, or violence. I once complained about what I considered to be overcharging, but this was naive of me; the entertainment world is expensive, unless one becomes a habitué, when special arrangements can be made. I never had the time for that.

Readers of such works as *Bachelor's Japan* by the irrepressible Boye De Mente, and, worse still, *Tokyo by Night*, by another American 'expert', will smile at some of the opinions I have just voiced. Discovering that I was single, a well-meaning businessman presented me with a copy of the former handbook soon after my arrival, as if to suggest that it were an indispensable work of reference. Like the other and more lurid book, it seems to me to be a typical product of American puritanism *à rebours*; and like all forms of puritanism which are bound up with prurience, I found it offensive. There is the assumption that every Japanese woman has her price, and that the entertainment world in particular is geared to the provision of nothing but sensual gratification. Yet if you read carefully between the lines, you realize that this is by no means the case. Except for those whose profession is straightforward prostitution, the Japanese girl would seem to be a good deal less compliant than some of the Anglo-Saxon creatures whom De Mente berates for their timorous attitude to experience. This contention is confirmed by some works by Japanese themselves. The director of the famous bookstore, Kinokuniya, Mr. Tanabe Moichi, sent me a copy of his curious book *Mayor of the Night*, a kind of autobiography of a ladies' man such as could only appear in Japan. It consisted of account after account of intrigues with women; but what struck me most forcibly was the frequency with which this expert met his match. Contrary to the view of some of my friends and to the accounts written by certain enthusiastic visitors to Japan, I ascribe the attraction of the Japanese entertainment world to the fact that it has a light, gossamer beauty which, if disturbed, would instantly disintegrate. I found it to be the least vicious of anything of its kind anywhere. Naturally, I speak of the general run of entertainment, especially the sort provided in the interval between finishing work and going home to dinner, when a man needs to unwind. Again and again, when I was on my walks or travelling from one engagement to another, I was impressed by the prevailing atmosphere of lightheartedness. This was the case especially when, in the hotter months, the windows of the restaurants and *sushi* bars stood open, and the pungent smell of cooking and the sound of merry chatter invaded the streets, while crates of empty bottles, stacked outside doorways and in passages leading to a warren of bars, testified to the enormous consumption of beverages.

I dissent from the view, expounded by D. J. Enright in his interesting book *The World of Dew*, that an enormous 'trade in flesh' goes on in Japan. At many large functions, hundreds of bar-girls are engaged to act as waitresses or hostesses, and such occasions are rendered colourful and gay by reason of their presence. It is inconceivable that the majority of these girls are prostitutes in disguise. If so, they were not merely on their best behaviour, but losing an opportunity to further their professional interests. On several such occasions, I was invited to the bar at which they worked, and if I followed up the invitation they seemed unaffectedly delighted. For these attractive young creatures had been trained for years to make themselves pleasant to men. Nor does such pleasantry consist in making heavy conversation. They were functionaries in the enormous and complicated organization whereby work in Japan is balanced by diversion. If the entertainment industry were to be cut down or abolished, the effect might even be psychologically harmful. I believe that, in this sphere, the Japanese have worked out, and maintained, a 'norm' of living which other countries are the poorer for being without. The nearest approach to the Japanese hostesses are the kitsoeng in Korea. They too can be delightful companions for an evening party, though their training is more like that of geisha.

III

Some of the most enjoyable evenings I spent in Tokyo were at a hall called the Shichi-go-san (literally 'Seven-five-three'). Here was true *family* entertainment. The hall must have accommodated several hundred people. They sat on the floor in long rows, eating and drinking at lacquered tables. At the far end of the hall was a large stage, where an orchestra played throughout the evening with tremendous gusto, varied with acts such as solo-singing, acrobatics or juggling. Among the relaxed crowd moved friendly waitresses, bringing dishes, replenishing glasses, and engaging in the *badinage* at which the Japanese servant is so adept. At times the noise of music and chatter was deafening; I cannot imagine how much *sake* and beer was consumed. But whether it was due to the presence of wives, or to the excellent but unobtrusive discipline of the management (one of whom, a most charming lady, was a drummer), the company was among the most orderly I have seen.

To geisha I have alluded, and I must rebut from the start the view that these highly trained entertainers are nothing but expensive *cocottes*. Fortunately, this impression is not so current as it used to be, but it persists. I will not go into details here about the training of these remarkable girls, because I deal with this in the chapter on Kyoto. One of the most interesting aspects of geisha life is that, as so often in Japan, age has its own consolations. To this the foreigner takes time to become accustomed, as a geisha past the junior stage need not necessarily be beautiful in the conventional sense; but she must retain her deportment and her wit, which time will usually have sharpened.

By good fortune, early in my stay I made acquaintance with one of the most cultivated of Japanese who, by reason of his birth, enjoyed access to some of the most exclusive geisha-houses; for such places are debarred save to those of a certain status, and it is idle to pretend otherwise. Apart from that, he was one of the best English speakers I met in Japan. The result was that I came as near to understanding what was going on in the geisha-houses we visited as the outsider may hope to do; for my friend took great pleasure in conveying to me his own enjoyment, which I trust was increased by being shared.

Just as I shall suppress the identity of my friend, so I will conceal the whereabouts of our favourite geisha-house; I record merely that it was one of several standing beside the Sumida River. An expert on *sake*, my friend insisted always on bringing his own variety, though there was more than one occasion when, running out of this most gentle of wines, we were obliged to resort to the house's supply. I used to worry at the little he ate during some of those evenings (which, needless to say, were well spaced throughout the year, as we were both very busy), whereas I was only too glad when the large plates of *sushi* were brought in.

As a rule, we were entertained by three geisha, two of a 'certain age' whom my friend had known for a long time, and one a good deal younger, who used to serve me. The elder ones wielded the authority, but all three got on as excellently with one another as they did with us. The younger one, whom I will call Michiko-San, was by contrast to many geisha a girl of some stature and of almost ethereal beauty. She knew almost no English; but apart from what I could convey to her and what my friend supplemented, she was an expert at communication by look, turn of head and gesture. As the evening wore on, I would forget that we were talking another language.

Apart from the conversation and the repartee, what used to fascinate me, until it became almost a haunting, was the unforgettable atmosphere of the place. The room in which we sat was small, though the *tokonoma* was graced by a *kakemono* of considerable value. In the summer months, the *shoji* on the riverside balcony were drawn back, and we had a view of the river and the winking lights far opposite. Sometimes I would adjourn to this little verandah and survey the calm scene. Down below was a small wooden jetty, from which in the old days parties could set off on an evening's excursion, but this kind of life had not survived the war. True, the river was polluted; but at the height of the balcony this was not particularly noticeable. On either side of me, the hesitant sound of the *koto* could be heard, and laughter and the clink of glasses. I would suddenly have the feeling, which was repeated in other parts of Japan, that such diversion was one aspect of the good life, and that our existence needed to be lightened periodically by enjoyment of this kind, which was the keener for being the most part concerned with the surface of experience. 'Gently dip but not too deep': Eliot's quotation in the short poem 'Usk' conveys exactly the right mood. In more rampant pleasures, the waters can so easily be muddied.

My friend would sometimes twit me about my affection for Michiko-San, and it is true that if she had not appeared (but she always did), I should have been disappointed. It is also true that part of my attachment, unless I were misled, was due to her 'inaccessibility'. She was like a lovely spirit who would appear and disappear in my crowded, somewhat tense, life. She, for her part, may have found my own quiet mood easier to tolerate than an alien thrustfulness. No doubt Michiko-San, like some of her kind, had a protector. At least, I was sure she would soon either acquire one or marry. These were private matters which I made no attempt to plumb. In any case, a sheath of mystery envelops the world of geisha, and the Japanese prefer it that way. All I know is that Michiko-San was the reverse of the easy woman. If anyone, including a Japanese, had become deeply fond of her, he would no doubt have been obliged to woo her with the same assiduity as any other member of her sex. Indeed, I doubt whether a foreigner, unless he had a good deal of time to spare and was well versed in Japanese customs, would have had much chance of winning her affections, quite apart from the problem of securing her release from her closely integrated profession.

As I had a long way to go home, I would often leave the geisha-house before my friend; and here again Japanese efficiency was brought into play. A comfortable car was always waiting at the door, supplied by the establishment and included in its charges. Michiko-San would come with me as far as the house where she slept. In the dimly lit street, I could never quite make out what sort of place this was. With a smile, she would vanish into her remote world. I fancy she was soon sound asleep on her *futon*. Indeed, she must have led a quiet, sober life, or never could she have appeared looking so healthy, serene and graceful as she invariably did.

On such nights, it was pleasant to be wafted home, in an 'executive' car with white covers on the seats, gliding through a somnolent Tokyo. Next morning, unless the *sake* had been too liberally taken, I would feel in better spirits than usual. On my way to work it used to amuse me to see the same kind of 'executive' cars passing in the reverse direction, with their wealthy and usually elderly passengers reclining half asleep, and sometimes wholly asleep, amid the recesses of the upholstery; for the Japanese have an excellent habit of taking rest when they can, and of using the drive to work as the last opportunity of making up for the exertions or dissipations of the previous evening.

In due course, I had glimpses of the geisha world, or rather small corners of it, throughout the length and breadth of Japan; but never did I see it at such close quarters as in that mysterious house by the Sumida River. There are geisha at Wakkani on the extreme north of Hokkaido, and there are geisha in the very different atmosphere of the southernmost island of Kyushu. There are geisha who perform what I can call Instant Tea Ceremony at Gion Corner at Kyoto; but this tourist attraction is really a travesty, like some other tourist exhibitions from which the spirit seems to be entirely absent. I shall have more to say on this subject. There are other professional entertainers, modelled on geisha and much less expensive to engage, which may in due course take the place of the traditional kind. Nevertheless, the geisha world still has its enthusiastic patrons in Japan, though chiefly among the older generation.

IV

It is by no means true, however, that men past the prime of life dote pathetically on the young. On the contrary, as I have said, the respect due to age extends to the geisha of advancing years. When I was in Osaka in 1962 with one of my London colleagues and his wife, we were taken to a restaurant by a gentleman of the old school who had engaged an elderly geisha for the evening. It was a memorable occasion, because this striking lady, though gaunt and lined, kept us spellbound by the impact of her personality, even though her sprightly conversation had to be para-phrased in a manner which must have deprived it of half its force. When we left, my colleague was profuse in his thanks to our host for introducing us to this mature lady. We toured the Kansai for several days, and on return to Osaka we happened to meet our friend again. He begged to be allowed to invite us out for another evening. Unfortunately, as we were leaving for Tokyo that same day, we were unable to accept. Greatly disappointed, our friend threw in all his inducements to prevail upon us to stay, adding to me *sotto voce*, and behind his hand as if to convey a more doubtful proposition: 'I have a wonderful *old* geisha.'

If I have spoken of the pleasures of Japanese leisure-time as being superior in quality to that elsewhere, it must be remembered that the lands of the Far East and South-East Asia are mostly too poor for the masses to have any comparable pleasures at all. The comparison, here as so often elsewhere, must be with the West. I suspect that what is sordid in the Japanese entertainment world is mostly due to Western importation. I have a strong dislike of strip-tease. The seedy little places where this sort of entertainment is given are not among the pleasanter haunts of Japanese towns; but owing to its vogue in the West, the Japanese feel they must follow suit. In Amano-Hashidate once, Francis King and I dropped into one of these places, and the view of the slight little bodies of the performers, mechanically removing their coverings, induced in me such a combination of pity and revulsion that I suggested that we should leave, which we did.

The example I give shows how the Japanese remain acutely aware of foreign influence and opinion, and how ready they are to assimilate such influence. Dating probably from the time when they first sent cultural missions to China, this tendency has given rise to the view that the Japanese are no more than clever imitators. I do not believe this to be true. Their genius consists, it seems to me, in making something of their own out of what may start out as thoroughly alien. Extreme sensitivity to foreign opinion can, however, sometimes lead to strange results. Among the vast preparations for the Olympic Games, there were a number of small touches which revealed the national character better than the major ones. In the Hanzomon district, not far from the British Embassy, there are two groups of statuary, one of three nude girls and the other of three nude youths. They are presumably meant to symbolize Youth, though carefully segregated. Shortly before the start of the Games, these inoffensive, and indeed slightly sexless, groups were carefully wrapped round with straw so that they came to resemble the trees which the Japanese upholster against the rigours of winter. I was told that this was in order not to offend foreign susceptibilities. I do not know of any country which would have displayed such solicitude.

V

Now I come to the Games themselves and the not inconsiderable part they played in rehabilitating the national morale. For a year or two Tokyo had been thrown into something like disarray, while the road drill shivered frantically through cement and cobblestones, and the thick steel articulations of concrete structures began to sprout. For months the disorder was such that, but for faith in the Japanese capacity to perform technological miracles, the inhabitants of Tokyo must have felt that the city would never be ready in time. A new road to Haneda airport was in construction, and beside it a monorail system. Gradually it became clear that by a clever weaving of overpasses and underpasses the traffic of the world's largest city would be able to run without the maddening delays which had become our daily experience. Meanwhile, in the Yoyogi district and in Kanda, some remarkable architectural structures began to emerge with almost biological inevitability. These were the athletic halls designed by Tange Kenzo. Finally, Tokyo was provided with several giant new hotels, inaugurated with great pomp, which put her among the best accommodated of capitals.

During 1964 Japan herself went on exhibition. One of the largest exhibitions of Japanese art treasures ever to be assembled was organized at the National Museum. Some remarkable publications appeared, under which head could be classed short guide-books to Japan, with all sorts of information thought to be of use to the foreigner, many written in 'Japanese English'. The clean-up of night spots went forward, which, if in some cases overdue, was in other cases overscrupulous; and special precautions were taken that the visitor should not be cheated. This latter measure proved largely successful; those who found themselves rooked were usually looking for something which would have been costly in any market. Finally, the Tokyo Metropolitan Government enlisted a host of interpreters and guides; and it was my constant worry that my staff, given its linguistic competence and charm, would be depleted. By good fortune, however, no one was beguiled by the attractive offers made on every hand.

The impact of the Games was felt throughout Japan. Officials were nervously anxious that such an international event should show above all else Japan's new dedication to the arts of peace. There was also a feeling, almost amounting to an obsession, that everything, from the organization of the athletic events to the welfare of the participants, should be conducted with unexampled efficiency. All these aspirations were realized. It was generally agreed that the organization of the Games was superb. Moreover, contrary to the forebodings of some pessimists, mostly foreigners, everything was ready on the dot.

I have certain recollections of the Games which form part of my abiding impressions of Japan. There was the sudden presence of fair-haired people. There was the meeting with friends, or friends of friends, among the British contingent; and entertaining our rowing team under Dr. Ray Owen. There was Dick Ellingworth, our Embassy representative, in a most becoming uniform. There were the pre-Olympic festivities at the Korakuen Football Ground. These included a performance by a girl's band, with majorettes in the American style for which, in my view, the Japanese female figure was unfitted; ladder-gymnastics by the 'Members of the Traditional Firemen's League of Tokyo'; music and dances by the 'Hayashi Music Preservation Societies'; and, more intriguing still, a 'Display of the Traditional Festive Mood through Carrying about a Tabernacle by Certain Folks of the Torigoe District, Taito Ward, Tokyo'—all of which were most entertaining.

Although there had been deluges of rain a few days earlier, the formal opening of the Olympics on Saturday October 10th, took place in almost perfect weather. In a stadium packed with 70,000 people, the teams paraded before the Emperor, in alphabetical order. I could not help being moved by the sight of the Commonwealth teams, most of whom carried Union Jacks. Many Japanese and foreigners were surprised to see that flag borne by teams which they had not realized to be British, so vague were their general notions about the Commonwealth. Some of the Communist teams, out to impress, produced little Japanese flags and waved them frantically at the assembly; I did not feel that this overdone gesture went down at all well. The Emperor's voice opening the Games came over clearly. Hundreds of balloons were released, which congregated in the air like bags of coloured sweets. Eight thousand pigeons were unboxed, and vanished in an inkling. The ceremony concluded with fireworks.

The Games came to an end with a magnificent ceremony on Saturday October 23rd. Admittedly, the final crowding of the athletes on to the field, with some exhibitionist clowning (chiefly by those who had not distinguished themselves), was something of an anticlimax. By contrast, the Japanese team maintained perfect order. To the singing of 'Auld Lang Syne', the Olympic fire was extinguished, and the Olympic March, by then so familiar, was played for the last time. That evening I wandered around Tokyo, as did so many others, and lingered in some of the places to which I had become attached. Here the minutiae of Japanese organization were again in evidence. The organizers had dispatched guides and interpreters throughout the city to lend help to visitors who were lost or otherwise in difficulties. Seeing me standing apparently in deep thought, one young man came up to me and offered his assistance. He was surprised and puzzled when I told him in Japanese that I wanted to stay where I was. At any rate, he seemed very uncertain whether I really meant what I said; but ascertaining that I was English and presumably attributing my conduct to mild eccentricity, he finally made off.

Although my life was busier after the Games and continued to increase in tempo, I soon became aware that I was living in a 'New' Japan. The country had taken a psychological leap forward, and only living through such a change in attitude convinced one that it could occur. Thereafter the people went ahead with the feeling that they had earned their passage, and from that time they did not look back. I have visited many countries of South-East Asia, and I am deeply attached to several of them; but I returned to Japan always with relief and with that sense of security much reinforced now that the people had this sense of confidence. I watched the growth of affluence, and observed at first hand, by visiting plants and factories, how much hard work the Japanese had done to deserve their commanding position. In terms of Gross National Product, this was soon third after the United States and Russia. The sense of achievement communicated itself to the man in the street; and, as I have argued, I believe that this exhilaration, though apparently material-istic, was responsible for a distinct and salutary shift in the attitude of the ordinary citizen to his own past. Now the average Japanese could look back, not with guilt and horror, but with pride that his four little islands had come to mean so much to the world.

VI

How many people came to see me in my Tokyo offices, I would not like to reckon. I had a very full engagement book. The Japanese pay calls out of politeness, and they know how long to stay, which, fortunately for those who have a load of office work to discharge, is not too long. And much effort is saved by their habit, now increasing in the West, of presenting cards, usually with Japanese on one side and English on the other, and frequently carrying a potted biography. One is thereby saved the agony of groping around for clues as to the visitor's background and rank. On tendering one's own card in return, there was usually a hiss of acknowledgement, and a rigid gesture as the card was held up for respectful scrutiny. Then the business could begin. As I have said, too much is made of the necessity for a preliminary exchange of commonplaces: this takes place less in conversation than in letters, where the hope is expressed at the start that one is in good health, and at the end that one will 'take it easy'. Perhaps the Americans have been responsible for this cutting down of formalities.

Into my office came many non-Japanese. These were often compatriots seeking employment, and others who had mistaken us for the British Consulate. Sometimes these people took their time, and mine. Then there were people whose nationality it was difficult to determine, and about whose sanity one sometimes had one's doubts. One visitor, however, I shall not easily forget. He was a short, bearded young man, a painter, who spoke excellent English. He wanted me to arrange an exhibition of his pictures; and although I explained that we only sponsored British displays, he would not take No for an answer, though in the most charming way. He called more than once, evidently hoping that I would change my mind, and he always left without resentment. The next I heard of him, several years later, was that he had tried to kill the Pope. He was Benjamin Mendoza Y. Amor of Bolivia. A gentler man it would have been difficult to find, seemingly incapable of wishing to hurt a fly, let alone the Supreme Pontiff. Yet, on his arrest in Manila, he stated that he had harboured this particular design 'for a long time'. I still find this hard to believe.

Of Japanese visitors, none was more remarkable than the man whose sudden display of violence, though directed against himself, shocked and puzzled the world. This was Mishima Yukio. Having long admired his work, I arranged to send him to England as a guest of the British Council. On the occasions when I saw him at my office or at his Omari home (a most un-Japanese-like place), he was the soul of politeness—quiet, modest, and of singular charm. Of his literary gifts I think there is no doubt. He was married with children, and it seemed that he had everything—happiness, wealth, reputation, and the prospect of still greater fame—that he could desire. But there was another side to him. As well as being homosexual, he was addicted to curious sado-masochistic practices or fantasies, which he did not attempt to conceal; for he went to the trouble of having himself photographed in poses which might have been 'gifts' for the clinical psychiatrist. Some photographs published after his death, together with the body-building pictures in his book *The Young Samurai*, have an underlying unpleasantness about them which I find hard to associate with the man I knew, except that some of his books, *Forbidden Colours* and *Confessions of a Mask* for example, are sordid in the extreme, with hardly a character who is not in some way repulsive. In a most revealing interview he gave to the *Figaro Littéraire* in 1966 (published in December 1970, after his death), he said that he was descended from both peasants and samurai, which may explain both his industry and his taste for heroism; and in reply to a question about homosexuality, he said that the practice in Japan was more ancient and natural than love between the sexes, but that—surely an exaggeration—this tradition had been 'interrupted' by American missionaries in the nineteenth century. At the same time, he said he remained faithful to his wife, a lady, as I recall, of great charm. He declared that he admired suicide, though he was afraid of death, and wished for a quiet one, if only to spare the feelings of others. This rather suggests that, towards the end, the complexities of his character produced a disturbed mental condition.

It is maintained that Mishima wished to revive the virtues of the Old Japan, and I do not say for a moment that his patriotism and devotion to the Emperor were insincere; but they also provided the means, it seems to me, whereby his sexual aberrations were permitted outlet. He often spoke of *seppuku* or *hara-kiri* as the supreme act of heroism, and his story *Patriotism*, is a noble and moving study on that theme; but if one views that last desperate act in association with his consenting to be tied up and stuck with arrows like St. Sebastian, and to be photographed in that posture, one tends to conclude that the climax was involved with a form of sexual 'expression' to which he was all along preparing himself. His conduct had a macabre logic about it; and we knew from the letters that he wrote to friends that he was moving towards a spectacular *dénouement*. Others, who knew him much better than I, may throw more light on this ghastly consummation. So far as I was concerned, he was a polite and punctilious gentleman. The last I saw of him was when he turned up at my farewell party.

VII

Apart from those made in the course of duty, encounters would take place at the oddest times and places. I was once strolling through Shimbashi, when I passed what seemed to be an ordinary chemist's shop. An elderly man behind the counter beckoned to me with a look compounded of furtiveness and amusement. Curiosity overcoming me, I stepped in. From a drawer beneath the counter, he produced a variety of rubber contraptions the like of which I had neither seen nor, in most cases, heard of. What the vendor chiefly pressed on my attention were aids specially designed for men of failing powers, in which Japanese ingenuity had reached a high degree of perfection. That he should have thought me to belong to this category somewhat abashed me, as I tried to convey my embarrassment; but this he took for foreign prudery and tried all the more to persuade me to make a purchase. I had difficulty in retiring with dignity, especially as he kept producing even more ingenious gadgets for my inspection, complete with detailed explanations as to their use.

A good deal has been written about this particular industry in Japan, and I have known professional 'mystics' who, in search of fresh sensations, have visited the country in search of just such articles. I doubt if they are in common use, though there is a long tradition in Japan, as in India, of associating certain aspects of religious belief with the erotic. I suspect that they go to make a good export trade. As to certain Japanese prints which some Westerners seek out, I was told by a man who knew what he was talking about, that these were not intended to be pornographic in the strict sense. In the days before there was any formal sexual instruction, or a readily available literature, they were primarily of educational interest. Mothers were in the habit of using them for the initiation of their daughters into the art of love-making. There *is* a pornographic industry in Japan, and there was such an industry long before the Western nations went in for it on the present scale themselves; but this again was directed chiefly at the export market.

A man on his own in a large city is an obvious target for the tout, the pimp, and the con-man. I was sometimes invited to visit establishments which, judging from the lurid descriptions given, were obviously the resort of hard-drug addicts; but it was a trifle sad to be offered girl students, though this happened to me more than once. A foreigner presumed to be English or American would be certain at one time or another to be offered boys: my revulsion often occasioned the go-between no little surprise, for he would hint at a flourishing business among the foreign community. Although prostitution was illegal, girls would accost one especially late at night, but sometimes also in daytime. Some of these young things had a sweet, almost childlike, approach, and they would accept a refusal with both politeness and grace. Some writers in Japan have described the *pam-pam*, as these girls are sometimes called, as the dregs of society. It is true that there are gradations of rank among those selling their favours, for the prostitute as such has not so bad a name in Japan as in the West; but there is something ladylike about most Japanese females, and in so far as my limited experience went, this applied to the sometimes frail little creatures of whom I speak. No doubt, the majority must have been, under the mask, both hard-hearted and acquisitive: I do not wish to sentimentalize them: but since so much of life is made up of stray encounters, it is pleasant when they leave behind a sense of decency and even dignity.

Then there were the bores who wanted company, and the beggars. The latter were very rare, far rarer than in America, where not so much the beggar as the drop-out or the bum would solicit the cost of a hamburger or a Budweiser, and return to their beat, often to make a second encounter a few minutes later. Finally, there were the eccentrics, whose motives for soliciting one's company were often difficult to grasp, but who grinned and slapped one gingerly on the back and repeated 'O.K.', either out of approbation or from mere exuberance. I have stood drinks to some of these creatures, when I had the time, which was not often; for I found that they were best evaded by leaving them standing happily at a bar. The bores, especially the articulate ones, were not so easily shaken off. At such times, one regretted the spread of the English language.

In this way, I came to know something of Tokyo and of human nature that would otherwise have been denied me. I do not regret my wanderings.

VIII

Now that I am so many miles away, what I recall vividly are certain glimpses of Tokyo which few other cities could have afforded. It might be at the barber's: a *Sumo* wrestler having his hair done in the traditional manner by means of curlers, or a woman standing with her baby slung over her back, while his hair was cut by the barber sitting down behind. Or at a temple, such as the one in Tokyo dedicated to the Fox and much frequented by geisha, where several fortune-tellers, one of whom was blind, seemed to be doing good business, and where I noticed a loquacious individual delivering his prediction through a microphone, while his client, a stocky peasant, listened through an earphone, though the two were separated by only a few feet. Or at Tsuda College, the fine institution for girls, where the school song is sung to the tune of 'Drink to me only with thine eyes', and in the front courtyard of which stands an enormous *Venus de Milo* (the real one came to Japan when I was there), an outsize example of Aryan womanhood dwarfing her Nipponese sisters. Or at a time of head-colds, when men and women went about with white masks (they used to be black), making them like 'spectres without noses': a practice, which, if somewhat offputting at first sight, is probably most hygienic. Or, in the centre of Tokyo, the construction of cliff-faces where would-be mountaineers could practise. Or in the street at Shoto-cho, the district of my last residence and rather a sophisticated one, where the early *tofu* man, abandoning his traditional conch, had adopted mechanical means of making his presence known. Or—but I could go on for paragraphs. 'What images return!' There can be few cities displaying the variety and contrasts of Tokyo; and if a Japanese should think it odd that I have singled out these somewhat unusual *vignettes*, I must reply that he, too, in London or New York would note the unusual, while dismissing the increasing and regrettable similarities.

In the end, despite the grey skies, the *smogu*, the traffic, the crowds, the difficulty of finding one's way, I was drawn to like Tokyo. There was always something new to be found, an alley with a little bar to explore, a shrine or temple to visit, an *o-matsuri* or local festival to view, and above all a home to return to. Sometimes I go back there in memory, and then life takes on that peculiar febrile excitement which I shall never know again.

CHAPTER IV

Climbing Mount Fuji

It was all planned at the eleventh hour. There were brief consultations with our office colleagues, some limbering up after the day's work along Tokyo's narrow, congested pavements, and then the six of us—three Japanese and three British—were off to climb Japan's most sacred mountain.

Fuji-San, as the Chinese *Kanji* character is rendered, means literally 'Rich Warrior Mountain', whereas the more familiar Fujiyama is the Japanese 'reading' of this character. The name Fuji itself is probably derived from the Ainu Goddess of Fire, Kamui Fuchi, and Mount Fuji is said to rival Cotopaxi in Ecuador for the title of the world's most shapely volcano. Every Japanese aspires to climb this 12,467 foot high peak at least once in a lifetime, though before the Meiji Restoration of 1868 it was forbidden to women. There is even a group of Shinto monks or *Yamabushi* who claim it as their special sanctuary; they are at the moment engaged in defending their rights in a complicated lawsuit. The number of recorded eruptions is eighteen, and one of them opened an enormous cleft down the side. The last of these took place in 1707. Rumours regularly circulate that another is due.

According to the experts, we were making the ascent at the ideal time —towards the end of July. The 'season' covers but two months, July and August. At other times accidents abound, and they are often fatal. Accidents in the season are due usually to the enormous crowds which surge up the slopes at week-ends, sometimes 25,000-strong, which means that you have literally to queue for the summit.

In a mood of quiet expectancy, we took the evening bus on a Friday evening from Shinjuku Station. Almost as we set out, the sky began to fill with brooding clouds, and soon it opened up with great vans of lightning, starting a frantic dance of rain needles on the road. The five hours' journey proved somewhat tedious; but, deskbound as we had been for so long, we had prudently decided to start the climb from the Fifth Station, which is 7,111 feet up. My neighbour, one of our two little secretaries, soon gently bent over into sleep, like a collapsing flower. Looking around me, I envied the Japanese ability to while away such journeys in placid unconsciousness. As the suburbs fell away, the houses grew dark, and the gaudy little bars put up their shutters, until at length we moved up the Fuji Toll Road, lurching and veering laboriously over the foothills. Then well past 1 a.m., there loomed before us an up-to-date caravanserai, the Fifth Station, ablaze with electricity. Bodies jolted upright, knapsacks were clawed from the racks, and we jumped down on to the cold, beaten soil. The rain had stopped, and we were revived by the newly washed air. Amid the sudden chatter of voices, we crowded indoors to make ready for our ascent through the small hours.

The atmosphere inside was one of great bustle and excitement. After eating our rations—a solemn little ceremony, the Japanese delicately picking from their *bento*, or food boxes, with chopsticks, and we consuming our crude sandwiches—we donned sweaters, acquired a variety of picturesque headgear, and purchased long staves for ceremonial branding at each station. Then, with injunctions to proceed at a measured pace and at all costs not to lose contact, we moved off into the darkness in single file. Carefree students; family groups; old men who had made the pilgrimage before and others anxious to do so before it was too late; here a father with his child slung on his back; there a giant blond American or German, loaded with sophisticated gear: we soon formed a long, straggling procession, waving our torches in slow rhythm, and, as the steepness began to tell, lapsing into meditative silence.

Mount Fuji is best climbed by night, so that the summit can be approached at sunrise, a superb and rewarding experience. The mountain is dotted with ninety huts, all told, which do a brisk trade in equipment, refreshments (including a variety of patent restoratives), souvenirs, and charms. Given the enormous numbers who make the ascent annually, we had expected the place to be defiled by rubbish; but we were impressed by its tidiness, perhaps the result of a campaign against litter. Of the five trails, we had decided to take the Funatsu path, pausing hourly for a brief rest. Fuji presents no complicated mountaineering problems; it is simply a case of persistent trudging, with some periodical negotiating of sharp rocks, strung with chains.

As the great girth of the mountain dimly displayed itself, the zigzagging path ahead was traced by hundreds of climbers, a mysterious flickering cavalcade. From time to time thin platters of mist would float down, isolating us from our fellows. The stiffest ordeal occurred when, with neither base nor summit visible, we found ourselves groping through an obscure limbo, encouraged only by the felt presence of our heavily breathing neighbours.

On one or two points the guide-books proved slightly misleading. A 'station', for instance, did not always imply one particular hut. There would be a string of sub-stations, and the times between them must have been computed by limbs fleeter than ours. On a sharp incline, one of our companions strained her leg badly; but she pressed on with typical Japanese grit, dragging herself up, a pretty slip of a girl. There were moments when we all felt very weary. Then, almost before we were prepared for it, the night air freshened, and, as we glanced back, the sky disclosed a crack, which soon split the horizon in two, diffusing an oily green, which slowly turned pale yellowish. Just as we were clambering to the Eighth Station at 11,000 feet, a brilliant coin of light began slowly to press itself through the widening cleft, and by 4.45 a.m. the sun was up. Heartened, we toasted our good fortune in thin refreshing Japanese tea. It was as if a great unveiling ceremony had taken place. We looked down to see a colourful concourse straggling over the mountain, a twisted skein of humanity, while below there was an expansion of fleecy, ribbed cloud, obscuring the valley.

Our original plan had been to snatch an hour or two's rest at the Eighth Station; but although we pressed into the hut and rolled ourselves gratefully into heavy coarse blankets—the temperature was well below 50°F—we were far too excited to sleep. A wind began to moan ominously and, fearing to be cheated of our goal, we were soon on our feet again, shaking off the tiredness and eagerly scanning the summit.

It was then that a two-way traffic began, as those who had watched the sunrise from the top began to pick their way down. We passed little parties sitting in a bemused state on stray rocks. A young woman was carried past unconscious. Here and there a victim of mountain-sickness was receiving a back-massage, the Japanese remedy for so many ills. As we plodded on, the rough path grew perceptibly steeper. Against an enormous outcrop were patches of brown-stained snow, like dripping. Then a *torii* came into view and, with renewed zest, we realized that at last the summit was within our reach.

I had been anxious that we should all arrive at the top together; and so, as we closed ranks, our sturdy chauffeur Nanaumi-San, the one member of the party who had climbed the mountain before, photographed us all assembled under the second sacred arch, which was flanked by two ferocious stone beasts, guardians of the sacred precincts. A few steps to the left and we found ourselves in a small market-place, full of merry folk, relaxing, drinking, writing postcards (for there is a tiny post office up there), and paying their respects at the shrine, which is dedicated to the goddess Konohama-sakuya-hime, or Asama. Watched with satisfaction and curiosity by the white-robed priests, we tossed ten-yen coins into the large offertory box, clapping our hands to gain the attention of the *kami*. Then in a nearby café, sitting on rough benches or lying on the *tatami*, we had a delicious meal of *soba* (noodle soup), while our staves were specially branded with the ochre lettering which set the seal on our arrival. The branding can be done in Japanese or in English; we decided that our staves should be bi-lingual.

On the spur of the moment, we resolved to make our way back by the Gotemba route; but before descending, we rested a moment in the small hut at the edge of the huge crater which houses a telephone exchange, and there we rang our office, causing much surprise and some mirth among our colleagues. Nearby is a radar station and observatory, which registers typhoons. Mount Fuji must be one of the best serviced of mountains! In fact, the descent proved a good deal harder than we had anticipated. We ran into unexpected bad weather. It suddenly began to rain in torrents, and volleys of hailstones beat us about unmercifully. Encased in poly-ethylene protectors, we must have looked like so many giant chrysalises. There came a moment when, marooned in a hut and soaked and steaming, we feared that we might have to spend another night up there; but in due course the storm ceased as abruptly as it had begun, though it was then a case of making our way down over tiresome rocks, which gave place to grey friable soil, somewhat thickened by the downpour, through which we plunged in ungainly fashion, a tax on unused muscles.

To add to our difficulties, the entire base of the mountain became suffused in thick mist; and, but for a trailing rope laid between tall markers, we should have lost our way. It was now past 5 p.m., and we had been on the march for fifteen hours, and without sleep for more than thirty. When the slope had gradually evened out and we realized that we had descended the mountain from top to bottom, we encountered a party of young Americans, men and girls, in their vivid shirts and blouses, who were attempting, on whose advice we could not imagine, to make for the summit up that most unrewarding of paths, They hailed us, and we shouted encouragement. They needed it.

On the Monday morning, there were our girls at their typewriters, calm and *soignées* as usual. But we all felt a little proud of ourselves. We had made our pilgrimage, and we even felt that we had some claim to be enrolled as honorary *Yamabushi*.

CHAPTER V

Kyoto and Nara

I

The Japanese have always been great travellers, at least within the bounds of their own country, and they have cultivated one art in particular, which is very important, namely that of travelling light. The ordinary Japanese may set out on a long journey carrying only a few necessities, wrapped up in a large silk scarf called a *furoshiki*; but there is in fact no need for him to do otherwise, as the inn or *ryokan* at which he stays will provide him with the articles he needs: that is, a *yukata* to sleep in, a toothbrush, dentifrice, soap in a celluloid box, and a small towel or *tanugui* with which to dab himself dry (paradoxically, it has to be dampened first).

Although I 'lived European' in Tokyo, save during the hot months when I would sleep on the *tatami*, I preferred to 'live Japanese' on my many journeys. The only difficulty was that many Japanese inns were becoming very expensive; I foresee a time when the ordinary Japanese way of travel will disappear, and with it one of the charms of country life. Many foreigners, while they enjoyed an occasional stay at a *ryokan*, found the food unappetizing as a regular diet. For my part, I came to be increasingly fond of it, until I looked forward to a good meal at an inn or Japanese restaurant as to a kind of ambrosia. After living Japanese for periods at a time, European food seemed both coarse and heavy, doing violence to the stomach and clouding the brain. And part of the pleasure of eating Japanese food was derived from the exquisite but essentially simple manner in which it was prepared and set before the guest.

Travelling is tending to become wearisome in the modern world;

but in Japan I used to enjoy the journey almost as much as the programme arranged for me at the end of it. With the exception of the horrors of travelling on the Tokyo Underground at rush-hour, public transport in Japan is comfortable, efficient and reliable. Indeed, if a train is late, the traveller is entitled to claim a rebate on his fare: a practice to be commended to some other countries. Moreover, the Japanese begin to relax the moment they are *en voyage*. Shoes, and, a blessing to men, coats can be removed. Food is always available. One of the most pleasant aspects of train travel is the regular passage up and down the corridors of healthy-looking peasant girls, lugging great baskets between them, from which food and drink (including beer and *sake*) are dispensed. The sight of these young creatures, announcing their wares in their musical voices, always raised the spirits, and a transaction with them could be an amusing experience. Japanese countryfolk always assume that a foreigner will know not a word of Japanese, so that it takes them a little while to realize that they are being addressed, however inadequately, in their own language. This may cause a good deal of initial misunderstanding and much resort to gesture; but once the words get across, there is delighted recognition, and often amused wonderment. Naturally, the amusement shown was not always due to linguistic problems: the Westerner's large body and in particular his outsize nose provide the Japanese with an irresistible source of diversion. (So does the hair on his chest, which enterprising bar-hostesses will sometimes investigate.)

True, this might suggest that the foreigner, on his journeys through the provinces, is subject to a certain amount of unwelcome scrutiny. It is certain that he is carefully and often meticulously observed; but for the most part this is done in a manner almost unbelievably discreet. There is a marked difference between the behaviour of people in Japan and that in, for instance, some Middle East countries, where at the sight of a stranger, eyes goggle and tongues loll in a kind of hypnotic fascination. Except in the case of school-children, the habit of staring is rare. Fearing to cause embarrassment or to be confronted with a situation with which he cannot cope, the average Japanese will sometimes avoid contact with visitors, even to the point of pretending not to hear an enquiry addressed to him. This habit can be annoying, but it is understandable; and it is much less common than it was.

On the contrary, the foreigner, especially if he is obviously English-

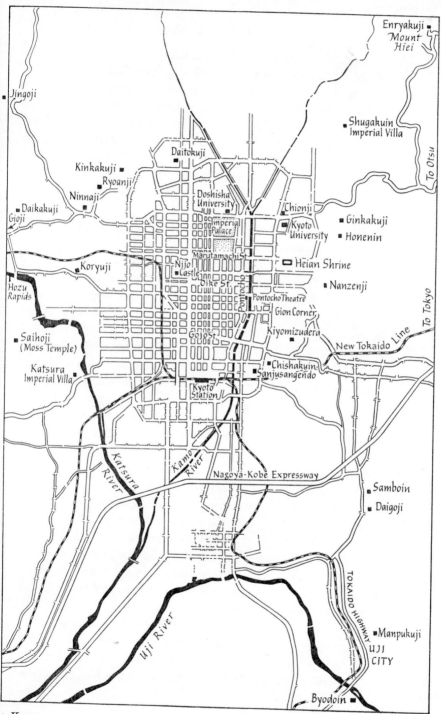

Enryakuji
Mount Hiei

To Otsu

Jingoji

Shugakuin
Imperial Villa

Daitokuji

Kinkakuji
Ryoanji

Ninnaji

Doshisha
University

Chionji

Kyoto
University

Ginkakuji

Honenin

Daikakuji
Gioji

Imperial
Palace

Marutamachi St.

Heian Shrine

Koryuji

Nijo
Castle

Oike St.

Pontocho

Nanzenji

Hozu
Rapids

Pontocho Theatre

Gion Corner

To Tokyo

Gojo St.

Kiyomizudera

Saihoji
(Moss Temple)

New Tokaido Line

Katsura
Imperial Villa

Chishakuin
Sanjusangendo

Kyoto
Station

*Katsura
River*

*Kamo
River*

Nagoya-Kobe Expressway

Samboin

Daigoji

Uji River

TOKAIDO HIGHWAY

Manpukuji

UJI
CITY

Byodoin

3. Kyoto

speaking, is approached on the most unexpected occasions, often by students hoping for a free and improvised lesson in English conversation. More than once this has happened to me on trains, where escape is difficult and known to be so. English, Japan's medium for contact with the outside world, presents considerable problems for the Japanese, and they slave at it with grim determination. Highly sensitive to phonation and intonation, they are quick to distinguish an English from an American accent; and, as the English accent has some scarcity-value, they will tend to seize to the full the opportunity of talking to British people.

Despite problems of communication, which dogged my early days, I never found undue difficulty in moving about Japan. Indeed, by the end of my stay, I had covered a great deal of ground, and I had learnt to cope with most of the problems. One reason why travelling proved to be so easy and enjoyable was the wonderful hospitality given me by Japanese. Usually these were from the academic world, and I could not but admire the scrupulous care which they took to meet me and see me off. I know of no country where kindness to visitors is displayed so unsparingly, and also in such a thoughtful and practical manner. Often it was a delegation that awaited me on the station platform, while outside a car or two would be drawn up, and, as often as not, a carefully typed programme handed to me by the administrative assistant who, when he was not telephoning or booking tickets or restaurant accommodation, would hover perpetually on the edge of the party. Sometimes, especially in the South and North, I would be the first Englishman to have visited a particular place or institution. If not, I would soon be told how often my predecessors or who else of interest had been there, all of which information had been faithfully recorded. As a rule, the programme would be fairly heavy, with at least one *zadankai*, or round-table conference, at which representatives of various Faculties would be present; but the Japanese, experts at the art of relaxation, would always include several communal meals, often an expedition to a famous beauty-spot, temple or shrine and, with great thoughtfulness, an hour or two of rest.

It was natural that I should pay early visits to Kyoto, because we had at that time a small office there. The whole Kansai area was supervised by Francis King, who, in addition to his administrative work, did a lecturing job at Kohnan University. At the time when I first met him, he had just

produced his novel *The Custom House*; and apart from the fact that I still
consider it to be one of his best works, even if he wrote it before he had
become reconciled to many features of Japanese life, I was amazed at the
insight which it showed into the Japanese character, despite its being
written under pressure during his first year. It was Francis King who
'introduced' me to Kyoto, and thereafter I became increasingly attached
to that city. I envied Francis his stay there, as I did that of Peter Martin and
his charming American wife, who succeeded to the Regional Directorate.
Under Peter, we built a new Cultural Centre, one of the best buildings of
its kind; and I owed much to him both for his support and for his
hospitality. He was always busy; but he found time to produce, in
collaboration with his wife, a book on Japanese cookery.

The visitor who hopes to 'do' Kyoto in a day or two will most
probably end up by being disappointed, especially if he arrives in bad
weather. He will find himself in an apparently modern town, graced with
one of the 'towers' of which the Japanese are so fond, swirling with traffic,
and seemingly more full of students (the boys in their drab, Germanic
uniforms) than any other city in the country. He will no doubt notice the
wide streets, intersecting at right-angles, and he may learn that the whole
place is laid out on the traditional Chinese pattern, that it has survived
repeated fires and rebuilding, and that, owing to the earnest plea of
an official of the Boston Fine Arts Museum, it was spared bombardment during the last war. He will see the 'show' places; he will visit
the meretricious Gion Corner; and, as often as not, he will end the day,
perhaps with relief, by patronizing one of the excellent steak-houses
which will remind him of home.

Everybody must discover his own Kyoto. I discovered, though I
never sufficiently explored, mine. As this is not a guide-book to the city,
or to any other part of Japan, I am free to indulge my whims and to give
free rein to my nostalgia for surely one of the most fascinating of places.
Usually I wandered about alone, but sometimes with Peter or a Japanese
friend, and once with a friend who shared my attachment to the 'Western
Capital'.[1]

Naturally, to appreciate Kyoto without some knowledge of its past is
impossible; and for me one of the attractions of Kyoto was that it once
produced a 'moment' in history of inexhaustible interest. This was the

[1] Kyoto means 'capital city', or 'capital of capitals'.

so-called Heian Period. The name is taken from the original name of Kyoto, Heiankyo, the 'City of Peace and Tranquillity'. Nothing comparable to this period can be found in the history of any other country, though I sometimes think that a similar 'moment' may have occurred during the reign of the Pharaoh Ikhnaton. Whereas, however, we know comparatively little about Egyptian court life at that time, we do know, even allowing for exaggeration and some idealization, a good deal about court life in tenth-century Kyoto. This is because of the work of two women of genius, Murasaki Shikibu, author of *The Tale of Genji* and Sei Shonagon, whose *Pillow Book* is possibly nearer to the facts.

Admittedly, the exquisite life cultivated at the Heian court was bought at a stiff price. Such a life could not have been sustained but for the labour of thousands of peasants and artisans. It is not easy to defend a social system which enabled courtiers to conduct their relationships by means of the exchange of delicate poems, or to seek salvation by copying the *Lotus Sutra*, while the ordinary people lived in ignorance and at subsistence level; but the inequalities of the past cannot be redressed. All we can say is that, in the conditions then prevailing, the upper class achieved an *art of life* for which there is no parallel. Nor is it likely ever to be equalled, or even approached, unless our civilization should take a sudden swerve from the direction it is now pursuing.

My attraction to the Heian Period, apart from its intrinsic interest, is due to the fact that, with all the provisos I have mentioned, it throws light upon some aspects of the Japanese character even today. This may seem a startling statement. We forget that human societies preserved a remarkable continuity until the age of industrialism, which has speeded up changes to a degree still psychologically difficult to assimilate. Even so, the changes have not invaded or transformed every aspect of life: I myself live in a part of Britain which, despite the telephone and electricity supply, has altered very little during the last centuries. Indeed, the more developed our technology may be, the *less* it may interfere with nature, whereas the first Industrial Revolution played havoc with many aspects of natural and social life. Japan's Industrial Revolution began a century later than that of the West; and although it has brought with it enormous and sometimes devastating changes, it may have, and I believe has, left undamaged the essence and continuity of Japanese life, though I would not like to say whether, or how much, it will spare that life in the future.

Many educated Japanese today, especially of the younger generation, display a surprising ignorance of their traditions, and even a contempt for them, though I have mentioned cases in which such verbal repudiation failed to match up with conduct: the only language, as Burke remarked, which never lies.

A few centuries after the Heian Period, Japan was racked by civil war and violence, so that a visitor from the West would have recognized, apart from certain superficial differences, a state of affairs to which he was not unaccustomed. But if that same visitor had been miraculously transported back to the Japan of the tenth or eleventh centuries, he would have found something 'almost totally unrelated to the experience of the West'.[1] In so far as he could understand the state of affairs at all, he would have remarked upon one thing above all: the apparent absence of the uncouth, the coarse, the vulgar. What would seem to have distinguished Heian Japan from the France of Louis XIV, for example, would have been the absence of overt debauchery. We have only to read the *Mémoires* of Saint-Simon to become aware of the coarse horse-play which took place, as a matter of daily occurrence, under the veneer of civilized life at the Sun King's court.

Now this fastidiousness of behaviour still seems to me to be a marked characteristic of Japanese life. Indeed, it is now diffused throughout society. In the Heian Period, it became, for a combination of reasons, almost a kind of religion, or perhaps a benign aesthetic growth on the religion of Buddhism. Granted, the existence of this exquisiteness and comeliness in Japanese life does not imply the total absence of opposite characteristics. These, as we know, are present too, and given the occasion they can erupt with atrocious results; but, somehow, and by good fortune, the gentle side of the Japanese character has managed to survive.

Kyoto is the place where the memory of this exquisite moment, of this particular art of living, is still best preserved; and where there is memory there is a kind of reality, or at least its 'permanent possibility'. There are other centres in Japan which give forth the same kind of atmosphere, though the reality is of a different order, and of much greater antiquity. Of these, Ise and Izumo are the most moving, as I shall seek to show. As for Kyoto, the town and its environs are so rich in monuments that no one without years to spare could come to know them all

[1] Ivan Morris, *The World of the Shining Prince* (1964) p. XII.

thoroughly; but this makes the need to discover, and sedulously to cultivate, one's own Kyoto the more imperative.

II

When I first visited Kyoto on Sunday, 28 January 1962, after a ride in the observation car of the Daiichi Tsubame Express, which afforded me my first run down the Tokaido 'highway' and my first view of Mount Fuji, I became conscious of a more relaxed atmosphere than that of Tokyo. I also found a warm welcome, due to the kindness of Francis King and to the hospitality of the Mayor, in whose car I was enabled to see the major sites after making a number of formal calls. There had been more snow in the city than for fifty years. As it lay about chiefly on the surrounding hills, it allowed me to gain an impression of the shape and contours of the city. The cold had even partly frozen over the lake graced by the Kinkakuji, or Temple of the Golden Pavilion. The next few days saw more snow; and this superimposed another layer of quietness.

In Kyoto, I was to find another quietness, the Shinto-Buddhist peace which virtually 'inhabits' certain of its temples and shrines. Only recently I had visited a number of shrines in Tokyo, including the Meiji shrine on New Year's Day: but this was among a jostling crowd of merry and slightly inebriated students, and we could not approach further than the entrance. My first experience of the other silence was in the San-jusangendo, or Hall of the Thousand Buddhas. This capacious hall, 200 feet long, in which the statues have stood their ground for 1,000 years, is a test case for the devotee; for the impression of rapt stillness which their varied countenances convey is sometimes brutally counteracted by a loud-speaker commentary. On the threshold of any exploration of Kyoto, therefore, I was confronted with one of the paradoxes of Japan: the juxtaposition of theophany and cacophany. At first, I found it difficult to conceive how the sensitive Japanese mind could countenance so violent an association, let alone deliberately engineer it; but gradually I came to understand that these people possess the capacity to think away distractions or, as in the case of the Sanjusangendo, to attend to the two things at once. As for myself, I never learnt to achieve such a dissociation. Whenever I visited the Sanjusangendo to find the strident tape being played, I felt that it was, in Max Picard's words, like 'a pistol shooting at silence'.[1]

Shooting, indeed, was not unconnected with this remarkable place. Archery used to be practised in the gallery running in front of the images, and the aim was to shoot as many arrows as possible in a given time. The marks of this exercise can still be seen. In 1686, a samurai shot 13,000 arrows, of which 8,033 reached their mark. But such feats of archery were more than a sport. They were in the nature of a spiritual discipline. The degree to which it achieved this result is explained, though perhaps not quite convincingly, in Eugen Herrigel's little essay *Zen in the Art of Archery*, to which the late Suzuki Daisetz contributed a foreword. Suzuki compares the discipline of Zen archery to that of the other arts, such as flower-arrangement and Tea Ceremony: disciplines which are designed to lead to an understanding of the essence of things.

The Sanjusangendo is part of a temple within a temple, belonging to the Tendai sect. The name of the first is Rengeoin, and the second Myohoin: the name Sanjusangendo refers to the spaces, numbering thirty-three (sanju-san), between the pillars. If you walk along the rows of golden statues, you realize, with a kind of crescendo of wonderment, that they are both individual and at the same time reflections or even emanations of the great central statue of Kannon, or Goddess of Mercy. The Goddess alone is seated; her expression is one of mystical serenity, which is taken up by those in attendance and around her. Many of them clasp some amulet or token. In addition to the 1,001 images ranged throughout the temple, Kannon has twenty-eight immediate disciples. She herself is '1,000-handed', and this impression is conveyed with great ingenuity. Before her there are always votive offerings, but these are rendered insignificant by her awe-inspiring authority. A man of eighty-two, Tankei, carved her in 1254. To my mind, the entire group, from whichever point it is viewed, is beyond anything in majesty of its kind that I have seen, even including Anghor in Cambodia and the Temple of the Azure Cloud in the Western Hills outside Peking, with its 508 *arhats* or ascetics; but it is majesty without obtrusiveness or assertion.

In a gallery behind the Buddhas, there is another parallel to it which contains some statuary in a very different style, representing, among others, the Storm God and the Wind God. Like some of the demons at

[1] Cf. *The World of Silence* (1948).

shrine or temple gates, these images convey an impression of unrelieved ferocity and horror. In fact, the Sanjusangendo itself is not without its horrific associations. During the conquest of Korea in 1596, at least 10,000 Koreans were put to slaughter. Their ears were severed and pickled in salt and *sake*, and the whole consignment of 20,000 was shipped to Japan and buried at the entrance to the Sanjusangendo, with a barrow and stone to mark the spot. In one's rapture, it does not do to forget such violent contrasts.

There is another wooden statue behind the great array, and this serves to mediate between the mystical company and the gods and deeds of violence. This statue is that of Basosennin. He was reputedly a hermit engaged in a perpetual pilgrimage throughout the world, followed by the 9,200 million souls he had saved from hell, surely the biggest missionary effort on record. His wonderful enquiring ascetic face and his emaciated body are admirably executed.

As the subject of Zen, and its claim to reveal ultimate reality or to produce enlightenment, will recur, I ought to make clear my own position in regard to it. When I was in the United States prior to taking up my work in Japan, I came across, especially in California, an astonishing amount of interest in Zen, especially amoung young people. This interest seemed to me to spring from a profound dissatisfaction with contemporary life, a spiritual emptiness, and a hunger for certainty. At the same time, I saw the beginnings of that *olla podrida* of mysticism, drugs, and sex which has since received such enormous publicity, giving rise to the flight of pop artists to the Himalayan foothills, and their antics, half serious and half ballyhoo, nearer home.

It is now some time since Arthur Koestler, in his *Lotus and the Robot*, spoke of a 'stink of Zen', and engaged in an argument with Suzuki, the famous Buddhist scholar, on the subject. I knew Suzuki slightly. He was a wonderful man; and it was only natural justice that when he wrote in 1953 of the Zen master as mirroring the universe for 'seventy, eighty or even ninety' years, he should have more than attained the latter age by the time of his death in 1966. On the other hand, the 'Zen' spoken of in the West would seem to have little or no connection with that blend of Taoism and Mahayana Buddhism which, called Cha'an in China, reached Japan first in the eighth century. Moreover, although I have visited and stayed in Zen temples and patronized Zen restaurants where a very nourishing vegetarian food (*shojin-ryori*) is served, I still confess to finding much of Zen beyond my grasp, which is perhaps as it should be; and what I have grasped of Zen seems to me to be either a fact of experience, or something indistinguishable from the mysticism of the other world religions.

Seizing on my first remark, the Zen devotee will pronounce me condemned out of my own mouth. What he will no doubt say is this: Zen is to be grasped or not to be grasped; and if you have not grasped it, you confess that you do not know what it is. Now this sort of argument has for me a familiar ring. It is evoked in defence of certain experiments in the arts. If you do not see what this artist is doing, say the partisans, then we can do nothing for you. You are beyond the aesthetic pale. Similarly, declare the Zen devotees, you must experience Zen to understand it; and if you do not understand it, this means you have not experienced it. Zen is what we understand by Zen.

This would be all very well if the devotees of Zen were content to stop there. But they do not. That is where they start. Having pronounced Zen to be inexplicable and indefinable, they proceed to write long books explaining what it is. In my Japanese library, I have a dozen books on Zen. Some of them are very well written; all are polemical. They are out to convey by argument what they have pronounced to be beyond argumentative reach.

On the other hand, I believe I do know in part what Zen is, and I believe it to be not quite so ineffable an experience as its devotees claim. Take the experience of Zen illumination called *satori*. In January 1963 when Sir Paul Sinker paid a visit to Japan, we spent a week-end of recuperation from official visits at the Hot Spring resort of Ikao. While Lady Sinker was busy sketching the scenery, Sir Paul and I set out to explore the frozen countryside. As Sir Paul was an indefatigable climber and walker, we penetrated further afield than we had originally planned. Finally, as darkness began to fall, we got lost. Seeing lights in the distance, we began to make for them at a running pace, when suddenly we slipped and fell down one after the other. I shall never forget the sudden 'shift' of experience which this mishap produced, and I believe Sir Paul would confirm the impression. As for me, I found myself lying flat on my back and looking up at the moon. It was as if I had seen the moon for the first time, and also as if she were looking at me, rather in the manner described in Hardy's poem 'Waiting Both'. The sudden 'thrill of recognition' which I experienced was unmistakable. That it flooded me with wisdom or a sense of rightness 'at the heart of things', I do not claim. It may have been just a moment of lunacy, as of course in part it was. Its value derived from its being an exquisite moment of *perception*, such as the traditional Japanese 'moon-viewing' parties afforded. That is what I would call the experience of *satori*.

The Zen *koans*, riddles, paradoxes or conundrums, seem to me to be designed to bring about just such a shift in experience as our propitious fall did that evening near Ikao. The *koans* are paradoxes on which to meditate. The expectation is that their deliberate violation of the rational order will enable the mind to jump free of this order, and to live, if only for a moment, on a higher level. Thus the devotee is enjoined to meditate on such ideas as the noise made by one hand clapping. Such an exercise may conceivably produce the result suggested, but I tend to think that the general outcome is simply to see things from another point of view, just as I saw the moon from a fresh angle while I was lying on my back. It is the 'doors of *perception*' that are 'opened'.

The practice of Zen meditation, called *zazen*, is devoutly followed by many Japanese, and the Zen tradition has produced some of Japan's most beautiful literature and art, as well as one of the most graceful of ceremonies, namely the *Chanoyu*, or Tea Ceremony. This ceremony, often occupying several hours and involving five persons, consists of making the beverage ritually from powdered green tea, and passing it round in a tea-bowl or *chawan* to be sipped by the guests, who thus participate in a kind of sacrament.[1] Every year, hundreds of young people follow a regime of meditation which puts our modern 'pop transcendentalism' in the shade. The devotee will usually spend a week in a Zen temple, beginning his day at 3 a.m. and ending it at 9 p.m., and devoting the time not spent in *zazen* or the recital of the Sutras, to ordinary housework. In some cases, there is the practice of living within the minimum space which a Japanese is supposed to need, namely one *tatami* mat. The food is of the simplest, namely rice or rice-gruel and pickles, the diet of the poorest peasants. The position most suited to meditation is the Lotus

---

[1] There are several schools of Tea Ceremony, and today it is largely secularized, but the aim is to promote calm of spirit. The utensils are simple but often of great value and beauty. A proper tea room consists of 4½ mats (see above).

Seat, that is to say, sitting cross-legged with the foot resting on the thigh, as in yoga, and with the eyes fixed on a particular point, while the breathing is subject to strict control.

In so far as it proved possible, I tried to discover what it was that the Japanese themselves found in this form of meditation; for I came to the conclusion that few Westerners were able to practise it in an authentic manner. I speak therefore as an outsider, despite my numerous discussions with adepts and postulants. My conclusion was that the result of prolonged meditation on the lines described is not so much a grasp of 'ultimate reality' as a sense of 'oneness' with nature based upon acuity of perception. This sense of 'oneness' is not of the Wordsworthian kind, for the essence of Buddhism is concerned with the transitoriness of the world. If the Zen devotee experiences what I have already mentioned, namely a heightening of his perceptions, and if he meditates on the transitoriness of the natural world, he at the same time appreciates more fully the phenomena as they pass. This surely is the basis of Japanese art, and of the cult of the cherry blossom, valued for its ephemeral nature. This, too, would explain why Buddhism was so comparatively easy to reconcile with Shinto. For Shinto, in deifying so much of nature, relishes the value of phenomena, even though they are passing.

To me, this is the true meaning of Buddhist enlightenment, understood in its Zen context: for the moment of *satori* is a way of 'seeing', with a very real visual basis. The meaning of enlightenment for other Buddhist sects, and its meaning for the Buddha himself, were no doubt very different. The Buddha's own enlightenment under the Bodhi tree at Bodh Gaya, India, was, we gather, a realization of the way of escape from the world of bodily pain: a way out that was supposed to lead to the total dissolution of the self. Although it is difficult (especially for a Westerner), to understand exactly what the Buddha meant by an *enlightenment* that led to *extinction*, we can be sure that, as a metaphysical belief, it needed underpinning by a more 'physical' one; for no popular religion can be nurtured on metaphysics alone. In any case, Buddhism grew up in the sixth-century B.C. in the matrix of a very elaborate Hindu faith, the metaphysical aspects of which, though rarefied, were themselves buttressed by a pantheon which was highly naturalistic. And when Buddhism, like most other higher religions, spread from the country of its birth, it not merely underwent a metamorphosis itself, but it combined itself with the nature cults which it encountered. Thus the aesthetic faith of Sakyamuni became the lofty theistic religion of the Mahayana, or the Great Vehicle, which arrived in Japan to find the indigenous cult of Shinto. The Japanese devotee of Zen is one who practises Buddhism in the light of a worship of nature made congenial to him from birth.

III

I began the account of my pilgrimages in Kyoto with the Sanjusangendo, because this was the first Buddhist temple to make an overwhelming impression on me. It was built after the Heian period, and somewhat before the systematic cult of Zen itself, which was due to the monk, Eisai. Although my digression on Zen may, therefore, seem anachronistic, I have singled it out because of its great influence abroad, and because it had become for many people the 'typical' form of mysticism outside the Indian or Vedanta tradition. Even so, it would be a mistake to assume that Zen was wholly unknown in Heian court circles, because it was continually making itself felt through the teaching of monks who had been trained in China. An influence can often be the more telling *before* it becomes systematized. Perhaps it is true to say that, in the realm of theology, the conscious effort at systematization is the final phase of real influence, which works best at the subconscious level. Once there are formulated creeds, there is explicit scepticism.

During Murasaki Shikibu's time, Buddhism in its Tendai and Shingon sectarian forms was becoming, or had become, an officially established religion.[1] These had evolved creeds and formal liturgies, whereas Zen never assumed such a rigid form, nor did the Taosim which so greatly influenced it. To a foreigner reading Lady Murasaki and Sei Shonagon, the little knowledge that he has been able to obtain of Zen may help him to understand the world which those ladies depicted.

Before describing some of the other remarkable places, let me dwell for a moment on two of the Zen temples in Kyoto which I got to know early and particularly liked. I should say at once that my account will be incomplete, even of the temples I describe; for most temples of this order

[1] Morris, op.cit., p. 104.

are in fact temple-compounds, with a large number of edifices, some devoted to secular purposes and some private.

Every tourist is told to visit the famous Ryoanji temple, sometimes misleadingly referred to as the Stone Garden. Its popularity is perhaps the great obstacle to true appreciation, because the temple is rarely free of tourists; and the Westerner, unlike the Japanese, has difficulty in putting aside distractions, the greatest of which may be the presence of his own kind.

Literally rendered 'Dragon-safe temple', this extraordinary place was begun in 1450 by a great feudal lord, Hosokawa Katsumoto, whose family still flourishes and some of whom I came to know. The main hall is approached past a pond on the left, which has two islets; and it is reached by climbing some wide and much worn stone steps. The garden, surrounded by low mud walls with a tiled roof on three sides, consists of an expanse of whitish sand-grit on which fifteen rocks, differing in size, and arranged in five groups, have been placed. Round these rocks the sand has been raked to form concentric circles, whereas elsewhere it is ruled straight. There are neither flowers nor plants, and not a single tree, though a little moss or lichen borders some of the rocks. The garden was reputedly the work of the great master Soami, who laid it out about 1499. Many consider it to be the most perfect example of the Zen philosophy translated into visible form.

I do not pretend to have grasped the meaning of Soami's design; but in the Ryoanji, as at similar temples, the golden rule is surely to adopt an attitude of *en hypomene*, Simone Weil's 'waiting in patience'. Of the fifteen rocks, fourteen are always visible from whatever direction you look at them, but the fifteenth remains concealed. Fosco Maraini, one of the few Europeans to have a deep understanding of Japan, calls the Ryoanji a 'poem in minerals and light', and he points out how, in relation to art, Japan's is 'our present, perhaps our future';[1] but he also finds the garden symbolic of 'the meaning of ultimate things'. Maraini is a Buddhist. I can work only from a point with which I am familiar, and to me the significance of the Ryoanji is that, whatever 'the meaning of ultimate things', it must be the reverse of the abstruse and the prolix; for I find it hard to reconcile myself to the view that, following the strain and stress of human life, the battered soul will be obliged to confront the kind

[1] *Meeting with Japan* (1964), p. 342.

of bureaucratic supernatural realm of which some modern esoteric thinkers have provided a draft prospectus.[1]

Soami was responsible also for designing one of the gardens of the Daitokuji, the Temple of the Great Virtue, a Zen edifice so large as almost to constitute an ecclesiastical township. It covers an area of more than twenty-seven acres. With its long lifted verandahs and its richly lacquered pavilions, the temple is unsurpassed in Kyoto for magnificence. Indeed, the riches of the complex are astonishing. There are screen-paintings by Kano and many other paintings by masters. There are the tombs of the great Shogun Nobunaga and his sons, together with that of the mother of Hideyoshi. There are masterpieces of calligraphy. But the feature which I found most exquisite was the garden of the Daisenin. This is held by many experts to equal Soami's own masterpieces at Ryoanji, and perhaps to be superior to it. To me at least, it is the more exquisite. Stones of menhir size, sand and trees, some of which are just sufficiently free in their growth as to banish the air of artificiality, adjoin the verandah and form part of the room.

I paid my last visit to the Daitokuji on Sunday, 30 April 1967. I took refuge there, partly to escape from the great heat which had fallen upon Kyoto, though it was towards the end of the afternoon, and partly because I knew by then that my stay in Japan was coming to an end, and I wanted time for reflection. Naturally, I had admired many other Kyoto gardens, particularly those of the Katsura and Shugakuin Detached Palaces, the Moss Garden, and the garden of the Samboin, the Daikakuji, and the Ginkakuji or Silver Pavilion. This latter is also reputed to have been designed by Soami; but of all the remarkable essays in grouping trees and rocks, that of the Daitokuji is the one upon which my memory lingers; and second to it is that of the Daikakuji, often confused with the former. So I spent a period at the one, and then went on to the other, trying to absorb into myself the spirit which had inspired the temple builders and garden designers. Fortunately, in so vast a temple as the Daitokuji, it is possible to evade the crowd, who tend to keep to the main paths; but at the smaller Daikakuji it was less easy. I soon encountered a wanderer. He was a toothless old man who, padding softly up to me, announced in tolerable English that he was a 'puritan Christian'. On

[1] I am thinking of such works as J. G. Bennett's *Dramatic Universe* (1956), based on Gurdjieff, with its strange terminology and complicated diagrams.

learning my nationality, he produced a very old mandolin on which he strummed a melody which I barely recognized as 'God Save the Queen'. Then, with the legerdemain which the loose folds of the *yukata* made possible, he whipped out an album containing photographs of Earl Attlee's visit to Japan, and he said he too was a World Federalist. I sat talking to him for a while. His presence had not in fact greatly disturbed me, because he was a kindly, simple soul; and with his strange equipment and his air of freedom, he represented something of the essential Japan for me. But I spent the time until the temple closed looking at the garden, and thinking of less human things than how to tame governments.

The Daikakuji, with its lake of perfect placidity, brings me gently back to the Heian Period. Although the building dates from the ninth century, it began as an imperial villa, and in due course it became the place to which abdicating sovereigns repaired. It was destroyed and rebuilt several times; but it still retains features exclusive to palaces, being liberally coated with lacquer even to the floors themselves. Some temples, and even more some shrines, are beginning to show signs of neglect, but the Daikakuji is maintained in excellent condition.

Abdication was not unusual in the Heian Period, even when the sovereign was obliged to resign in favour of a child; and for that reason the Period is sometimes called that of the Cloistered Emperors. Another such abdication palace was the Ninnaji, which stands not far from the Ryoanji; but the Emperor who built it in 886 died before he could arrange for his own departure thither, and it was left for a successor not merely to finish the building, but to turn it into a temple, and to become its first abbot. This set a precedent, followed until the Meiji era, whereby a member of the imperial family governed the temple and the lesser foundations associated with it. I was fortunate in seeing the Ninnaji at the cherry blossom season. As might be expected, this is a festival time throughout the country, though some of the open-air evening parties can be spoiled by the interfering rain, and the visitor is inclined to tire of the paper cherry blossoms which deck every lamp-standard, lending a meretricious air to an otherwise joyous, if brief, season. In its precincts the Ninnaji has some remarkable cherry trees, the age of which is very great. Their trunks are squat and hunched, like traditional pictures of Japanese peasants, but their multifoliate blossoms are, I understand, unique.

Consequently, they attract a concourse of admirers who may show little curiosity about the temple.

It was in the reign of the Emperor Kammu, who lived from 794 to 806, that the capital was removed from Heijo to Heiankyo. The transfer of capitals in those days was not unusual; it became an obligatory act when some auspicious event had occurred or when a ruler died. There were indeed practical reasons for this particular move: Heiankyo was nearer to the most convenient route to the provinces, and this lent greater importance to the Tokaido highway. A sign of the new times was the discontinuance, after 838, of the practice of sending cultural missions to China, whereas sixteen such missions had been dispatched between 607 and the final year. This end of direct Chinese influence undoubtedly led to the development of the unique Heian way of life.

One of the secrets of the 'Heian moment' was no doubt that the court began to concern itself less directly with politics. Some of the men continued to hold impressive titles, but these were only nominal. The resulting mode of government, with the Emperor reigning and a powerful family ruling, became a pattern for many centuries to come. The family to dominate the throne at this time was that of the Fujiwara. As they maintained their influence for well on a thousand years, they were evidently a clan of remarkable ability and pertinacity. Originally named Kamatari and given the martial name of Fujiwara after helping to oppose another powerful family called the Soga, they obtained their hold over the imperial court by providing wives, or if necessary concubines, for the Emperors. Indeed, they managed to maintain this practice until the present century, when it was broken by the initiative of the reigning Emperor. Although the origins of the Fujiwara are obscure, it is thought that they were descended from a tribe called the Hata, which, coming possibly from that sensitive area, the Chinese-Russian border, was incorporated into the Japanese state by naturalization as early as 390. The Hata are credited with having introduced the making of silk cloth (*hata* means 'loom'), and their original dwelling place was the area now occupied by the great Koryuji temple. This temple is therefore of particular interest, being reputedly the oldest in Kyoto. Certainly its lecture hall, built in 1165, is the most ancient building in the city, though this is because it has been spared the ravages of fire. The temple itself was built by one of the Hata tribe in 603 for the repose of the soul of one of the greatest figures in Japanese history, Prince Shotoku (573–621), who, almost single-handed, established Buddhism in Japan.[1] At least two of the statues are supposed to be likenesses of the prince, and even to have been carved by him; but of equal, if not greater, interest is the Miroku-Bosatsu, the Buddha or Bodhisattva in a 'thinking' posture, also carved from wood. This statue, the oldest in Kyoto, was damaged by a student in 1961; he snapped off its fingers, which, carved with extreme delicacy, represented the symbol of meditation, the first finger lightly touching the top of the thumb. The statue, which may possibly antedate the building of the temple itself, was covered originally with gold leaf affixed with lacquer; and today one can see how skilfully the material was worked, e.g., the grain shaping the cheek and turning perfectly round the knee. Although tradition has it that it, too, was the work of the saintly prince, it was most probably done by a Korean sculptor.

IV

On 7 January 1967, I went with Peter Martin to Otsu to visit the Homyoin, an adjunct to the Miidera temple. My purpose was to locate the tomb of Ernest Fenollosa, the remarkable American who had first come to Japan in 1879, some years before Lafcadio Hearn. He taught at the Imperial University of Tokyo, and finally became a Buddhist; but his great work was that of interpreting the Noh drama to the West, and his influence upon Ezra Pound and Yeats was, as we know, enormous. Although Fenollosa died in London, it was his wish that his remains should be buried in Japan.

As I had had something to do with promoting the first visit of the Noh to London—by the Umewaka-Hashioka troupe—it seemed to me appropriate to pay a tribute to Fenollosa's memory; and our visit to the Homyoin was in order to make the preliminary arrangements. On this occasion, we were received by the pleasant young assistant abbot, who was knowledgeable about Pound. We saw Fenollosa's workroom, and then the tomb itself. Around it a number of memorial stones had been set up: the donors were American, French and British, the latter being Lawrence Binyon.

[1] It is difficult to exaggerate the part played by Prince Shotoku in Japanese tradition. His portrait still graces some Japanese banknotes.

The temple commanded a fine view of Lake Biwa, though, alas, the shores were dotted with a number of huge and rather ugly new buildings, whereas, to the right, there was a typically Japanese tree-covered hill. It was a case of taking in the new and the old Japan at the turn of a head.

We were back at the Homyoin on 30 April, and I noticed how rich and green everything had meanwhile become. In the temple a young man was delivering a lecture on Fenollosa. We squatted down at the side near an altar, which was loaded with offerings—chiefly apples and beancakes—while on the wall above there was Fenollosa's picture. After the lecture, I was called upon to make a speech, and I explained the reasons which had brought us there. Then, moving into the open, we formed up behind a procession headed by the Abbot of Miidera and his attendant priests, Peter carrying our offering of a wreath of lilies. Not merely was the weather idyllic but the temple was looking at its best: the occasion had been chosen specially, as it was in fact the temple 'day'. Still in single file, we walked up the steps to the grave, whereupon the temple group entered the little stone enclosure, and began to chant Sutras. At a certain point, a sign was given for me to go forward. I placed our wreath on the gravestone, and deposited a few grains of incense on a burner nearby. Finally, the Abbot himself knelt down and prayed.

After the ceremony, we grouped round a platform covered with a white sheet, which had been set up for the occasion. Here Mr. Kongo, director of the Kongo Noh school at Osaka, performed a *shimai* or ritual dance from the play *Kakitsubata* (*Iris*), which Fenollosa had translated, while four of the chorus sang. It was amazing to watch this performance close to. The dancer seemed to generate strength or to draw upon some power within, so that as he moved his whole body tensed and throbbed. Watching a Noh play from a distance, one does not always realize with what controlled energy the stylized movements are made.

After another speech, the programme ended with a Tea Ceremony held on the terrace overlooking the lake. Then I distributed gifts to those who had been chiefly responsible for organizing the ceremony. That evening I again read through Fenollosa and Pound's pioneer little work on the Noh.[1] Like many foreigners, I could not at first reconcile myself to this form of drama, even after repeated attendance and much reading; but there had come a moment when I began to look forward to the

[1] *Noh, or Accomplishment* (1916).

performances, and thereafter this sense of expectancy and excitement never diminished. The fact that the Noh has the longest history of any dramatic form, perhaps being in continuity with vegetable and fertility rituals, must reflect something in Japanese culture which is not present in any other.

V

Both Tendai and Shingon, the two most powerful sects during this period, were 'mountain sects'. The one had its headquarters on Mount Hiei, and the other on Mount Koya, two religious fastnesses. I visited the temples on Mount Hiei several times: once only did I go to Mount Koya, for the formalities for entry are complicated.

Mount Hiei, or 'chilly mountain', dominates Kyoto. At one time it was covered with a network of temples, built to protect the town from the north-east direction, which, according to the Bureau of Divination, though not to strict Buddhist teaching, was unlucky. Many of the foundations were presided over by members of the aristocracy. The joint-holding of secular and sacred office was by no means un-common in the Heian Period and thereafter, as it could have the effect of exempting property from taxation. For some reason, the monks of this mountain acquired a taste for violence; and, contravening all the laws of the Buddha by wearing swords beneath their robes, they would descend periodically upon Kyoto and terrorize the inhabitants. What is more, they would engage in combat with other sects, in which their violence became even more extreme; though it must be said that such sectarian feuds were usually less about doctrine than about property-rights. Finally, Nobunaga slaughtered the lot. In those days, the way up the mountain was both difficult and dangerous. Today you may go up by funicular or by car. I went up with Peter Martin, and I remember being greatly taken with the Enryakuji temple, and the reverence with which a young priest showed us around. Never was there a more authentic 'dim religious light', conjured out of the darkness round the altar by oil lamps. In this numinous atmosphere, it was difficult to imagine the scenes of cupidity which had at one time disgraced the neighbourhood.

My visit to the headquarters of the Shingon sect on Mount Koya was one of the highlights of my stay in Japan. I set out on Saturday, 8 April

1967. Peter Martin had obtained all the necessary permits for me, and he saw me off from the Namba Station. Koya-San lies a good way to the south-east of Kyoto in the Kii mountains. The train was a modern one; but although we were given hot towels by a demure young lady, there was nothing to eat save peanuts, which I washed down with Kirin lemonade. Slowly we moved out of the more hideous parts of Osaka into sunny country made exquisite by profuse cherry blossom. Then, beginning to climb, we passed through scenery immemorially associated with Japan: wooded knolls, geometrical paddy fields, and peasants in traditional straw hats, bending to till the soil. We were in Wakayama prefecture. Gradually the scenery grew wilder, and finally we swung up a very steep incline, with the coaches in front moving at an angle. Although I was in the mood for a pilgrimage, I had not learnt the lesson that moods should not be arranged in advance; for as we arrived at Koyashita, or Mount Koya station, the strains of 'Auld Lang Syne' began to break on our ears. But that was not all. Lugging my heavy case up a stone staircase, I entered the cable-car planted flush against the steep mountainside. During the journey, as if to resume the musical commentary, we were entertained to 'Funiculi-Funicular', a song associated with my mother's generation: and with this we were regaled until the top station, situated at nearly 3,000 feet.

Although the journey by cable-car had lasted only a few minutes, and despite this distraction, the view which had opened before me was breathtaking. By contrast to those in the Ninnaji, the cherry trees were of enormous size, certainly the biggest I had seen. On arrival, slightly dazed and bewildered, I was met by an attractive girl in slacks who, querying 'Eikoku-Taishikan?' ('British Embassy?'), popped me into a taxi. The operation was so swiftly carried out that I hardly knew that it had taken place until it was over. I never saw the girl again; she was one of those emissaries who move in and out of Japanese life, with baffling anonymity. The taxi rapidly described a long arc, and I was deposited at the temple headquarters, the Kongobuji. Here I was greeted by the Naijo-cho, or Chief of Internal Temple Affairs, Mr. Ueda. He took me along smooth wooden corridors to a parlour which, the moment I saw it, reminded me of a reception room in one of the larger monasteries of Mount Athos. In fact, apart from the presence of women and female animals, Mount Koya called to mind repeatedly the island of the Panayia. (Women were banned from Mount Koya until 1873.) Seated in a luxury Western chair, I was served with tea and *tofu*. Like many other monasteries, Mount Koya had its specialities, and this delicious bean-curd preparation was one of them. Indeed, the claim is made that the delicacy originated there. After meeting a kindly priest, Mr. Moru, I was taken by a student to my quarters in the Ryokoin Inn. The room gave on to a small Japanese garden, laid out in the Tokugawa style. As the temperature was fairly low, a charcoal fire was brought in, and this was followed by more sweetmeats. The main food on Koya-San is vegetarian.

There are still 120 temples on the sacred mountain, and it remains a place of pilgrimages, catering for at least a million visitors annually. Fortunately, the rush had not begun, and I was able to wander about in peace. It is strange that although so many people in Japan show indifference to Buddhism, they haunt temples and shrines in vast numbers. The great popularity of Shingon-Buddhism, however, may be due to its great artistic appeal. Just as the doctrine of the Trinity has gained a measure of intelligibility through religious art, so the exalted ideas of Shingon were similarly conveyed; and there was certainly need for such interpretation. The theology of Tendai (T'ien-t'ai: or 'Heavenly Terrace') was derived from China: that of Shingon (Chen-yen: 'the True Words') was of largely Indian inspiration. This Indian spirit pervades both Shingon art and the Shingon liturgy, which at Koya-San is to be seen at its richest and most elaborate. Another clue to the awe which Shingon Buddhism inspires, especially in the foreigner who by background and knowledge is so far removed from it in spirit, is the fact that its inner doctrines (or, to use Sanskrit terminology, *Smriti*) are supposed to be secret to all but a group of initiates. These secret laws concern body, speech and thought. As to the body, Shingon developed some peculiar, though not necessarily perverse, sexual teaching; I referred earlier to the connection between religion and the erotic, but details of this side of Shingon are not forthcoming. Hence the need for another medium of communication, the aesthetic. The first teacher of Japanese Shingon, Kukai, made this clear: 'The esoteric scriptures are so abstruse', he declared, 'that their meaning cannot be conveyed except through art.' The result is a splendour, and above all a symbolic richness, surpassing almost all other forms in the Buddhist tradition.

As the weather was deteriorating, and as I did not wish to be cheated

of the beauty of Koya-San by one of the storms that can periodically
scourge the mountain as if in chastisement of its sensuousness, I set out
forthwith to view some of the temples. First, I visited the Kompon Daito,
or Great Central Pagoda. This holds some of the rare treasures of Koya-
San, namely, the five sacred images of the chief Buddhas, though
repeated damage by fire makes it difficult to know how old they are.
Next I entered the Kondo, or main hall, which suffered the same fate in
1926, and then across to the Daishi Kyokai, in front of which some young
men were practising baseball. Sliding the enormous screen doors aside, I
stepped in and found a modern structure for holding ceremonies,
sermons, and, in summer, dancing. All this, interestingly enough, was in
the compound pronounced as *garan*, or 'holy', and it is traditionally the
area chosen as sacred ground by Kobo Daishi, the posthumous name
given to Kukai and meaning 'Great Teacher'.

Kobo was more than a religious innovator. As might have been
expected, he was a considerable artist, which meant a great calligrapher.
(To write, to draw, and to paint are rendered by the same word in
Japanese.) He invented the syllabary known as *Hiragana* (*Kana*), or so it is
believed: the characters are supposedly Indian in origin. If that be the
case, this holy man was partly responsible for the production of such
works, not uniformly holy in content, as *The Tale of Genji* and *The Pillow
Book*. For the use of the *Kanji*, or the Chinese character, was regarded as a
male monopoly: women wrote in *Kana*.

Passing clumps of Japanese cedar and trees peculiar to the mountain,
called Koyamaki, I revisited the Kongobuji. This 'Temple of the Daimond
Mountain', consists of a succession of rooms many of which have panels
painted by Kano. It also contains an image of the founder. In one room
(O-chigo-no-ma), there are secret closets where guards were stationed
during important visits: for the danger of ambush, treachery, or delation
was not the less acute in temples to which fugitives would repair, and
where even amorous assignations were arranged. After contemplating
the gorgeous decoration of these chambers, I found myself suddenly on
the threshold of one of the largest kitchens I had ever seen. Over the rice-
oven there was a shrine, an appropriate fixture for the spot where the
most sacred of foods was prepared.

It was a long walk downhill to the great cemetery of Koya-San, called
the Okunoin. This is a place to stroll through at leisure, pondering upon

the meaning of the Buddhist attitude to death; but a quick eye is needed in order not to miss some unique sight or vista. Some of the monuments, and also the trees, were adorned with little coloured 'aprons', a sign of the attention of the faithful and of their expectations of divine favour. Certain of the larger trees were scooped out to form hermits' living quarters; but explore as I might, I found none of them occupied, nor was I plagued with beggars, which one guide-book mentioned as being the bane of the visitor. I did locate the extraordinary replica of the Nestorian monument at Sian in China, which an Irishwoman, Mrs. Gordon, formerly a lady-in-waiting to Queen Victoria, caused to be set up in 1911. Although this was an oddity, it did not jar on the mind in a country so full of contrasts. Nevertheless, I was struck by the liberal views of the authorities who had gratified the lady's whim; and I wondered how many Christian cemeteries would have admitted a Buddhist monument, and a heretical one at that, to be set up among the slabs, crosses and mounds. In fact, there is a remote connection between Nestorianism and Kobo Daishi. When he was in China, he studied Sanskrit under an Indian who, it is said, had worked with a Nestorian monk named Adam.[1]

My final visit that day was to the mausoleum of Kobo himself. Before reaching the shrine, I was confronted by a row of bronze statues of the seven Buddhas and Bodhisattvas. Beneath them, elderly women were reverently depositing wooden tablets, which had been purchased at a little office close by. Here they were inscribed with the names of family and friends, and I lingered to watch the beautiful calligraphy coming lightly off the brush and travelling down the length of the thin pieces of wood. According to tradition, if water be sprinkled over the tablets, the dead will derive special benefit; and as it was raining, there was an unusual bustle of activity. I passed the Torodo, which contains the gifts of devotees in the form of several thousand lanterns. This abuts on the Gokusho, where the formal presentation of such gifts is made. Adjoining this again is a building called the Kotsudo, or Hall of Bones. As there is merit in having one's remains deposited near those of the saint, this reliquary was built next door to the mausoleum itself, which stands on raised ground within a cluster of very old pines and cryptomeria. Here, since the year of his death in 835, Kobo has been awaiting the coming of the Buddha-to-be, Maitreya.

[1] Sir Charles Eliot, *Japanese Buddhism* (1964), p. 236.

When I returned to my quarters, I was invited by a student to take a bath, which I found extremely hot even by normal *o-furo* standards. A vegetarian meal, accompanied by two bottles of beer, was awaiting me. Before I had time to begin it, the student, aided by a strapping girl in a white overall, began making up my bed on the floor. Normally, a servant supervises one's meal, and this could be a welcome opportunity of practising one's Japanese; but on the present occasion I was not displeased to be left to myself, as I wanted to examine the volume on Mount Koya's art treasures which had been presented to me by the guest-master. Reflecting on what I had seen, and studying the reproductions in one of those albums which Japanese publishers produce with such skill, I understood a little better how the 'good people' (as they called themselves) of the Heian court acquired their interest, almost their obsession, with aesthetic taste, which lightened their otherwise somewhat monotonous amorous intrigues.

These thoughts were going through my mind when I heard a hesitant pattering on the roof. This intensified until I was aware of a steady downpour. The hypnotic sound soon induced sleep, so that I awoke the next day greatly refreshed.

In order to shave, it was necessary to walk along a narrow wooden platform, hardly more than a ledge, to an open wash-house. This was situated almost opposite one of the temple 'chapels'; and here a priest was reciting the Sutras, accompanied by the ringing of a soft-sounding gong. As I peered inside, I beheld a sight even more awe-inspiring than that in the temple on Mount Hiei. There were candles, lamps, and offerings which brought out the strong burnish of the brasses. When I was ready, I nervously entered the precincts and became, so far as I could see, the entire congregation. Needless to say, the meaning of the chanted words were beyond me, quite apart from their being intoned in a special manner. I felt there was something just a little mechanical in the way in which each strophe ended with a kind of grunt, like the turning off of a tap. This intoning had, in fact, become a stylized practice, not unlike certain recitals of the Mass; but so far as I could gather from talking to the faithful (an opportunity not easy to come by) the exact meaning of what went on was by no means clear. The efficacy resided in the recitation itself; and as this was better done by a professional than by an amateur, the faithful were content to attend in respectful incomprehension.

Next day I spent going over the temples I had already visited in order to fix their several characters in my mind. What struck me was the amount of building work taking place, together with a general air of affluence not usually found in such centres, at least in Japan. I also visited the museum, which contains some priceless treasures, chiefly *kakemono*. Two exhibits particularly attracted my attention. One was a magnificent Buddha, before which, as in front of some other sculptures (all 'National Treasures'), members of the public stopped to pray and also to deposit small coins. Neither practice had I witnessed in a museum before. Nevertheless, I was depressed to observe the preponderance of 1 yen coins (a sum worth a good deal less than an old penny), when I thought of the 'tribute' these same people were ready to cast before more worldly images. The other noteworthy exhibit was a remarkable Nepalese mandala, which emphasized the link between Shingon and India.

When finally, having taken leave of my kind hosts and having presented a donation in an envelope, I descended the funicular, there was no sound of music. For this I was thankful, as it would have spoiled the scene which presented itself: the mist creeping among the tall pines and softening the mountain contours, so that I seemed to be blending with the landscape. There was an hour to wait for the Limited Express and as it was cold I was glad of the station-master's invitation to share his cosy little office.

I wondered how long Mount Koya, like Mount Athos, would last in a world rapidly becoming secularized. Its air of prosperity might be deceptive, because many of the pilgrims went there to see national rather than spiritual treasures. The recruitment of Buddhist priests was as much on the decline as is that of Christian ordinands. In the sphere of religion, however, the unexpected is always recurring; and I have a feeling that a century from now, the funicular to Mount Koya, with or without canned music, will still be in service.

VI

A favourite Shingon haunt of mine in Kyoto was a temple called the Chishakuin, or the Temple of Increasing Wisdom. Fortunately, I visited it, as most places should be visited if there is a chance of coming back, before I read it up in the guide-books: for you are tempted to look upon a building and its treasures with a different eye if you know that what you are seeing is a modern replica of the original. Built originally in 1598, the Chishakuin was burnt to the ground in 1947 and many priceless treasures, including some beautiful screens, were lost. For me, the famous Golden Pavilion also lacks something, because it too is a restoration after being set on fire by a neurotic acolyte of whom Mishima wrote in his novel *The Temple of the Golden Pavilion*. In point of fact, this reverence for ancient fabric is in some respects a superstition. Many places in Japan, including the Ise shrine, are as modern as the houses in a New Town. What proved initially attractive about the Chishakuin, however, was the warm welcome I received there. On the threshold, as if he were on sentry duty, I was met by a gay old man with a goatee beard, who took me round and introduced me to some of the community of forty or so monks. No doubt it was their presence, together with the sense of communal living according to a rule, that generated such atmosphere as I felt. Nor was I the less impressed on learning that my host, instead of being the abbot or priest, was a retired engineer. He had once been rich. He struck me as a man who had at last found the contentment for which all his life he had been seeking. Never had he been happier, he assured me, than in following that simple mode of life. He would sit on the floor for hours meditating and reading, often looking out into the garden, which could be viewed by removing a small panel from the wall. Happily, the garden was genuine: it had been designed by a famous tea-master, Sen-no-Rikyu, who lived from 1522 to 1591; and it was beautifully tended in the strict Buddhist manner.

Another temple I shall not forget, this time of the Tendai sect, was the Chionji, which I visited first with Peter Martin on 14 July 1965. This was also, so to speak, 'in action'. To our surprise, a large congregation was beating on gourds (carved into the shapes of fish) with long-handled mallets, and at the same time shouting vigorously. This hubbub was going on when we arrived, and it was still going on, with equal pertinacity and enthusiasm, when we left. The practice had been followed annually since 1331. In that year, a plague raged through Kyoto, and the Abbot of the Chionji held a special service at which he enjoined his people to repeat the invocation to Amida Buddha a million times. Perhaps the number was nominal: we do not know. In Pure Land Buddhism, espoused by the Tendai sect, the faithful needed only to call upon the name of Amida (which means the 'measureless light') to discharge the obligations of their faith, though repetition made the practice more efficacious: for apart from more temporal favours, the greater were the chances of being reborn in the Pure Land or Paradise in the West.

Despite the attraction of temples such as the Chionji (and the number of foundations in Kyoto runs into hundreds), there are few in my estimation to compare, apart from the interior of the Sanjusangendo, with the exquisite Byodoin and Samboin. I would escape when I could merely to glimpse these places. They were so large and full of detail as to deserve far more study than I could hope to give them. The Byodoin, which became a monastery dedicated to Amidism at the beginning of the eleventh century, seems to hover over the water in which the whole is reflected; for its Phoenix Hall is in fact designed to represent a bird in descent (not, as we might suppose, rising). Standing on the edge of the lake, the Hall spreads out its wings with a grace which is a triumph of architectural subtlety; and the wings are rendered transparent by the elimination of all but bracketed columns joined by a low railing, though the wing-tips are surmounted by a curved 'drooping verge' roof, pagoda-like on the left, which provides a touch of asymmetry giving precisely the illusion of 'landing'.

Inside the Phoenix Hall is a gilt statue of Amida, seated on a lotus and backed by a canopy covered with lacquer and mother-of-pearl. The surrounding walls are decorated with scenes representing the descent of Amida and the Pure Land paradise, while higher up there are pictures of angels seated on clouds, performing on musical instruments.

The Samboin, part of the Daigoji temple complex and a Shingon foundation, is, despite its riches and its paintings by Kano, best appreciated, at least to begin with, by contemplating the garden. This is an example of 'naturalistic' art at its best, with little stone bridges, water, and indeed cascades. Tradition has it that it was designed by Hideyoshi himself. If so, that powerful soldier and ruler must have had a remarkable aesthetic sense.

The interior of the Samboin contains room after *tatamied* room, the vistas of which give an extraordinary impression of sweep and cleanness of line. This is particularly true of the *Omote-shoin*, or formal reception room, part of which can be used as a Noh stage. Among other things, the

Samboin is a school for mountain ascetics. It antedates the garden, having been founded in 1115.

VII

Few people have entered the mind of another age so successfully as Arthur Waley. His translation of *The Tale of Genji* is a masterpiece, even in the eyes of many Japanese. Nevertheless, it does not always make easy reading. As it is extremely long, though still not the whole (Waley omitted one book), it might be best digested by being read aloud by several persons in rotation, as it was first to the Emperor Ichijo. Nevertheless, Murasaki Shikibu's romance, which Donald Keene compares to Proust's *A la recherche du temps perdu*,[1] became a classic almost as soon as it was written, and its influence has perhaps been greater than that of almost any other single work of fiction.

It is difficult for a book of this kind, even one placed deliberately in another age, not to reflect something of the time in which it was written. The world of Prince Genji, as portrayed by Lady Murasaki, was not supposed to be a duplicate of the world in which the authoress lived; but in being an idealized story, it tells us a good deal about the mood of that time. And from her own diary, and those of her contemporaries, we can build up a convincing picture of life at Heiankyo.

That Japanese women have succeeded in exerting unusual power, while remaining socially inferior, has already been argued. This paradox is well illustrated by Lady Murasaki's work, and indeed by the fact that, as Ivan Morris says, 'during the period of about one hundred years that spans the world of *The Tale of Genji*, about every noteworthy author who wrote in Japanese was a woman.'[2] There can be little doubt that this great outpouring of feminine observation, ardour, wit, criticism, spite, sense of *taedium vitae*, and above all the passing of all beautiful things, called in Japanese *aware*, has exerted a profound influence upon the Japanese mind, and consequently upon the behaviour of the ordinary Japanese. Morris goes on to point out how *sure of themselves* the Japanese women in *The*

[1] *Japanese Literature* (1953), p. 75.
[2] Op.cit., p. 199. It may be mentioned that the *Lotus Sutra* is the only one in which Buddhahood was offered to women.

Tale of Genji are, even though they were a prey to anxiety on account of the repeated infidelity of their menfolk. He also stresses that most of the features we commonly associate with Japanese culture—Noh, Tea Ceremony, Kabuki, many familiar dishes, etc.—are all post-Heian. All the more surely, then, have the manners of Heiankyo proved their influence, because these still seem to be part of Japanese social life, and are those features which most forcibly strike the foreign visitor. In short, the 'rule of taste' still prevails, though it now has to contend with an increasing vulgarity. Even the still deep-seated habit of communicating by letter, which in some countries is almost a lost art, recalls the world of Heiankyo; and the pouring out of emotions on paper, by both men and women, is part of a tradition which was established, though at a superior social level, in the tenth century.

During a visit to Kyoto in October 1967, I realized that I had never visited the temple most closely associated with Lady Murasaki, namely that at Ishiyama. The official guide-book to Japan states that 'it is here that Murasaki Shikibu (975–c.1031) is said to have written her classic romance, *Genji Monogatari*.' Well, there is a rather attractive effigy of the lady in one of the rooms, with her writing equipment, inkstone and brush etc.; and on the day that I visited there, in company with Peter Martin, a crowd of enthusiastic sightseers had assembled. Yet it is more than doubtful whether the romance, or even part of it, was written here. In fact, the temple began to be venerated a good two centuries after Lady Murasaki's death; and although a special window has been preserved, no view of Lake Biwa is visible from it, as tradition maintains that it was, though you can see the lake from the grounds. Living in retirement at home after the death of her husband in 1001 (the marriage was a brief one), Lady Murasaki probably began the work soon after, and she must have continued it on her appointment, some time after 1004, as maid-of-honour to Emperor Ichijo's principal wife. Lady Murasaki died between 1025 and 1031, having perhaps reached the age of fifty; but whether, as tradition has it, she entered a convent during her last years we have no means of telling.

In fact, the association of Lady Murasaki with the Ishiyama temple dates from the time of the first *Genji* commentary. This relates how the priestess of the Kamo shrine sought the advice of the Empress Akiko concerning a suitable story written in the phonetic script, which might beguile her leisure. The Empress is said to have commissioned a work from the lady-in-waiting whom she considered most talented. The chosen one, Murasaki herself, then went to the temple at Ishiyama and prayed for inspiration. As it was 15 August, when the moon was held to be at its best for ceremonial viewing, her mind was exalted, inspiration came swiftly and she began then and there to draft some early chapters. For writing material, she 'borrowed' the scroll of the Great Wisdom Sutra, and later, in order to make reparation, she recopied this Sutra and presented it to the temple, where it may be seen today. Considering the length of the Sutra and of *The Tale of Genji* itself (it has fifty-four books and runs to more than 600,000 words), the magnitude of her labours, taking into account the Diary kept for about two years from 1008, outdoes that of most writers. For although there have been scholars who deny her authorship of the novel, they have failed to make out a very good case.

The tradition that Lady Murasaki paid a special visit to the Ishiyama temple in connection with the writing of her romance is not out of keeping with the habits of the time. That she should have sought divine inspiration for the composition of a story concerned mostly with love intrigues is no more absurd than that the Vestal of the Kamo shrine should have hugely appreciated it, as we gather she did. In due course, a school of *Genji* studies appeared which treated the romance much as the early Church treated the *Song of Songs*. Even today, temples are used for purposes which would be frowned upon in churches, despite recent experiments. With all their philandering, the characters in the romance behave, if not with chivalry, then with consideration for one another's feelings; and many of them retire to temples and convents when passion begins to wane. In contrast to Sei Shonagon, Murasaki Shikibu seems to have led a life comparatively free from emotional complications. There is a revealing passage in her Diary which, if any part of that work is a record of her feelings, may perhaps reflect them accurately. This is how it runs: 'All things in this world are sad and tiresome. But from now on I shall fear nothing. Whatever others may do or say, I shall recite my prayers tirelessly to Amida Buddha. And when in my mind the things of this world have come to assume no more importance and stability than the morning dew, then I shall exert all my efforts to become a wise and holy person.'

The interest of this passage, apart from its dignified ring, is in its reference to Amida. It is noteworthy that Murasaki Shikibu, who owing to her scholarly father's influence was immensely learned in the Chinese classics, should have clung at last to an essential 'simple faith', shared with the common people whom she was inclined otherwise to despise or to ignore.

On that almost perfect October day, with Kyoto bathed in sunlight, Peter and I went on a drive down the river valley, passing Nango Spa and crossing the new bridge, in order to visit the famous Mampukuji temple. This is a Zen foundation. Covering as many as sixty-three acres, it is built in the Chinese style, having been founded in 1659 by a Chinese priest. On this occasion, great preparations were afoot for a festival, and sacred dances were being rehearsed. In order to emulate the Zen spirit, we repaired to a restaurant almost opposite called Haku-un-an, where we had a vegetarian meal in some of the most beautiful surroundings in which it is possible to eat in Kyoto. This was our last talk together in Japan, save over the telephone, and I think we both realized how, in our different ways, we had become devoted to that country.

This final visit was in fact the result of another celebration, which had taken place the previous day.

After a discreet and indeed secret courtship, one of our British lecturers at Tokyo University, Martin Collcutt, had become engaged to a secretary in our office, Doi (Morinaga) Akiko, who combined intelligence and sensitivity with a rare, fragile beauty. I was pleased with this match, as of the other Anglo-Japanese alliances which took place within my orbit, because I believe the two peoples have much to give each other. Akiko-San was deeply attached to an uncle who was Abbot of the Daishuin temple, and it was natural that the couple should have wished the marriage to take place within those precincts. The Daishuin is part of the Ryoanji, and therefore my account appropriately links up with that of the first Zen temple of which I have spoken. Of no less interest was the fact that I was to assist at a wedding conducted according to Buddhist rites. This was an uncommon practice, as almost all weddings are performed with Shinto ceremonies, though the latter custom is not so old as is sometimes thought.

It would be difficult to imagine a place more idyllic in which to be married than this little temple standing by its lotus pond. Much re-arrangement had been necessary; but the structure of such buildings, with their easily removable screens and partitions, lends itself to quick changes, and there was a happy atmosphere as friends of bride and bridegroom arrived under a sky streaked with soft cloud. We gathered finally in a large *tatami* room, open on two sides, providing that blend with nature which Japanese so much prize. We knelt in two groups, friends of the bridegroom on the right and those of the bride on the left. The priest, who had formally adopted Akiko and given her his name of Morinaga, performed the ceremony, with the couple standing before an altar, which was heaped with votive offerings. Both Akiko and Martin were dressed in Japanese traditional costume. Four Sutras were sung, and these were interspersed with short remarks by the Abbot which were by way of sermons. The ceremony culminated in the formal putting on of rings.

So simple and yet so carefully ritualized a service was very impressive. I reflected on the conjunction of people which had brought us to join in it: Akiko's family, Martin's mother and myself, the group of professors from Tokyo University with whom Martin worked and many other friends. There seemed no barrier between us, and yet I should have thought such a scene scarcely conceivable had it been described in a work of fiction.

The ceremony over, I recall being helped to my feet by Professor Shumuta, also my friend from Todai,[1] because I had determined to maintain the correct sitting posture for so solemn an occasion, even though it entailed something of an ordeal. While the room was being prepared for the wedding breakfast, we wandered round the temple grounds, including the little cemetery. The weather had held, though there were a few showers, which left the greenery taut and fresh. Japanese wedding breakfasts are always festive occasions, but there was something special about this one. We were served with Zen food, exquisitely prepared. The Abbot said it was right that the living should partake of the food of the dead; he was referring, I suppose, to the offerings on the altar. *Sake* was in plentiful supply, and within a short time our mood of quiet devotion had been changed to that of open good fellowship. After a while, Akiko, who had been sitting with Martin with the Abbot on her right and Mrs. Collcutt on his right, left the gathering to change into a kimono, and on her return we were all set for speeches.

[1] i.e. Tokyo Daigakku (University).

While these were being delivered, new dishes were set before us, and each had some particular form of symbolism, e.g. two thick pieces of seaweed woven together. At one point, the chef was invited in the explain the menu, to which it was evident that much thought had been given. Finally, about 4.30, after many group photographs, we broke up, and having paid a farewell visit to the Ryoanji, I wandered home on foot.

VIII

In relating some of my experiences and impressions in Kyoto I have made one omission, which I must now repair, especially as I referred to the subject in the chapter on Tokyo. Kyoto is the headquarters of geisha. A sheath of mystery surrounds the geisha world, and the Japanese prefer it that way. In Kyoto the geisha quarters are Gion Kobu and Pontocho; of the two, Pontocho is, to my mind, the more attractive and certainly the more shrouded in mystery. The escape from the modern streets into this alley of wooden houses, heavily shuttered, and always quiet, lit with Japanese lanterns by night, was to enter another world. Above the doors were little wooden tablets on which the names of geisha were inscribed, with a 'chicken' sign. Sometimes, though the sight was rare, a door would slide open and a geisha in all her finery would emerge, to disappear quickly on an assignment, her *geta* or open wooden clogs clicking as she went. Most beautiful of all were the junior geisha, or *maiko*, as they are called in Kyoto, whose hair-style was more elaborate than that of their seniors, and who wore long trailing *obis*.

The distinctive geisha make-up, which includes a very white face, an elaborate wig stuck through and through with combs, and a peculiar double-tongued marking on the nape of the neck left bare of white powder-paste, is not perhaps at first sight very appealing to the Westerner. Naturally, this opinion is not shared by the Japanese, for whom the neck has an almost irresistible fascination. For this reason, the collar of the kimono is rucked back to afford a better view.

It is often forgotten that geisha receive a long and strict training, like any other artist in Japan; and if the word geisha means 'entertainer', this does not imply that the entertainment is not a form of art. In Pontocho there is a centre, the Nyokobu, consisting of a geisha school, a medical office, and the headquarters of the geisha association. This latter is very powerful, and there have on occasion been geisha strikes.

Unless the foreigner's Japanese is extremely good, most of the verbal entertainment provided by geisha is inevitably lost on him. An educated geisha will have at her finger-ends a knowledge of the Chinese and Japanese classics, with which she makes great play by means of apt quotation, puns and innuendo.

Many, but by no means all, geisha have protectors. They are known by some such epithet as 'Mr. Twice-a-Week'. On the other hand, it is extremely expensive nowadays for a married man to maintain a geisha; but the practice of having a geisha wife to do the entertaining was not without its advantages. The Japanese have an attitude to sexual morality different from the Western one, but it is doubtful whether the latter can be considered morally superior. When in 1964 Air France invited some geisha to Paris, their Mama-San endeavoured, though without success, to insure their virginity at Lloyds.[1] I wonder how many other Madames would be in a position to consider such a measure.

It is doubtful whether there is much future for geisha, simply because the expense of hiring them is very great; but if the institution were to die out, something precious would surely be lost. I should be sad to see the little houses of Pontocho changed into ordinary bars or shops. Kyoto would be deprived of some of its magic.

When I look back on what I have written of Kyoto, I realize how hopelessly inadequate it is as an account of the things I myself did and saw there, and of the extraordinary power which the city assumes over those who come to know it. Although you have to go in search of Kyoto, the search is always rewarding. I recall so many other unexpected moments: discovering the Jingoji temple, with its long view over the trees and its rapt silence; watching the Daimonji festival from the roof of the British Council office, with Carmen Blacker, the distinguished Japanese scholar, the Martins, and many Japanese guests; being taken by the Marquis of Hosokawa round his beautiful estate (I was to be present later at the wedding of his son to Princess Yazuko, the daughter of Prince and Princess Mikasa); watching the Jidai Matsuri, a sort

1 Cf. Elizabeth Dufourq, *Les Femmes Japonaises* (1970), p. 186. Madame Dufourq's husband was French Cultural Counsellor in Japan while I was serving there.

of historical pageant of Kyoto, in which Murasaki Shikibu features prominently; participating with my sister and my son in a Tea Ceremony at the house of a friend, Mr. Matsuoka, when we were televised on a nationwide circuit; drinking late in a geisha-house with a great friend, Mr. Nakamura, who revered Edmund Blunden and who had translated long English historical works; and not least wandering by the Kamo River in the hot summer evenings, with the lanterns reflected line after line in the water; and again, from the vantage point of some high building, observing how the modern city, ablaze with light, was somehow relieved of its garishness by the deep clusters of darkness, irregularly spaced, which indicated the presence of a temple or shrine. I know well that the visitor like myself can idealize Kyoto, and that many of the people who crowd its streets think little enough about the dark clusters and what lies enshrouded in them. The foreigner looks for what he is unaccustomed to seeing, and it is natural that he should do so. But I am convinced that this ancient Kyoto still means much to the Japanese, even though the significance may be below the level of consciousness.

IX

One of the earliest of my visits was to a city which Japan took for one of its earliest capitals, Nara, originally Heijo. That I was able to see from the beginning something more than the tourist's Nara was due to the kindness and generosity not merely of Japanese hosts but of a foreign resident, Patrick James. Patrick had a beautiful Japanese house not far from Tenri, where he taught at the university established by the extraordinary sect of Tenrikyo. Patrick, himself a Japanese scholar, had taken the vows of a Buddhist priest, though he had a dispensation regarding the tonsure; but somehow the more Japanese and Buddhist he became, the more American he remained, this Americanism being in turn tempered by a good deal of Englishness, for he was a Cambridge graduate. During my stay in Japan, he married a Japanese girl of imposing appearance and much charm. As he had become so thoroughly imbued with Japanese traditions, he had insisted that his marriage should be 'arranged', as indeed a number of marriages in Japan still are. One could only say that it was very well arranged, for he seemed the happiest of men.

The 'Nara period', which lasted from 710 to 794, was one of the most creative in the country's history. Nor is it paradoxical to affirm that it was the epoch of predominantly Chinese influence. Nara today is a rather sleepy little place (which has nothing to do with the proximity of that horror called Dreamland, an amusement park); but in the days of its greatness, it was a busy populous city, though situated a good deal to the west of the present one. It was at this time that the great national chronicles were compiled, the *Kojiki* and the *Nihon Shoki*, meaning 'Records of Ancient Matters' and 'Chronicles of Japan' respectively; and the impulse towards compilation produced also one of the earliest anthologies of Japanese poetry, the *Manyoshu*. But perhaps the most significant achievement of the Nara period was the building of the great temples, among which the Todaiji is the earliest, and the foundation of affiliated temples and other religious houses, including many nunneries.

If you wish to appreciate a temple like the Todaiji, or 'Great East Temple', you need to know something about that complicated development of Buddhism which gave rise to the Six Nara Sects, but particularly that named Kegon, the Fifth Sect; for the Todaiji is its headquarters. The theological ideas behind Kegon are of a complication seemingly foreign even to the Japanese mind; but this indicates the extent to which it *is* foreign, having come from India via T'ang China. Orthodox Buddhists, though not a Zen priest whom I met, believe that there was an historical figure, Sakyamuni, or Gautama of the Sakya clan, who lived in the sixth century B.C.; but according to Kegon belief Sakyamuni was merely a manifestation in the temporal dimension of an eternal or universal Buddha, a cosmic being called Vairocana or, in Japanese, Roshana. To venerate this universal Buddha, and also to express thanksgiving for deliverance from an outbreak of smallpox which occurred about 735 (its first appearance in Japan), the Emperor Shomu caused a colossal statue to be cast; and this effigy, the largest bronze statue in the world, has survived, though after much damage and reconstruction, as the Daibutsu or Great Buddha.

To visit Nara without seeing the Great Buddha is like visiting Kamakura, seat of the ancient shogunate, and omitting to see its own Daibutsu. Nevertheless, I confess that I prefer the Kamakura Buddha to that at Nara: the latter seems to me to lack the compassionate expression of most Buddhist images, and even to wear a slightly cynical look. But perhaps the effect of the Nara Daibutsu is spoilt to some extent by an impression of being severely cramped. Seated on its enormous lotus and surrounded by a halo decorated with the incarnations of the cosmic Buddha, it seems to be irked by its restricted wooden hutch. In fact, the present building is a good deal smaller than the earlier one, which twice suffered from fire, though it remains among the world's largest wooden buildings. Granted, those who planned and cast the Daibutsu (the original artist is supposed to have been a Korean of the imposing name of Kuninaka-no-Muraji-Kimimoro) had in mind the Buddha who escaped all dimensions and transcended all categories; and so the elaborate adornments surrounding the head and shoulders was intended to convey a sense of infinity. It is said that when, in 752, the ceremony of 'opening the eyes', or inauguration, of the Daibutsu was held, no less than 20,000 members and officials were present.

Most of the Todaiji itself was ruthlessly destroyed in 1180 by the Taira or Heike clan, which had acquired a powerful position at Court; and it was a priest, Chogen, who, with great effort, succeeded in rebuilding it, employing a style adapted from southern China. One of the surviving parts of the reconstruction is the Great South Gate; and its double curved roof, which seems to compress the supporting pillars with their heavy brackets, reveals something of the power of the new technique. In the same style is the so-called Worship Hall, where the roof is sustained by another set of complicated brackets. This is the oldest surviving building of the Todaiji. It contains a beautiful statue of the Goddess of Mercy, presumed to be the work of a priest-artist, Roben. The statue is surrounded by a kind of body-halo, shooting out metal prongs. This goddess, depicted in a praying attitude, is accorded special reverence on account of her supposed power to relieve suffering. Round the statue are many smaller ones, as well as a figure with a look of ferocity, expelling evil forces. A Bell House, of a slightly later date, is partly influenced by another Chinese school but associated with Zen. It holds a huge bell, nine feet in diameter. Cast originally in 749, it was wrecked in a typhoon: the present one dates from about 1239.

Another structure dedicated to Roshana stands not far away. This is the famous Shosoin, or Treasure House, built of huge logs. The Emperor Shomu had abdicated in favour of his daughter Koken, and it was as Empress that Koken was present at the 'eye opening' ceremony. The

Dowager Empress, Shomu's widow, celebrating the crucial forty-ninth day after her husband's death, had decided to donate all his treasures to the Todaiji, including those used at the opening ceremony. As the collection was a particularly valuable one; as it has no parallel elsewhere; and as it includes objects originating from outside Japan, the Shosoin contains a collection which is beyond price. It is now under the control of the Imperial Household Agency. I was fortunate enough to visit Nara on one of the few occasions when the treasures were open for inspection. Their preservation is no doubt due partly to the fact that the building was placed on piles which hindered dampness. Even so, it has been thought best to build additional storehouses, and these, made of concrete, and of no great attractiveness, stand a short distance away.

We then went to the Kofukuji temple, which dates chiefly from the ninth century, though its museums contains statues and examples of printing from the eighth century and even earlier. It would seem that printing from copper plates began in the eighth century (perhaps the earliest example in the world is in the Tenri museum), and woodblock printing, which requires rice paper, from the thirteenth century. The Kofukuji, head temple of the Hosso sect and family temple of the Fujiwaras, means 'happiness-producing' temple. It is an enormous complex; but of its original 175 buildings most have been destroyed by fire. Dating from the fifteenth century is the lovely five-storey pagoda, though fire has damaged it too: there are statues of the Buddha on every storey. A three-storey pagoda, not less attractive than the other, is nearby. Of all the buildings, the Nan-endo, an octagonal hall with an elaborate ceiling, is perhaps the finest. This holds a statue of Fukukenjaku, the goddess revered in the Worship Hall of the Todaiji.

We passed on to the Chuguji nunnery, which has an exquisite contemplative statue of wood considered by some to be the work of Prince Shotoku; but perhaps the highlight of this part of the excursion was the Hokkeji nunnery, with its wooden statue of Kannon with eleven heads. Here, because of Patrick's knowledge of the place, and the respect he had won, we were invited to take tea with the Abbess. She was a fresh-looking lady, probably about thirty-five but looking much younger, with a completely shaven head. She talked with much animation. The nunnery, under imperial patronage, is run by four sisters. Both on this occasion and on my second visit some years later, also in Patrick's company, I experienced some rare moments of serenity. Part of this feeling of satisfaction and completion was due, I felt sure, to the meticulous order, simplicity and elegance of the small rooms which we inspected. Apart from the Abbess, we saw only one other sister, an older woman who was waiting on us; but with the pervading quietness and decorum, there was everywhere a feeling of industry and dedication.

Finally, making our way back to the more conventional route, we visited the Horyuji temple, which is situated about seven miles out of Nara. Here, disposed over a very large area, is a foundation superior in many respects to any other in Nara. Originally established by Prince Shotoku, it would seem to have been rebuilt at a later date a few miles away. The Horyuji is one of those temple-complexes to which years of study could be devoted. Before I even set foot in its precincts I came to the conclusion that I would try to learn from it one thing at least, so that a torrent of impressions should not prevent the formation of a coherent picture. I found that this 'selective appreciation' was the only approach possible for a layman to what Sacheverell Sitwell has called 'giant art'. In the case of the Horyuji, the aim, I felt, was to try to grasp, or even simply to contemplate, the great achievement of the Japanese in constructing, on their own soil, and out of the materials available to them, works of art which, though Chinese in inspiration, possessed an authentic and original character, and in doing this without the prolonged process of trial and error which submission to foreign influence usually entails. In China, which I was soon after to visit, there are remarkable edifices of stone of which even the present regime is proud; but the wooden structures are almost all gone, whereas the Japanese, who from the start used wood rather than stone, have been successful in preserving a great many of their temples despite the three afflictions which they have been obliged to live with—earthquakes, fire, and the occasional madman. Thus there is nothing of wood in any country to compare with the Horyuji for antiquity; and, until the fire which severely damaged it, the Golden Hall of the temple must have preserved the oldest and most perfect examples, of their kind, of Japanese Buddhist art. In 1949, the famous frescoes on the walls were severely damaged, though this time as the result of an electricity fault; and it was necessary, in order to save them from total destruction, gently to slice them off, backed with a thin layer of clay. Their restoration, which was undertaken with some foreign help, proved a triumph of patient industry; they can now be seen in the museum attached to the temple. What is particularly interesting about the depictions of the Bodhisattvas in these frescoes is not only their stylistic resemblance to the traditions of T'ang China, and their consequent links with Indian art, but also the hint they give of the traditions of Greece, or rather Hellenism. Never afterwards does one see faces and drapery so reminiscent of classical art, which is often assumed to have taken an exclusively Western direction.

This allusion to the West prompts me to reflect upon the pace at which influence in the artistic sphere can be exerted. Whereas the Hellenistic tradition had extended its influence as far as the remote islands of Japan by the eighth century, and probably earlier, the Westerly influence upon which we dwell so much in our education and which constituted the basis of upper-class formation until recently, was comparatively slow in making itself felt. Moreover, the difference between this Western drive and the *Drang nach Osten* was that most of the classical influence was carried West by invasion, whereas there has been no successful invasion of Japan in historic times. The Eastward movement was an example of cultural assimilation undertaken for its own sake.

It is the serene faces of the Buddhas and Bodhisattvas which have given consolation to the disciples of Gautama, warming hearts that would otherwise have remained unaffected by the intricacies of sect and doctrine; and although I have rarely seen in Japan such 'homely' scenes in temples as I have witnessed in other Buddhist countries, such as Thailand, I believe that if temples such as the Horyuji and nunneries such as the Chuguji and the Hokkeji were secularized and turned into museums, their impressiveness as works of art would be reduced, just as I feel that art itself will disappear if, *per impossibile*, the religious impulse were altogether to die out. Although Rudolf Otto's 'numinous' is not the whole of religion, it is an essential part of it, and therefore a psychic necessity. As we desert our churches, so we darken our discotheques.

Thus although today we inspect the temples of Nara and Kyoto and elsewhere chiefly as works of art, it seems to me that there is a great deal of cultural snobbery about such a practice. We dare not return with the admission that we have *not* seen this temple or that, this statue or that, this garden or that. Yet how much does it really mean to us? A good deal is written, and some mention has been made here, of architectural techniques; but such techniques are no more than means to an end. The end was the worship of the Buddha, and to provide in the statuary and in the imagery the means whereby to assist such adoration. Unless we try to put ourselves in the frame of mind of the worshippers, we shall come away with little profit. If indeed we cannot make the necessary mental adjustment, or if we regard the whole attempt at worship and contemplation as so much waste of mental effort, I do not see what point there is in traipsing round ancient buildings, except for the purpose of studying the material forms assumed by delusion and credulity.

Such a digression reflected my thoughts as I viewed the temples of Nara. I was driven to such reflection because, with all their majesty, I found these places slightly less attractive than those of Kyoto, which were on the whole not so heavy and overwhelming. I can imagine the enormous concourse that assembled to witness the unveiling of the Great Buddha; I see the Byodoin or the Sanjusangendo in Kyoto as places to which to withdraw. Nara was the place where Buddhism arrived as a militant religion, out to conquer: Kyoto was the place where the essence of that religion was quietly distilled.

X

Although Patrick had taught for so long at Tenri University, he had never felt drawn to the faith which animated its founder, though he did not underestimate the hold which it had upon its adherents. I was anxious to see something of Tenrikyo at first hand. Nakayama Miki was an ordinary Japanese housewife who, in 1843, suddenly received an illumination which convinced her that she was God incarnate. Such an idea has been entertained by more than one person, but it has remained usually a particular obsession. With Mrs. Nakayama it was different. Against enormous odds, one of which was her female status, she succeeded in convincing first her family and then a group of friends that she possessed unusual and unique spiritual gifts, and in due course her power over others was such that her followers began to suffer persecution. She wrote down many of her ideas; the Tenri scriptures are a combination of Shinto, Buddhism, and even Christian doctrines. This body of doctrine was intermingled with a rather strange mythology; and it must be admitted that some part of her teaching, which includes the notion that the human race began as a group of beings a few inches high, had proved a stumbling-block to sophisticated modern believers. The death of the foundress caused more immediate difficulties. Can God incarnate die? The faithful decided in the negative. She was declared to have remained alive, and in the world, though no longer visible to human sight. Consequently, her home still remains in the temple which she founded, and she is looked after in rotation by the faithful. She is served regular meals, of which she eats the subtle part, and she is put to bed regularly at 9 p.m. Now known as 'God the Parent' or 'the Blessed Parent', she is considered to be the mother of all followers of Tenrikyo, who number several millions, including many in Korea and among the Japanese communities of South America.

The proper attitude to a religion wholly outside one's own tradition is, it seems to me, to take it as seriously as it will allow. If you regard its adherents as a pack of crazy fanatics, you will learn nothing and perhaps miss an important experience. So it was in the former frame of mind that I paid my first visit to the Tenrikyo headquarters and called on the Patriarch, the Rev. Nakayama Shozen, a direct descendant of the foundress. I was escorted round by an earnest American nisei girl, Miss Uchida, who showed me the prayer room and the temple, and in whose company I attended that part of the evening service, a moving one, in which the foundress formally 'retires' for the night. Kneeling on the *tatami*, we could see into the far inner sanctum in which women in kimonos were going quietly about their business. The temple, now a huge and somewhat elaborate building, must certainly be one of the largest wooden structures of its kind. The atmosphere was devout; and the ritual I was witnessing, though curious, had nothing absurd about it. In the precincts, workers, all volunteers, were tending the paths and the garden; and I had the impression of a solidarity which is so integral a part of the Japanese character. Each worker wore a special tunic with the Tenri crest or *mon* on the back. I gathered, even from persons hostile or indifferent to Tenrikyo, that the standard of public dealing was, like that of the Quakers, of a high order. One adherent, a quiet and efficient girl, joined my staff in Tokyo.

The Patriarch was a large man, somewhat resembling Wyndham Lewis in his last years. He was a judo champion, and perhaps more a man of the world than some of his predecessors. His manner was affable, open, and quite without *hauteur*. The lunch over which he presided could not be regarded as ascetic. Apart from his duties as head of a still flourishing sect, he was a great collector, and the Tenri museum and its adjoining library of 750,000 books possessed an interest quite independent of the tenets of the religion. It contained many collected editions of English authors which are today hard to come by.

What struck me about Tenrikyo was its robust, cheerful, yet essentially simple approach to life. Before my first visit to Tenri I saw a large crowd one day on a station platform in Tokyo and I was impressed by the sight of enthusiastic, happy faces. As I learnt afterwards, they were followers of Tenrikyo seeing off the Patriarch.

My last visit to Nara was on 13 August 1967. I went with the incidental intention of seeing the great Lantern Festival at the Kasuga shrine. Once more I put up at the Nara Hotel, with its Victorian atmosphere, which, because of its convenient situation, I preferred in this case to a *ryokan*. First I wandered round the deer park. This customary stroll was always obligatory on a visit to Nara; but I confess that I never greatly took to the deer, who, despite their being 'divine messengers', were a rather irritable crew, and who, in the rutting season, could be a trifle diabolical. Then I sauntered up to the great shrine, and watched the preparations for the evening festival. The men wore a most attractive lightish green *hakama*, and there was much bustle. Before returning for the festival opening at 7 o'clock, I wandered around the numerous mini shrines and also visited that called the Kasuga-Wakamiya, sacred to the Shinto deity Ameno-oishikumo-no-Mikoto. At the appropriate hour, having purchased a garland and a miniature lamp, I joined a large crowd to watch the *Bugaku* dances. As darkness fell, the 2,000 bronze and wooden lanterns were lit; and with the half-moon in a clear sky, the scene was slowly transfused with an unearthly brightness. Even the mosquitoes, which were numerous, did not detract from the glory of the scene. There were many children present and a large concourse of the 'faithful', and I observed how, as usual, gravity and cheerfulness were blended. Somehow I did not want to be borne home by the surge of people, so I slipped away before the end, wandering past the lanterns, which seemed to be links in a chain of flame. This suddenly gave way to a moonlight-diluted darkness, and all was still.

It was not merely the lantern festival that I had come to see; I had wanted to locate the famous pine tree which, according to tradition, provided the background of the original Noh drama, and which is reproduced on the backcloth of all Noh stages. Could I find that tree? I could not. Nobody knew where it was, though an *o-sembe* man had at least heard of it, and waved me towards the entrance to the shrine. Next day, determined not to be thwarted, I telephoned the shrine office, whereupon I received precise and very simple instructions. The *o-sembe* man was not far wrong. The pine tree stood by the first *torii*, on the greensward to the right. There I snapped it in brilliant sunshine. It is a tall, gaunt tree, very different in shape from its conventional representation. A simple fence protects it, and a commemorative plaque is affixed nearby. Perhaps this is not the original tree, though I saw no reason to doubt its authenticity. At least we know that the earliest Noh drama was acted at or near this place, because the guilds (*za*) of Saragaku actors attached to the Kasuga shrine and the neighbouring Kofukuji temple were those whose genius developed the Noh drama as we have it today.

Attendance at the Lantern Festival and locating the Noh pine tree proved a fitting farewell to Nara. That evening I thought much of the time when this part of Japan had seen the birth of a unique culture, with which modern Japan preserved a direct continuity. But my mind also went back to a more remote period still; for it was on the Nara plain, the region known as Yamato, that the earliest Japanese state was founded.

CHAPTER VI

Returning to the Source: Ise and Izumo

As soon as I could so arrange my engagements, I decided to go to Ise and Izumo. In a way, this was one of the most important visits I was to undertake, a veritable *pélerinage à la source*; and I do not think it possible to arrive at an understanding of Japan unless a visit is paid to this fascinating region.

Before 1945, Japan had no prehistory. Instead, she had a mythology. To our eyes this mythology is so strange, and even preposterous, as to prompt the question whether any Japanese could genuinely have believed it. This depends upon the significance attached to the word belief. It would seem that the ordinary Japanese did not debate the question as we might debate a scientific theory. As the national myth was the orthodoxy of the time, they let the subject rest by not presuming to question it. The central aim of the myth was to establish the position of the Emperor as the divinely appointed sovereign of Japan. It did not originally imply that he was himself divine. Most people were prepared to accept his divine right. As for the myth, it could look after itself. The attribution of divinity to the Emperor's *person* came later.

What is the myth of the origin of Japan? I will do my best to present it in intelligible terms. First, it must be explained that some elements in the mythology are at variance with others. The story begins with two persons, sister and brother, Izanami and Izanagi. Together, they left the upper regions, and, arriving on earth, produced by their incestuous union the islands of Japan and also a number of other gods. In giving birth to the God of Fire, however, Izanami died. She descended to the nether regions. Here her brother paid her a visit; but Izanami was so ashamed to be seen in a state of decay that she prevailed on Izanagi to leave. Izanagi then set about purifying himself; and from the clothes which he relinquished, as well as from the parts of his body which he cleansed, many new gods were formed. These gods were of great power: they included Amaterasu, the Sun Goddess, a Moon God, a God of Destruction, and a host of others. The God of Destruction, named Susa-no-o, ascended with Amaterasu to the highest heaven, and here they begat a fresh series of gods. A most peculiar episode followed. True to his nature, Susa-no-o caused devastation in his sister's rice fields, and also befouled her residence. This caused her to hide herself, in consequence of which the entire world was plunged into darkness. The other gods then decided to coax her into the open again. They held a party at which one of the female gods did a provocative dance which brought the Sun Goddess out. The god originally responsible for the trouble, Susa-no-o, was thereupon judged by the assembled deities, and summarily exiled. This meant going down to the earth and—a point of importance— settling at Izumo in West Honshu, a town of which he became the ruler. He also went to Korea, bringing back with him a sword. Later, the descendants of the rulers of Izumo intermarried with the descendants of the Sun Goddess.

In due course, the grandson of the Sun Goddess, Ninigi, landed from heaven on the territory of Kyushu, the southernmost island. With him he brought the traditional regalia of the rulers of Japan: a bronze mirror, the iron sword which Susa-no-o had originally obtained from Korea, and a curved jewel.

Finally, Ninigi's own great-grandson, gathering together a large host, began a campaign of conquest which took him from Kyushu up the Inland Sea to the area known today as the Kinki region. Here, in Yamato, he established his authority by overcoming successively all the local gods. The date given in the annals for this conquest is 660 B.C. Calculated according to a Chinese system of chronology, the date marks the symbolic beginning of the line of Japanese emperors. The founder of the line received the posthumous title of Jimmu, which means 'Divine Warrior'.

What is interesting about this story is that it begins with a mythological phantasmagoria and ends with something like recognizable history: for at some point the historical line of emperors begins. In the mythology, we can disentangle certain archetypal myths, such as that concerned with solar eclipse. We can detect also an attempt to reconcile, in retrospect, the competing claims of the authority of Ise, the centre in Yamato where the Sun Goddess is still revered, and that of Izumo. The myth goes on to relate how the authority at Izumo finally submitted to that at Ise. The annals comprising the *Kojiki* and the *Nihon Shoki* are historically un-reliable for perhaps the first thousand years which they purport to cover; but from or about A.D. 400, when the Yamato court invited some scribes from Paikche—one of the states into which Korea was divided—to keep proper records in Chinese, we possess a chronicle which, so far as the main events are concerned, is in many respects accurate and can be checked from independent sources. For example, the great tumuli which are still to be seen in the Kinki region are almost certainly tombs of historical rulers of the fifth century. These rulers exercised authority over the whole of Kyushu and what is now called the Kanto region, and over part of Korea as well. That the present Emperor is linked with them by descent is indubitable. Indeed, the present dynasty is thought to go back to a date between A.D. 300 and A.D. 400.

One of the three items of the sacred regalia, the mirror, was removed to Ise. It was supposedly taken there from the imperial court, and a royal princess was reputed to assume responsibility for it. According to the *Wei Chih*, an early Chinese chronicle, the state of Wa, as Japan was then called, had a female ruler who remained unmarried. Himiko or Pimiko by name, she is described as ruling over an area called Yamatai. I will not discuss the theories which would make a distinction between Yamato and Yamatai: the current presumption is that the two refer to the same locality. If, as is also supposed, the queen's name meant 'Sun Princess', this would tend to identify her with the High Priestess of Ise. It would also suggest that the guardianship of the shrine of the mirror at Ise and the wielding of political authority were combined in the same person. Although today the Emperor of Japan is neither the direct supervisor of Ise nor the political ruler of his country, he remains both the reigning monarch and the Chief Priest of Shinto, of which Ise is the centre.[1] Ise

[1] In 1971, before the Emperor's journey abroad, the Imperial Household Agency or Kunaicho issued the following statement: 'The Emperor observes, in his private capacity, the traditional faith of the Imperial families, which takes the form of Shrine Shinto, and conducts the ceremonial rites of the Court. However, the

still has a Grand Priestess, the present incumbent being Mrs. Kitashira-kawa Sachiko.

Unlike the 'higher religions', Shinto grew up without a name and without a theology. Names, theologies, systems of metaphysics, are needed when there are faiths in competition. Thus it was that when Buddhism was introduced into Japan in the sixth century (the exact date is probably A.D. 532), the need to distinguish it from the popular faith became imperative. The latter was accordingly called the 'Way of the Gods' (Shinto), as opposed to 'The Way of the Buddha'. Between the two there was in the end no direct opposition, though some initial popular resistance to Buddhism was put up. Gradually, however, the multitudinous gods of Shinto were incorporated into the Buddhist pantheon, and the chief among them were regarded as avatars of the Buddhist divinities.

Although shrines and temples were usually kept distinct, there are few temples today which do not display Shinto influence; and the ordinary Japanese finds no incongruity in being married according to Shinto and buried according to Buddhist rites. When it is realized how old Buddhism was when it first entered Japan, the blending of this complicated system of beliefs with a communal 'nature religion' was the more remarkable. At the same time, a collection of folk-beliefs, many of which had sunk into the subconscious, provided a substructure powerful enough to help to promote the survival of Buddhism itself.

Although in the period before the Second World War Shinto had developed into a violently nationalistic religion, and although as a result it was 'disestablished' under American direction after the defeat of 1945, there is reason to think that it is the *religio perennis* of the Japanese people, and that it will never die as long as the Japanese community endures.

On frequent visits to shrines in the company of Japanese (some of them highly sophisticated people and some of scientific eminence), I was interested to observe how they would spontaneously perform the requisite, if simple, acts of reverence, clapping their hands to 'attract the attention of the god', saying a brief prayer, and throwing an offering into the repository placed before the inner sanctum.

Emperor has no special status, as head or otherwise, in either Shrine Shinto or Sectarian Shinto.' (*The Times*, 24.IX.71.) One may perhaps say that this statement was for overseas consumption.

Undoubtedly, Shinto was propagated by the Yamato emperors with the overriding object of securing the subordination of all local deities to the Sun Goddess; and this campaign of divine imperialism was almost completely successful. It reflected a similar conquest or assumption of authority in the realm of government.

I paid my first visit to Ise on Sunday, 10 June 1966. I wish only that I had gone before, as it would have enabled me to gain a true understanding of Japan much sooner. Flying to Osaka and taking the Kinki Express to Uji Yamada, I arrived at a place which, as I soon discovered, differs in character from any other in the country. Over the whole Ise area, though excluding the commercialized Pearl Island, there is a pervading atmosphere of the sacred and the immemorial. I would even contend that if the visitor does not feel this, he has lost a 'sense' which must be among our oldest psychic faculties. Why I do not scruple to be dogmatic on this subject is that, in my own case, I was quite unprepared for such a reaction. I had not long before visited some parts of Japan which, far from evoking the sensation of wonder promised by the guide-books, filled me with horror, chiefly at the desecration which modern building and commercialization had brought about. So Ise took me by surprise. Ise was unspoilt. Which is as it should be.

Not having fixed upon a hotel, I went first to one of the semi-open-air restaurants which are such a delight in Japan; and, having had a good meal, I asked if I might leave my customarily excessive impedimenta there. The woman-proprietor of the Misugi, in her white smock, was only too obliging. This welcoming attitude is found all over the country; but it is especially striking in certain places, Ise being one of them. I then set out to visit the great shrine-complex, or rather complexes, armed only with a camera and a note-book. As I strolled up one of the great alleys, lined with tall cryptomeria, I began to experience a sense of elation. I felt as if I were going back to the 'beginning'; and even if it were not my own racial beginning, the sheer serenity of the place infected my alien spirit.

The entrance to a shrine by way of a *torii*—the arch usually made of wood with two or more cross-beams, and conforming to one of six main types—was by now so familiar as to pass almost unnoticed. But here the *torii*, three in number and well separated, were of vast size. They led to a cluster of trees which was as near to being a sacred wood as I have known. Then, with an unexpectedness for which I had been prepared only by the superficial experience of reading, the outer shrine or Geku of Ise came into view. No building in Japan bears any resemblance to this or to the inner shrine or Naiku, some distance away. The reason is that these structures preserve with exactitude the earliest design of the shrines set up at this spot by the Yamato emperors. Such scrupulous preservation is due not to physical maintenance but to rebuilding the shrine, not on the exact spot but in a place adjoining, every twenty years. In historical times at least, this practice had been maintained regularly and with only a single break (in 1900 when water during a fire fell on the roof of the Naiku, and desecration was feared) and this may well have been the case since the beginning. The result is that we have a reasonably good idea of what the earliest building of shrines, and perhaps also of royal palaces, was like. Nor is there wanting further confirmation of the accuracy of the reconstruction. The designs of buildings on some of the bells belonging to the Tomb Culture correspond in a remarkable way to what, after all these centuries, is to be found at Ise.

Viewing this strange but simple structure, resting on piles and covered with straw, no doubt a style of architecture found in early China, it dawned on me how the tradition of periodic reconstruction as a method of preservation may sometimes be superior to the patching up, buttressing, concrete-injecting treatment of an ancient building, such as is practised elsewhere. But this depends upon the preservation of atmosphere: that is capital. The sight of Ise, with its cypress wood gleaming in pristine newness, had a unique, if simple, grandeur. As so often in Japan, the old and the new worked in collaboration, producing a result *tam antiqua et tam nova*.

Indeed, what struck me above all about the Ise shrines, and about their immediate environment, was the sense of salubrity, as if the whole place had been subject to the kind of regular lustration that most Japanese give to their persons. True, the sun was shining, as it was on all my subsequent visits, and I had escaped for a while from the murk of Tokyo; but I could imagine how, even in the prodigal Japanese rain, the timbers of Ise, tipped with gold, would have gleamed more brightly still. They had the living colour of that 'orient and immortal wheat' spoken of by Traherne.

The outer shrine is dedicated to the Goddess of Agriculture, especially rice, and sericulture. On 24 June a ceremony called 'The Divine Service of the Rice' is performed. The building is constructed in a style similar to the inner shrine, which, as the holy of holies, is dedicated to Amaterasu, and holds the precious sacred mirror. Neither building contains a single nail, and the design is of extreme economy, save for the extraordinary cross-beams surmounting the thatched roof, like stylized antlers. As the innermost buildings are surrounded by a rough stone wall surmounted by a protective wooden fence, the impression given is that of a group of gentle animals waiting patiently in their pen. The cross-beams, or *Shigi*, have been the subject of speculation since (and that is not so very long) the architecture of the shrine has been systematically studied. At one time this place was considered so sacred that it could not even be photographed.

It is useful to get one's bearings at the Geku in order to approach the Naiku with greater familiarity. Between them, the distance is about four miles. The Naiku also should be taken in stages, following the pilgrims' traditional route. At once, the impression of spaciousness struck me, even though it was necessary in visiting the 'water purification' area to enter another 'sacred wood'. Many shrines and temples in Japan are approached through narrow lanes or passages, as is so much else that is sacred, such as a Tea Ceremony room; but Ise is laid out on the grand scale, without seeming over-magnificent.

Next, I passed the Saikan or purification hall, followed by another place of purification, until I came to the Kaguraden, where special sacred dances are performed. On payment of a fee, it is possible to see a performance by the shrine-maidens. I came next to two buildings reserved for ceremonial cooking, then a large empty space, beyond which—the climax of the walk—I found myself on the threshold of the inner sanctuary. Climbing up some steps and passing under the second *torii*, I confronted a curtained gate. This is the point beyond which none but members of the imperial family, their envoys and some priests, may go. As the pilgrim is already on holy ground, he is expected to behave in a suitably reverent manner. The injunction is scarcely necessary, for the surroundings of themselves command a mood of devoutness. Nevertheless, in 1888, Viscount Mori, then Minister of Education and previously Ambassador to Washington and London, raised the inner curtain with his stick, wishing to demonstrate his scepticism. He paid for his enterprise by being murdered the following year by a fanatical Shinto devotee, Nischino Burtara, whose tomb in the Yanaka cemetery is still revered.

Some fortunate people have been able to take advantage of a breeze to catch a glimpse beneath this tantalizing curtain. Although nothing of the sort happened to me, I was able to see through the fence at the side, where it was possible to make out a number of courts dominated by the main building in the centre, with two smaller buildings 'in attendance'. These were the treasuries.

It was then that I realized that the area adjacent to the sacred compound was that set aside for the new main shrine. So far as is known, the reconstruction has taken place fifty-nine times; and the last occasion was 1973. A special ceremony called *Sengu-no-gi*, or the 'spirit-moving ceremony', is performed on the occasion of each reconstruction; and this must be one of the world's oldest rituals to have been preserved unmodified.

Is the sacred mirror really there? That is a question often asked. There is good reason to believe that it is. Moreover, the claim that it has never been seen by a human being is almost, if not quite true. It is reported to be wrapped in a brocade bag, and when this begins to show signs of wear, a new and similar bag is drawn over it. When the first bag was put on, someone must have seen the mirror, though it may only have been viewed from the back. The brocade bag and its contents are now protected by a golden-decorated box, covered with a silk mantle. A similar mirror is preserved at the Geku shrine, but again little is known about it, save that it too has remained invisible for many centuries. The mirrors to be found in all Shinto shrines are symbolic of those at Ise: that their function is to remind the worshipper of the duty of self-knowledge may be a later rationalization. Presumably these mirrors, like the ones found in so many ancient tomb-mounds, symbolize the sun disk, and therefore Amaterasu herself. They are of course of polished metal.

At crises, the Emperor will repair to the shrine to consult his ancestors: the last crucial occasion when he did so was following the 1945 defeat, but another occasion was before he went abroad in 1971. The prime minister will also come here to report national events of significance. Finally, the people of Japan come here, because this is somehow the spiritual centre of their country. In the past, Ise Associations were formed, with special Ise agents acting as liaison officers, so that farmers especially could make the pilgrimage, the individuals being chosen by lot and escorted to the village boundary by rejoicing peasants. I do not for a moment suggest that these pilgrims came, or still come, in the mood of their ancestors, who worshipped the Sun Goddess and the Goddess of Agriculture; but Ise means to them more than Canterbury has ever meant to the people of Britain. As the centre of Shinto devotion, the importance of the place is measured to some extent by the fact that until the Meiji Restoration no Buddhist priest or nun was allowed access to it. At the *mitarashi* or water-purification place down by the sacred Izuzu River, I watched people, mostly women, rinsing their hands (but not, I noticed, their mouths, as, strictly speaking, they should). In the courtyard of most shrines there is a washing place; but at Ise the river is the traditional spot for ablutions, and the act seems appropriately elemental. Indeed, nothing at Ise is used without the most elaborate precautions against impurity. Even the fire employed for cooking has to be ritually raised by drilling into a slab of cypress wood.

One of the most attractive shrines 'affiliated' to that at Ise is dedicated to the Wind God. It is called Kazamiya. Nearby is a graceful bridge, with views on either side of unsurpassed loveliness. The Wind God is supposed to shield the country and the people from the scourge of typhoons, or at least from their worst effects.

It was something of an anticlimax when, after another day's explora-tion, I left Ise for Toba to visit Pearl Island, with its squat statue of the industry's founder, Mr. Mikimoto; but there is a limit to sustaining every mood. Even so, Pearl Island is by no means lacking in interest. From a kind of lounge-observatory, I was given an exhibition of pearl-diving by women. They slid into the water gracefully, turned over like dolphins, and drew down their legs together like an undercarriage. When after about a minute they bobbed up again, they rolled their ropes deftly round their twirling wooden casks, and climbed into rowing-boats. These women divers are supposed to emit a strange sort of whistling noise called *isobue*, the 'whistle of the beaches', or *isonageki*, translated some-thing like 'the solitary sound of the beaches'. My privileged position was due to an encounter with a young lady-guide, who later took me to see the insertion of the nucleus or irritant in the oysters. This was done by girls who had an excellent command of English. My guide had good English too, and finally it transpired that she had attended the Seishin or

Catholic University at Okayama, where three years before she had heard me lecture.

II

Ise I regard as one of the most compelling places I ever visited. More and more was I driven to explore the other sacred spots which afforded some clue, if always a tantalizing one, to the origin and nature of the Japanese people. For this reason I made up my mind, as soon as my duties should permit, to explore that part of the Japan Sea coast which includes the prefectures of Tottori and Shimane. For here was another shrine, Izumo. The first opportunity occurred in the spring of 1967. It was a propitious moment to traverse the verdant valley of the Oi; and through most of this visit I enjoyed the kind of weather which transfigures the Japanese countryside. There must be something about the Oi which enables it to grace the earth with particular bounty; for its passages through Ishiyama, near Lady Murasaki's temple, causes the hills to blaze with the cherry and the maple, and this effulgence continued all the way up to the coast. At Ayabe, we changed directions, and so came to Maizuru, which was shrouded in cloud. Here I stopped for lunch. This busy port has an excellent and well-protected harbour, and it has developed close trade connections with Russia; but I was glad to take the new line to Amano-Hashidate, which brought back memories of a Summer School held there three years before, which Francis King had directed. The famous resort is known as the 'Bridge of Heaven'; and it is so called because, according to a version of the 'sun mythology', Izanagi and Izanami landed here, bringing into being the islands of Japan. I remember so well staying at Miyazu, not far away, and watching in the early morning the holiday-makers in their *yukatas* strolling along the beach. Like the Koreans, the Japanese take a particular pleasure in early mornings, whereas they lack, at least according to Fosco Maraini, an appreciation of sunsets. Nevertheless, I noticed that my staff always found the view of Mount Fuji from our office windows beautiful, perhaps because of its rarity.

I had not much time on this occasion to spend in Amano-Hashidate; and, it being the Golden Week holiday, when everybody likes to travel, I wanted to escape the conventional tourist routes. I was therefore glad to

be embarking on a journey across the Okutango peninsula, which few
visitors have time to explore. We veered south-west to Toyooka, where
90 per cent of Japan's osiers are grown, and to which the few remaining
storks in the country have stubbornly clung. At present, the main manu-
facture is that of wicker trunks. Here, our seats were swung round in a
manner which, given the confined space, never ceased to surprise me. We
passed Gembudo, noted for its three lofty basalt caves, and Kinosaki spa,
famous since the seventh century, where the wooded scenery and the
opulent soil, contrasting markedly with vast areas too poor to cultivate,
grew even richer as we skirted the coast. Suddenly on our right there was
a serene little bay, with narrow tiered sides, then an ear-compressing
tunnel, then a wider valley with flooded paddies, another bay, another
tunnel, and then a smaller bay containing a tiny humped island, as if it
were its private pet. We passed Kasumi, with its famous Daijoji temple,
containing paintings by the landscape artist, Marayama (1733–95), and
then more tiny bays with their tame islands. After more ear-compressing
tunnels, the train began riding higher and higher, until I was almost
relieved to stop at the little station of Kutani (not mentioned in the official
guide-book), even though only for a few minutes. This permitted a more
composed view of the tree-decked, folded, crumpled hills, interspersed
with some few which were, by contrast, shaven and honed. Then we were
off past Yayoi, to be reminded of the modern world by its steel bridge,
the most lofty in Japan, and on to Hamasaka, with its spring of such high
temperature that the villagers use the water for cooking. In some ways,
the last stretch was the most splendid. We moved through low, tiered
hills, catching glimpses every so often of the sea with more pine-islands,
until we came to Iwami, a place almost fizzling with hot springs. Here the
sun, suddenly emerging, caused the waves to dance dazzlingly. Only
after this radiant scene did the country, composed of flattening valleys,
revert to the sombre aspect which presages a modern town. And so we
arrived at Tottori.

As promised, I am keeping references to my official work to a minimum; but I cannot forbear to mention the warm welcome I received
at Tottori University, and the audience of 400 keen students who
assembled for my lecture; the *zadankai* held with the staff afterwards; and
the kindness shown me by so many people, especially Professor Yoshida.
After work, I was taken to see the Ochidani shrine, dedicated to

Ieyasu, the founder of the Tokugawa Shogunate, and both a Shinto and a Buddhist deity. This was a small but serene spot, with a *Kagura* hall for sacred dancing in front, and, behind, another shrine of great beauty, decorated in gold and bearing the Tokugawa emblems, and having a criss-cross roof-projection not unlike that at Ise. Then we visited the Kannon temple, where we were given ceremonial tea in a room affording a delightful view of the garden. In this garden I was shown an object of great curiosity. It was a stone intagliated with a kind of stunted cross shape, below which was the figure of a woman. This was a Christian symbol, though of studied ambiguity, set up during the long period when the Shogunate proscribed Christianity with relentless ferocity. The woman presumably represented the Virgin. We also visited the Folk Museum, with its remarkable Korean ware, particularly chests and medicine boxes.

No one can pay a visit to Tottori without seeing the renowned sand-dunes, rucked and dotted with the occasional pine tree, and always changing in colour. Here I benefited from the expert knowledge of Professor Ochi, a botany specialist and an expert at dune-control, who had studied in London. I understood that some skeletons dating from the Jomon period had been found there.

Next day I awoke to the same resplendent sunshine, and in this glow I set out for one of the most renowned places in Japan, Matsue. On either side of us stretched a neat, husbanded countryside with low hills on our right and a range of high ones, slowly turning bluish, on our left. We passed the placid Lake Koyama, where people were fishing as immobile as effigies; and there followed miles of paddies, with rice tufts sprouting from them. All at once the sea appeared, like a swiftly ruled line. Among stretches of clover were old farmhouses, some thatched and many with crinkly tiles. All this while I was on the lookout for another sight, which soon came into view. This was the Daisen range, with the mountain itself, streaked with snow, and looking not unlike Mount Fuji. Daisen, one of the most famous mountains of Japan, contained in the past about 100 temples of the Tendai sect, but most of them were destroyed by fire. Although it is much smaller than Mount Fuji, a magnificent summit view can be obtained of the Oki islands and of the Inland Sea. It is still haunted by bears.

On my arrival at Matsue, I was met by Professor Kobayashi, who took me to one of the best of *ryokans*, the Horai-so. It was obvious what I should expect to be shown in the town, and soon I was off to see the places associated with its most renowned son, Lafcadio Hearn.

Whatever we may thing of Hearn's writings, we have to admit that he was a man of remarkable, if complex, personality. In view of the success he achieved as an 'interpreter' of Japan to the Western world, it is interesting to reflect that he lived in the country for no more than fourteen years, and that he died at the age of fifty-four. Two of these years, probably his happiest, were spent at Matsue; and if you visit this lovable little place today, you will understand what an impact it must have made upon a young, lonely and highly impressionable man, who was setting foot in the country for the first time. For Matsue, still largely unspoilt, must in those days have been as truly Japanese as any provincial town, and the Matsue idyll was the measure by which Hearn judged the rest of the country.

Today, many, perhaps most, experts on Japan regard Lafcadio Hearn as an incorrigible sentimentalist. On that account his interpretations of Japan are said to have done a disservice; for the reader who never visits the country may be seriously misled, and those who know Japan are often so alienated by his views as to miss the artistry with which he expressed them.

There is much truth in the contention that Hearn was a sentimentalist, if we define the sentimentalist as one who, having an excess of undigested emotion, looks for an object on which to discharge it. By upbringing and experience, Hearn was a wanderer in search of a place to settle, for there are few persons for whom wandering is an end in itself. He had tried, and written about, other countries; but it was not until he arrived in Japan, and in one of its loveliest regions, that he realized he had found the goal he was seeking. This experience, which can take place at several levels (*sero te amavi*), is apt, as I say, to release an excess of feeling. And this release can have its reaction. It assuredly did in Hearn's case, though his love-affair with Japan was never quite broken off, and he died still in a state of mild infatuation. Here it may be pointed out that, until he acquired Japanese citizenship, Hearn was British. There is a widespread belief that he was an American. Of course, he spent much time in the United States; but he was the son of an Irish father and a Greek mother (hence his two names). I once suggested that he ought to be included in a handbook on English literature on which I had been asked to give advice; but the editor refused to admit him in the conviction, impossible to budge, that he was non-British. And I have met the same stubbornness elsewhere, not least in America.

When Hearn became a Japanese citizen, he took a Japanese name too. Writing to a friend, he said: 'I am going to be called Y. Koizumo (Koizumi Yakumo). The old people chose the name, and I guess it will do. It is a reminder that I belong hereafter to the province of the gods.'

Where I think Hearn tended to over-sentimentalize Japan—and it is an easy thing to do—is in believing, on the strength of the Matsue idyll, that Japan was a kind of vestal virgin whom alien associations must inevitably corrupt. Hence his revulsion against the Westernization which, in his comparatively short stay, he observed to be encroaching. He felt his own predilections threatened. He made a hard-and-fast distinction between authentic Japan and Westernized Japan. I would suggest, on the contrary, that except possibly for some part of the prehistoric period and not necessarily then, there never has been an authentic Japan which was not also a Japan avid to assimilate outside influence. That *is* the authentic Japan. Needless to say, the pendulum has on several occasions swung too far. One such occasion was the Tokugawa Shogunate, when the swing was towards extreme isolation; other occasions were the period after the Meiji Restoration and after the 1945 surrender, when the swing was towards extreme Westernization. But the balance has repeatedly been restored. My point in this book, and in my choice of title, is that Japan has succeeded in remaining a traditional community while moving to the forefront of the modern technological powers. This is a very difficult thing to do, and therefore a very remarkable thing to have done. But it is a fact open to inspection. If you read old books on Japan, especially by foreigners who were in residence for some years, you will be struck often by their claims that the Japanese, having finally repudiated their old traditions, are nothing but a mass of acquisitive materialists. The verdict is repeated today, especially by newspaper correspondents commissioned to write a 'series of articles'.[1] There are statements that such customs as Tea Ceremony are extinct; that the

---

[1] Cf. Anthony Carthew, *Daily Mail*, 21.IV.69; 'The Japanese are a collection of people gathered together for the exclusive and unanswerable purpose of making money. . . . What they want is to be left in peaceful command of a cherry-blossom-decorated cash register merrily ringing up the profits.'

kimono is relegated to the attic; and that both Shinto and Buddhism are dead. And yet, after my six years in Japan, I arrived at the conclusion that none of these claims was true. In short, the 'realist' interpretation of Japan seem to me to be just as one-sided, just as affected with sentimentalism *à rebours*, as the 'idealist' interpretation.

Notwithstanding Lafcadio Hearn's undoubted sentimentality, he produced some of the most interesting and readable books on Japan. His industry was prodigious. He had a heavy load of teaching; and when he was transferred to Tokyo University this load was greatly increased. He travelled extensively; and, being something of a local celebrity, he 'received' numerous visitors, a time-consuming occupation. He learnt a certain amount of Japanese, and he could write it after a fashion; and anyone who has tried to do this after the age of forty knows what an excruciatingly difficult task it can be. With all this, he wrote article after article, together with one distinguished book, *Japan, an Interpretation*, which, however controversial its central theme, is most rewarding to read. Of the collected pieces, my favourite is *Kokoro*. Not least important, Hearn wrote flowing, supple English prose; and I could wish that more Japanese aspirants to English composition would imitate his style rather than some other models, Carlyle for instance—an inexplicable favourite.

Back at the *ryokan* on the evening of 3 May, I was delighted to have the opportunity of welcoming two of Japan's Lafcadio Hearn experts: Professor Kajitani and Assistant Professor Tsunematsu, who, with Professor Kobayashi, entertained me for hours in talking about the celebrated writer.

In retailing Hearn's achievements, I have not mentioned one of the greatest importance, namely his marriage to a Japanese. How was it, I enquired of my guests, that an unknown foreigner, not long arrived, ignorant of the language, and living in a society of much stricter conventions than now prevail, could have succeeded in courting and winning a Japanese lady, and making an apparently outstanding success of the alliance? My guests admitted that this was no mean achievement; but the more we mulled over the question, the more it seemed apparent that, in this case, the normal Japanese conventions *were* observed. In short, the marriage was arranged. This is not such a strange custom as we in the West sometimes suppose. It was not, and it rarely is, the equivalent of making a particularly drastic and permanent 'blind date'. It implied that other people's views of the mutual compatibility of a pair were taken into account besides those of the two themselves. In this particular case, the lady, like Hearn, was something of an outsider in that she was a divorcee. There was no question of an alliance with an inexperienced girl, dragged from the bosom of her family. One of Hearn's colleagues at the Shimane Middle School, realizing his loneliness, brought about the meeting which was to have such fortunate results. His wife, who never learnt more than the rudiments of English, proved to have all the Japanese female virtues: loyalty, affection, and strongmindedness. She bore him children who, after his death, held his memory in the same veneration as she did. On the Buddhist shelf in the home, a light was always kept burning, for Hearn was himself a convert to the faith.

The house in which Hearn discovered so much about Japan is well preserved, and part of it is still lived in. This I found somehow fitting. The sound of a child practising on the piano lent an air of homeliness to the place. Much of it is kept as far as possible as it was in Hearn's day. There is the high table-desk, an unpretentious affair, at which he toiled. This is no cliché, as Hearn had lost an eye, and he put the other one to such strain that it underwent marked hypertrophy. In the museum next door there are glass cases full of diverse manuscripts and relics, including the great man's underclothes. I noticed a carefully composed letter written to one of his pupils a few hours before his death. His wife's photograph suggests a woman of no particular beauty, but of considerable depth of character. She was, as Hearn proudly claimed, of samurai descent. Despite her devotion, I wondered what in her heart she made of this man who had come so unexpectedly into her life. From some remarks she let drop after his death, we know that she occasionally found him baffling. Nor is it surprising.

Hearn's own fine description of Matsue castle was enough to make me want to gain a view from the top, and so we scaled the many stairs, pausing to inspect the exhibition arranged on every storey. In these enormous structures, which seemed to possess wings which keep them aloft yet stationary, it is possible to judge the great power wielded by the *daimyo* or feudal lord. The castle at Matsue is one of those which have been reasonably well preserved, whereas so many were destroyed in the war and are replicas. Only from the height of our great cathedrals have I witnessed a similar breadth of view.

III

The next day, in pursuit of early Japan, I visited some of the places Hearn knew, belonging to 'the province of the gods'. First, I went to the Yaegaki shrine. This is another of those structures which preserve an air of mystery, as it seems to point to a period when even Shinto was in its infancy. In fact, there is reason to think that this shrine may be one of the oldest in Japan, older perhaps than Ise and Izumo. There are associations with fertility worship; and if the enormous wooden trunk, roughly sculptured at the top, which is planted behind one of the smaller shrines on the left, does not represent a phallus, it is difficult to see why it should have been preserved. Over many centuries the shrine has been frequented by those about to wed, or by those in hope of securing a marriage-partner; for the gods associated with it are believed to influence the course of true love. The building behind is the older of the two larger ones; and in order to preserve some remarkable old pictures, a storehouse has recently been built. On my return to Tokyo, I was surprised to find so little written about this place.

At the time of my visit, the precincts of the shrine were echoing with the chatter and gay laughter of those whose personal destinies were as yet unripe for the attention of the tutelary gods. I found myself surrounded by school-children, some, mostly the boys, still preserving the rosy cheeks which make Japanese infants so adorable. As usual, they fired off in quick succession the contents of their little arsenals of English; and, intent on obtaining my autograph, they produced every scrap of paper on which they could lay hands, including sweet-wrappings. So great was the clamour that I could not get away until almost every little fist was left clutching its memento.

Taking a rural path, I came to a holy well, round which more children were gathered. They were launching 10 yen coins on little scraps of paper. Tradition says, with some prudence, that those whose votive offerings sink quickest will obtain good fortune: there were a good many happy faces around. Not far away, up a path of large flag-stones, was another shrine, the Kamosu. It was built on stilts, and it too had a roof resembling that at Ise. In front was an open, *tatamied* ante-chamber. With trees on three sides, it presented an appearance of extreme antiquity, though it would seem to be a good deal younger than the Yaegaki. Even so, the present building dates from 1346. In charge was an affable, mustachioed priest who told us something about the district. According to him, we were in a part of Japan different from any other, and the history of it was still very obscure. Far away on some hills to the left stood once the citadel of an old city. A good deal nearer were a series of shrines and temples mentioned in few books. Of these the Takeuchi was clearly a popular shrine, and children were busy drawing, seated on the stone steps leading up to it. The Gessoji was a temple, or rather the vestiges of one, containing the tombs of the great Matsudaira family, which has given so many statesmen to Japan. These tombs were slightly forbidding in appearance, perhaps because of the desolation into which they had been allowed to sink; but the covered gateway was adorned with some notable wood-carvings of leaves, dragons and tigers. I noticed the incongruous presence of some stick-on labels, which, adhering to the lintel, must have been propelled into position by an enterprising advertiser. I concluded my itinerary by a visit to the Me-me-an teahouse, situated on a high eminence. This had all the requisite buildings for Tea Ceremony, including a waiting room with lavatory, and a stone basin for washing. In addition, there were several ceremonial rooms, and we were served tea in the proper, if abbreviated, fashion. The teahouse had recently been restored. I asked if it were much patronised, and was told Yes; I doubt whether there would have been a demand for such a place twenty years ago.

In order to see more of the country, I stayed one night at the little spa of Tamatsukuri, where I had some of the best Japanese food I could remember. Imagine the relaxation (for I had done a good deal of lecturing and visiting) of taking a piping hot bath, and then, sitting in a *yukata* on a cushion before the low lacquered table and eating *sashimi* (raw fish), surely one of the great delicacies, and having *sake* poured out by a slim, motherly woman. All around there was the clear but sufficiently removed sound of more social revelry. Later, while I was sitting in a basket chair by the window reading, the bedding was hauled out of the cupboard, a lamp placed near my pillow, and, as the *shoji* slid shut, I was bidden *sayonara* in a soft, musical voice. There was tea left in a thermos; and with the good, fresh smell of the *tatami* in my nostrils, I turned in and dropped asleep.

I was to return to Tamatsukuri after my final visit to Matsue in October of the same year. I recall the *yukata*-clad crowds, and again the convivial atmosphere which never seemed to degenerate into rowdiness. The spa consists of one long 'street', which was in fact two paths on either side of a concrete-lined river bed, crossed by bridge after concrete bridge, which had mellowed enough to have acquired some patina. *Ryokans* with hot springs line the paths. At the end of the 'street', the canal becomes a river again, descending in a little waterfall. The whole place is a steaming, bubbling centre of relaxation and restoration, full of towels waving on clothes lines, and echoing with the hollow sound of the wooden washing-bowl on bathroom tiles.

This time I had gone to Matsue for the Shakespeare Society Conference. It had meant an early rise in Tokyo, the usual bumpy flight to Osaka, and a rush to catch the Towa plane to Yanago. As we flew over verdant islands and the placid Japan Sea, I was able to relax a little. At the station, a pleasant young woman approached me with a request to 'practise English'. I told her I was going to Matsue; and when the train came in I hopped on to it, the girl—who had suddenly produced a husband—preceding me. I found myself sitting next to them. She was a student at Osaka City University and was specializing in Jane Austen. Her husband was, as usual, much less forthcoming. After a little rather strained conversation, they asked me again if I were really going to Matsue because, if so, I was on the wrong train. Mine had been due a moment or so after. There were hurried consultations with the conductor, and I was put off at the next station, where I took a taxi at great expense to my intended destination. Here Professor and Mrs. Oyama had been awaiting me; but they were replaced after a time by Professor Tada, who took me to the Nozu Hotel.

Professor Tada and I, as old friends, had a long talk over beer, sitting in dazzling sunlight at the window. Just below us was a house with a miniscule Japanese garden, but containing a stone lantern and a Noh pine tree. In them seemed to be concentrated all Japanese home life. It was difficult to drag ourselves away. For me, the highlights of this visit were my election as life-member of the Japan Shakespeare Society, and the dinner in the enormous *tatami* room at the Suitosei hotel. This was one of those occasions in which the Japanese take especial pleasure, and in which they expand in good humour and fellowship, making many speeches interspersed with recitations, both prepared and spontaneous.

My last view of Matsue was, perhaps fittingly, of a sunset over Lake Shinji. There was an incandescent haze with that particular yellow shade for which the phenomenon is renowned. It gradually paled and melted away. By way of postscript, let me add that Matsue, despite the respect it excites in lovers of old Japan, is by no means a museum piece. The place is ahum with life; an air of prosperity prevails; and its bridges and canals are still functioning as in the days of the rickshaw and the pleasure-boat.

IV

It was in the company of Professor Kobayashi, a young English expert, that I set out one fine morning for the equally famous Taisha. My spirits were high: for the more I saw of this coast, the greater had become my affection for it. Along the way were thatched houses protected by palisades of very tall pine trees; for the west wind blowing off the Japan Sea can carry all before it. In no other part of Japan did I see anything resembling such enclosures.

Taisha is famous for the grand shrine of Izumo, which together with that at Ise, is a national sanctuary, and perhaps a good deal older. A special permit had been obtained for me to enter parts of the shrine not normally open to visitors, and on arrival we were received by the Chief Priest in an upper room of a wooden structure encased in concrete, modelled on the style of the oldest residences of Japan. The priest was a genial, grey-haired man, who reminded me of a don. After the normal civilities, we cleansed our hands and put on short white tunics, resembling in cut Oxford undergraduate gowns. We were then solemnly 'asperged' by a Shinto priest in full vestments, who made a kind of semaphore sign across us with a wand to which paper streamers were attached. Only then were we permitted to enter the threshold of the inner shrine. At this point, I was presented with a pine frond which I was required to lay, stem forwards, upon a little wooden altar at the entrance. Next, we were led into a small courtyard, littered with clean white pebbles, which is said to prove that at one time the sea was there. Beyond this spot we were not permitted to go, for in front of us was the inner shrine itself. At the foot of the steps the Emperor may stand; but he is forbidden to ascend them. Never, indeed, in the history of the Japanese state has any emperor penetrated to the inner shrine of Izumo.

I was eager to ask the Chief Priest more about the shrine, and he was willing to satisfy my curiosity, at least up to a point. He informed me that he was authorized to pay regular visits to the inner shrine; but within this shrine was another, more sacred than the rest, and this might be entered only once every sixty-one years, when a special festival was held. It happened that the time for such a festival had occurred during his own incumbency. Bound to strict secrecy, he declined to say what was within the 'holy of holies'. He mentioned, however, that the sacred objects or relics, or whatever they might be, had been temporarily removed on the occasion of some recent repairs, but this had never been known to happen before.

The shrine at Izumo differed from that at Ise in being in much less good condition, for at Izumo there is no tradition of periodic reconstruction. The present outer building was put up in 1874, and there have been several fires since. The wood had an anaemic look, as if covered with mycelium. On the right, there was a small shrine, dedicated to the wife of the founder; and on either side, to the fore, there were two tiny shrines on stilts, like raised chicken coops. Photography is normally forbidden, but I was allowed to take one picture. As we turned to leave this sanctuary, we noticed that a young girl had silently taken up a position by the gateway; and before we left, we received from her a cup of sacred *sake*. Dressed in white, she was exceedingly beautiful, with a most dignified and solemn bearing. In none of my many visits to shrines and temples in Japan did I feel in such religious constraint as before this young vestal. The cup in which the *sake* was served was presented to me, and this treasured possession reposes on a shelf behind me as I write.

Just before leaving, I noticed a room above a gateway with a brocade canopy rolled up. This was where the priest said the prescribed prayers in inclement weather. We returned to the upper room, where we were presented with mementoes. Then we wandered about the large court-yard, where groups of people were strolling in the sun.

On both sides of the main hall stand long wooden buildings divided into rooms like monks' cells. In point of fact, they are not cells for monks; they are cells for gods. The month of October is known throughout the rest of Japan as the *kannazuki*, or the 'month without gods'. This is because all the Shinto deities are presumed to have gone to Izumo, where October is accordingly called the *kamiarizuki,* or 'month with gods'. As there are at least eight million Shinto deities, the accommodation provided is purely symbolic.

But why do the gods go to Izumo? This raises one of the most interesting speculations about early Japanese history.

In speaking of the foundation of the Yamato State, I mentioned how the Sun Goddess of Ise came to exercise domination over all the other local gods and how the god Susa-no-o was banished to Izumo, where he set up a state on his own. Another legend says that it was a *descendant* of Susa-no-o who set up the state in Izumo. This descendant's name was Okuni-nushi-no-Mikito, who is reputed to have introduced to mankind such arts as those of fishing, sericulture, and medicine. Even so, he was obliged in due course to abdicate his throne in favour of one of the Yamato rulers. But he did so on one condition. This was that he should maintain permanent religious authority over the Izumo region, and that the Yamato emperor should henceforth have no right to challenge it. These myths are not simply an exercise of the imagination of a 'primitive' people; they are more probably a deliberate way of symbolizing an important historical occurrence in the manner in which history was then conceived. And so today, the Emperor of Japan still may not enter the inner shrine of Izumo.

Furthermore, it seems possible that the Shinto gods, many of whom are mobile, are thought to go to Izumo for one month in the year for the purpose of 'revisiting' the shrine which at one time competed for their allegiance. Most myths are invented for a purpose. Until recently, special ceremonies, which may originally have been harvest rites, were held in many places for dispatching the gods to Izumo and for welcoming them back again.

Shinto was, and still is, a kind of proto-religion. And it is very much alive, even at the intellectual level. In June 1967 I was a delegate at the second Shinto International Conference in Tokyo. The first such conference had been held at Claremont, California in 1965. At the meetings I attended I was able to learn some fascinating details about Shinto, and particularly about its practical character. There were passionate pleas for an understanding of Shinto as something other than primitive magic or animism; and it was pointed out how erroneous was the view that Shinto had no moral teaching. One of the speakers quoted a Shinto injunction which might have been uttered by a Hebrew prophet: 'What pleases the Deity is not material offerings. The true offerings are virtue and sincerity' (*Shinto Gobusko*). Thus even so learned and sympathetic a scholar as William Aston was in error when he said that 'the weakest part of Shinto is the almost total absence of a definite moral element.' I was greatly impressed by the address of Father Dumoulin of Sophia University in the course of which he said: 'Historians of religion, by penetrating more profoundly into the religious reality, have come to recognize that former generations have misjudged polytheism. What they understood to be "idolatry" was never practised in this manner by any religion. Religious people, by worshipping a variety of objects, always intended one thing, the SACRED, which they expressed in many forms.'

That is what I believe too.

When the gods assemble in Izumo, they are said to perform, among other things, the office of arranging marriages. Consequently, October is a month during which the locality tends to be thronged with young people. Izumo is thus associated with traditions similar to those of the Yaegaki shrine; and this association again suggests that the area was at one time the centre of important fertility rites.

Although the Izumo shrine is very large, the original structure is thought to have been larger still. Like the Kamosu, it was probably built on stilts, and modelled after the palace of the original ruler. The entrance to it is at the side, thereby permitting the god or gods to enjoy their privacy. Possibly some of the early Yayoi dwellings were built in this manner, and a great expert has gone so far as to declare that 'Izumo is therefore Yayoi in character.'[1] This would certainly make it in parts one of the oldest surviving shrines in Japan. It is thought that the Kamosu shrine may have preserved features nearer to the original Izumo foundation than the present structure.

As I was on the Japan Sea coast of Honshu, it seemed to me a good opportunity to pursue my journey southwards, particularly as the universities and schools of the area had so rarely been visited by foreigners. So I had made my plans already to push on to Hagi, where I had friends. After Hamada especially, the magnificent view drew my eyes from the books I had brought with me; and, partly hypnotized by the unusually

[1] Edward Kidder, *Japan Before Buddhism* (1966), p. 204.

smooth shuttle of the train, I watched the calm sea turning from blue to jade green (it was afternoon), and sending up from time to time a vertical jet of spray, which, with the sound 'shut off', looked like some spontaneous eurhythmic. We passed through Iwami-Masuda, where the great artist Sesshu (1421–1507) died. Long sandy beaches came into view, and then great stretches of grey sand, from which bricks were being made. By the time I reached Hagi, the sun had swollen into a fiery ball, and I felt I had arrived at a kind of *ultima thule.*

At the station was my old friend, Mr. Miyamoto, whom I had met in Tokyo four years earlier. As usual, he was the soul of hospitality. I put up at the Tomoe, a genuine traditional *ryokan*, and the next day, after the usual official visits, Mr. Miyamoto took me round Hagi. First, we drove to the summit of Mount Tatoko, where there was a view of pine islands, with Mishima, its radar station prominent, in the distance. Then we visited the Shoin shrine, built in the Izumo style, which is dedicated to a remarkable young man called Shoin Yoshida, who opposed the Tokugawa Government by teaching 'modern thought', and suffered for it as a corrupter of youth. Yoshida is the subject of an essay in Stevenson's *Familiar Studies of Men and Books*, and the local Japanese are very proud of this tribute. As I had not read the essay, Mr. Miyamoto lent me his copy and I devoured it that evening, reposing in my *yukata*. The school which Yoshida set up, the Matsushita, is still to be seen. It is a one-room building of somewhat Spartan appearance, whereas the building to which he was consigned in disfavour struck me as not an uncomfortable place in which to languish. Finally, Yoshida was executed by the Tokugawa, and the bitter vengeance of which he was the victim certainly showed him to be a man of singular courage. Nor was he alone. His friend Kusakabe suffered a similar fate. If it is true that, on being led to the place of execution, he quoted quietly from a Chinese poem, then he too must have possessed a noble character. The passage in question was: 'It is better to be a crystal and broken, than to remain perfect like a tile upon a house-top.'

Finally, we drove out to the peninsula of Shirayama, with its tiny extinct volcano, commanding such a view as I was not to see equalled until I went to Hakodate in Hokkaido. The weather had again held; and if I use that expression not for the first time it is that the climate of Japan, being even more precarious than that of Britain, is something which one receives with gratitude if good, and learns not to lament when bad.

Unlike the British, the Japanese do not complain about their weather, any more than they complain about their earthquakes. These things just happen.

To visit Hagi without paying a call on the famous potter, Mr. Miwa, would have been to miss an important experience. Pottery-making in this district is at least 350 years old, and the present kiln is 100 years old. Tradition in such matters is very important; many Japanese potters like to invoke an apostolic succession, even if it is sometimes of doubtful authenticity. Years of instruction and practice are required. Skill cannot be obtained simply by being 'revolutionary' or 'abolishing the past'. I much liked the *Hagi-yaki* pottery, though it was a little on the heavy side, and the tea-bowls were expensive. Having spoken of tradition, I must hasten to say that this is not incompatible with experimentation. Mr. Miwa's son, recently graduated from Tokyo University of the Arts, and about to join his father in the business, had his own studio. Here, contrasting violently with the paternal conservatism, were pots with breasts and lips under them, with large vulvas under these, and a series of objects made in the shape of high-heeled shoes, which, save that Mr. Miwa junior seemed a sunny, open young man, made me inclined to turn for elucidation to the works of Freud. An exhibition of young Mr. Miwa's work was shortly to be held at the Isetan department store in Tokyo.

I well recall the last restful lunch I had with Mr. Miyamoto at the Kanko (tourist) hotel. It overlooked both the little fishing village of Koshigayama, and a lagoon which, because of its variety of salt-water fish, is now a specially protected aquarium. To be able to have a Japanese bath prior to the meal, and to eat in comfortable Japanese style, was a solace. If physical happiness possesses a value in itself, then I have enjoyed myself more in Japan than anywhere else. By contrast, sitting bolt upright and jammed to the table next to a fellow guest in equal constraint, makes many Western formal meals a misery. And as for the bath before lunch, can there be a more admirable practice?

To wind up my visit to Hagi, Mr. Miyamoto took me to his beautiful house, with its large orchard of orange trees. Mrs. Miyamoto, whom I had also met before, was there to receive me. As usual, I noticed the taste and economy with which the house was furnished, and yet there seemed to be a place for everything. I then fulfilled my last duty of the day in giving a talk to the boys and girls, and some staff, of the Senior High

School. The headmaster, Mr. Takamatsu, welcomed me with green tea and sweets. I enjoyed this experience, both because the children put some most intelligent questions, and because there was a good deal of laughter, which is a sign, particularly in Japan, that one's words are being understood, assuming that it occurs at the right points. Sometimes, back in Tokyo, surprise and often incredulity were expressed to me that I should lecture to audiences of this kind without an interpreter. Admittedly, it required some practice; but I found always that, provided there was a good-sized blackboard and that I wrote up an occasional keyword and employed diagrams, communication was not merely possible but rewarding. The Japanese tend to await a foreign lecturer determined to be perplexed, and this initial barrier needs to be broken down. Many, as on this occasion, had neither seen an Englishman before nor heard 'British English' spoken. Gradually, as a kind of rapt atmosphere developed, I used to know that I had established contact. At the Hagi school, I recall that the use of a map of the world, produced by the headmaster, on which Britain appeared twice, caused much mirth, and this initial reaction put me at my ease.

As darkness was falling, we drove through wooded country to Yamaguchi, one and a half hours away. I put up at the Beizanso *ryokan*, and with the traditional Japanese solicitude Mr. Miyamoto took a room there himself. Two officials of the Prefectural Board of Education called on us, Mr. Kumano and Mr. Miyoshi. We had a Japanese meal in my room, enlivened with a most stimulating conversation, especially as Mr. Kumano was an historian with a particular interest in prehistory. Mr. Miyoshi had been in America and Hong Kong, but it was the first time Mr. Kumano had met a European.

I woke up early the next day, and, finding the *o-furo* empty, I took a cold shower. This caused a mild sensation among the staff, for whom it was a novelty, and placed me among the great eccentrics to have patronized the inn. The Japanese revulsion from cold water for washing dates back a long way. Townsend Harris, the first American consul after the 'opening up' of the country, reported from Shimoda, a town situated at the tip of the Izu peninsula, that his own daily practice caused astonishment and even concern in his household.

As we were a little way out of Yamaguchi, we set off soon after breakfast, as I was interested to see as much as I could of a place with such historic associations. St. Francis Xavier came here, and I visited the church dedicated to him. His statue is near by. I was later to follow the steps of his journey. Repeatedly I thought of the magnitude of his achievement, undertaken without any engines of publicity and I was struck, then as later, how proud the Japanese are of foreigners who have reached their shores, so long as their mission appears to have been disinterested. Alas, that last condition has not always been fulfilled. The later history of Christianity in Japan, though not without its moments of grandeur, is on the whole a melancholy story, providing a terrible lesson on the evils of sectarianism.

Under the leadership of the great Mori family, Yamaguchi played an important part in the Meiji Restoration, and at the time of my visit there was a full-scale exhibition being held at the Prefectural Cultural centre. The city had indeed 'got in first', for the rest of Japan was not celebrating this crucial event until the following year. The history leading up to the Restoration is complicated. The Shogun originally resigned all his functions in favour of the Emperor, and he took up arms only when there was a rebellion against his authority in the South. Not everybody of liberal persuasion was on the side of the Emperor; Fukuzawa Yukichi, the founder of Keio University, and a man of great enlightenment, did not at first favour the Restoration. But what strikes me, above all, as interesting about the struggle between the Emperor and the Shogun was that, once the imperial power had been restored, the Tokugawas and their followers were pardoned. There was even an alliance between the two families. Today, the Tokugawas hold respected positions in society, and one of the most active spirits in Japan-British co-operation is Tokugawa Yoshitomo, from whom I received many kindnesses. When one reflects upon the ferocity shown to fallen rivals by some other conquerors in the modern world, this act of conciliation, which has paid handsome dividends, stands out for its nobility.

Even so, it must not be thought that the Emperor Meiji[1] was successful in asserting his power from the moment he established his new order in Edo (soon to be renamed Tokyo). Looking back, it is possible to discern a remarkable achievement of reform and pacification; but there was more than one challenge to the imperial rule, the most notable and tragic being that of General Saigo of Satsuma in 1877. There is all the more reason to

[1] This was in fact his posthumous name.

commend the Emperor's breadth of mind in making his peace with the family which had dominated Japan for two centuries. It is a case of the man and the hour matching up. For what reason was there to suppose that a young man, nurtured in conditions of extreme artificiality, and habituated to public life only in the form of traditional ceremonial, should show himself in possession of outstanding political sagacity and administrative grasp? Again, what reason was there to suppose that his consort, the Empress Haruko, should turn out to have qualities matching his own, not least the gift of compassion?

Before leaving Yamaguchi, I was taken to the Akiyoshi cave, the second largest grotto in the world. As the entrance was flooded, we had to remove our shoes and roll up our trousers to wade through it. I shall not forget how one of the officers of the Prefectural Board carried my shoes throughout the whole afternoon. This was a little touch of kindness which I pause to mention because the Japanese have a taboo against touching footwear. Hence the long shoehorns they often employ to enable them to don their shoes without stooping to put them on manually.

The Akiyoshi cave has stalactites as large as the columns of a cathedral, produced by the ooze of the crystalline limestone of the walls; and indeed the whole place resembles a gothic structure, with a good deal of (artificial) dim religious light. Over the aeons the rocks have acquired grotesque formations, to each of which has been given a name, duly translated into English. In order to penetrate the interior, it is necessary to climb up some steps and then a huge ramp; and the final access, leading to a depth of nearly 1,000 feet, is very slippery, so that a chain is provided (which did not prevent the descent from being extremely hazardous). In summer, a welcome coolness prevails, and I was told that it was comfortably warm in winter. We must have spent well over an hour exploring this huge cavern, starting up echoes as if we had surprised some dormant spirit. Many legends cling about the place. Among other creatures, a dragon is supposed to have lived there. Another legend has it that the whole cavern was tunnelled out in one minute by Kobo Daishi, of Mount Koya fame. Hence it is sometimes called 'Kobo's Spring'.

From Yamaguchi to Okayama, one passes through Hiroshima. This was a city to which I was frequently to pay visits; but as it stands for so much in contemporary history, I shall speak of it in the same context as

Nagasaki (Chapter VIII). Okayama I also visited several times, and the welcome I received there remains vividly in my memory. In any case, Okayama is situated in a region which links up historically with Ise and Izumo.

The University in Okayama for which I retain special recollections is the Catholic one, Notre Dame Seishin. This belonged to the same Order as the great Sacred Heart University in Tokyo. I say 'great', because that institution has always possessed special distinction, which becomes apparent as soon as one sets foot in the spick and span vestibule. A graduate from the Sacred Heart shows it in her bearing; I was not surprised to learn why parents were so anxious to send their daughters there.

To walk up the 'aisle' of the large lecture room of the Sacred Heart, whether in Tokyo or in Okayama, and to become aware of hundreds of grey-costumed girl students silently bowing in waves as one passed, was to feel at once humbled and exhilarated. Here I wish to record my gratitude to the students and staff of the University, and to pay tribute especially to the memory of Mother Britt (who died so tragically following an accident, in my last year), for many hours of happy contact spend under their hospitable roof. No less a tribute would I pay to the Sisters and students at Okayama. I first met many of the latter on 16 June 1962, when they were in the audience at Okayama University, and I was glad to accept an invitation to go to Notre Dame University the following year and the year after that. After my lectures, there would be tea with a few select students, and these occasions, though brief, were a source of unusual enjoyment. Women's colleges, as I have found the world over, are good at provisioning: and the buns and cakes pressed upon me by eager girls were so liberal in quantity as almost to prevent me dealing with the questions which they pressed upon me with no less eagerness. As a rule, the Japanese girl is more articulate than the Japanese boy, and I found I was expected to provide information on a great variety of subjects, from the home-life of the Queen to some technical detail of British industry. Sometimes a Sister would be present, and I recall one tall and rather beautiful one whom I was to meet more than once, until she suddenly returned home. She always struck me as a woman of unusual charm and intelligence; and, interestingly enough, the young guide I met at Toba spontaneously voiced the same opinion. On one of the occasions when the girls were left to entertain me on their own, they ventured to ask about 'boy friends' (almost a Japanese composite word by now), and we had a conversation which, as I hope, was both adult and innocent at the same time. On return, the Sister, noticing the bright eyes and vivacity of her charges, jumped to the correct conclusion, and I noticed a look combined of amusement and sadness cross her face. After I had had a good deal to do with these institutions (with which I must link the Jiyu Gakuen School in Tokyo, another Christian foundation, directed by Miss Hani), I came to the conclusion that, leaving aside all doctrinal considerations, Buddhist and Christian decorum combined, produces an amalgam which, in girls at least, worked miracles of breeding; and I speculated what a purely secularized education would do, especially to that half of the human race which needed the training of feeling as much as of intellect. The Crown Princess, I may add, is a graduate of the Sacred Heart University of Tokyo.

Okayama was a place where the cultural officials were anxious to receive speakers of all nationalities, and many visitors besides myself must have been grateful to Mr. Yoshii of the International Cultural Centre for his exertions on their behalf. Between official duties, I was taken to the Korakuen Park, one of the three great parks of Japan, and reminiscent of the garden of the Katsura Detached Palace in Kyoto, with its several teahouses, its lotus pond, its miniature shrine, and its replica of the fifty-three stages of the Old Tokaido Road. With me were Professor Ikigami and Professor Katsumo, who, besides being very hospitable, had between them a pretty wit. We all dined in the garden with the newly elected President Hattori; and then I met many other university men, especially Professor Goh, who was an expert on Korean, Mongolian and Ottoman Turkish.

In Mr. Yoshii's company, I visited the famous Bizen pottery, the director of which, Mr. Fujiwara, is called a 'Living National Treasure'. He had studied English at Waseda University, and as late as the age of forty he had decided to become a potter. His son was a potter too, and it was hoped that his son likewise would follow the same calling. I was struck by the devotion of the family to their art, and by the fact that they believed themselves to be pitting their energies against the current of the modern world. A robust Canadian girl, with Indian blood, was serving an apprenticeship with them. Although it is true that this craft has deep roots in Japan, the fashion to denigrate traditional activities was affecting the potter's life; and the revival of folkcraft was a recent movement, to which Bernard Leach had made a distinguished contribution. Leach paid several visits to Japan while I was there, and I was always amazed to see the respect amounting to veneration with which he was regarded.

In speaking of Bernard Leach, it is a natural transition to move a little way from Okayama and to find oneself in Kurashiki. Although this is an important industrial centre, it contains an area south of the city almost in another time-dimension, where the arts and crafts are given special reverence. Here there are the Ohara Art Museum and the Japan Folk Craft Museum, both of great fame.

Looking out of a train window one day, I saw a stately figure, bare footed and in pilgrim's robes, who introduced himself to me as Mr. Tonomura. He was the Director of the Folk Craft Museum which I had been coming to see. Formed from a group of old granaries, the place itself is admirably arranged, containing a collection of ceramics, fabrics and furniture. Nor are the exhibits confined to Japanese craft, though this predominates; there are some foreign exhibits, including English.

Had I glimpsed Mr. Tonomura only on the station platform, I might have supposed him to be a starry-eyed idealist, seeking the restoration of a way of life vanished beyond recall. Although the gap between his outlook and that of the ordinary man was less extreme in Japan than it would be elsewhere, save perhaps in hippiedom, he struck me as a tough, sensible man with no illusions about the way the world was going. His career had been interesting. He had started off as a Methodist preacher. Now, at sixty-five years of age, but seeming a good deal younger, he could look back upon a lifetime of devotion to traditional crafts, especially weaving. He did his stint at the loom every morning, as a rhythmic start to the day. There were several looms in his house (once the property of a rich merchant), and both he and his wife gave instruction to seven pupils. With this delightful couple, I spent a lunch discussing the mental climate of Japan, with delicious Chinese *sake* to promote conversation. Mr. Tonomura was downright in his criticism of some aspects of the revival of Zen. Indeed, he agreed wholeheartedly with what Koestler had said about it in *The Lotus and the Robot*. Koestler had stayed with him a year or two earlier. He felt that the Buddhist revival was in large part due to foreign influence. Nevertheless, the apparent indifference of the young to their traditional beliefs rather puzzled him. We continued our talk during a drive along the Inland Sea coast. Soon we reached a prominence from which we could see, beyond groups of islets, the island of Shikoku, appearing dimly through the mist.

Mr. Tonomura, who had been to England, introduced me to a side of Japan into which Bernard Leach and Hamada later gave me increasing insight. (There is a Leach Room in the Ohara Museum.) I was later to visit Hamada in the company of Eric Newton, the art critic. It became increasingly clear to me that although the craft revival had been to some extent artificial, the true foundations of craftsmanship in Japan had never been destroyed, or brought to such a state of decay as they had been in the West. Consequently, the craftsmen, and particularly the potters, to be met with throughout Japan were not a minority of superannuated bohemians. There was no real war between art and technology, and the 'modern world' against which the Fujiwaras of Bizen felt themselves to be pitted was a philosophy of life largely imported from the West.

Indeed, Japan is perhaps the one Asiatic country which may be able to resist, though no doubt after a struggle, the mechanistic *outlook*, while developing to the full the potentialities of mechanization. She will in that case have given a lead to the Third World, which rejects the outlook of both America and the Soviet Union. A struggle there will surely be; I saw for myself how quickly Japanese *moeurs* were changing on the surface, and how affluence had begun to destroy that dignified economy of living which was the best aspect of the samurai ideal. But I saw also that movement towards the restoration of certain traditional ways of which I spoke earlier; and it is in this that I put my trust. I believe that men like Mr. Tonomura and Mr. Hamada are seeking to maintain that norm of living without which the peculiar happiness of the Japanese people might vanish almost overnight.

As I had decided to wind up this part of my journey with a few days' leave, I took the train to the little town of Mihara, where I hoped to climb a mountain or two not mentioned in the official Guide. When I arrived outside the station to catch a taxi, the weather had broken, and I felt forlorn and lonely. Suddenly, to my great surprise, and despite a leaden sky, it seemed that the rain had stopped. I looked up to find that I was under the shelter of a tiny umbrella. I glanced around. After my eyes had travelled quite a long way down, I saw looking up at me a girl's chubby face, smiling shyly. I was deeply touched, and I wondered whether a man would have thought of such a gesture. What is more, the girl soon found me a taxi and ushered me inside. All this while not a word had been exchanged between us, save for my *domo arigato gozaimashita* ('Thank you very much'). Soon I was in the Kanko hotel, and immersed up to my neck in the *o-furo*, but warmed above all by this little incident.

As it was off season, the hotel was undergoing reconstruction, and the place was rather disorganized; but the Japanese, like the French, have a great capacity for *se débrouiller*, and I was well looked after. There was much coming and going, and I stayed up until 2 a.m. reading and drinking beer. Next morning the view from the window was of rather dismal factories, beyond which lay the grey Japan Sea. I had intended to climb Mount Fudenge, but the weather was so dull that I was obliged to cancel it. In charge of the hotel was an amusing old woman, who besides smoking incessantly, seemed very fond of *sake*. She was also short of breath, and, as if to emphasize what was fairly evident, she tapped her chest from time to time in comical self-commiseration. She had a smoker's cough which sounded like the noise of shingle under a receding wave. Through this obsession with her ailment, she was dilatory in securing me a taxi, and I only just managed to catch the train for Hiro, where I changed with one minute to spare for Aki-Kawakita. Here, as the conditions were better, I began a leisurely climb up Mount Noro. The rain had reduced the reddish wet clay to such a binding paste that my shoes were soon caked with it. The mountain had just begun to be 'tamed', and a road was being pushed up it, while new houses were burgeoning on the foothills. As it was Sunday, there was hardly anyone about, though I saw a few lumber-jacks at work in the valley. Again, a great loneliness came over me; and although I obtained a magnificent view of the Inland Sea, I was glad to come down again. In the little township, I found a café where a cheerful Mama-San was doing good business, especially with beer and *sake*. Her clientéle of villagers had reached the state in which an addition to their party, even in the shape of a puzzling foreigner, was heartily welcome. Mama-San gave me a good fish meal, and she insisted on having my shoes off so that she could restore them to something like their original shape. About 3.30, a number of schoolgirls swarmed in, disappearing without trace, except as regards audibility, into an interior room where they appeared to be having high tea. By this time I was on such good terms with my companions that I ordered beer all round. Mama-San was delighted, as well she might be, though, in marked contrast to the old soul at Mihara, she would not herself touch alcohol. We had a full and frank duscussion of most of life's problems, or at least that is what I assumed we were elucidating in our mixture of Japanese and English. I regretted it very much when my train fell due, and I had to make a dash for the station, followed by a chorus of *sayonaras*.

CHAPTER VII

Snow Country and Sado Island

I

I have said that many Japanese, not obviously devout, behave at shrines and in temples with the reverential conduct expected of the faithful; but the formal practice of religion, save at weddings and funerals, is probably less common today than in Anglo-Saxon countries. I still believe that this apparent indifference is not a sign that the Japanese are irreligious. They practise a natural religion more assiduously than they would admit, and perhaps at a level deeper than we ever do. If it is in the academic world that one finds the most apparently free-thinking people, as well as those most anxious to repudiate their past, this is no doubt a legacy of the time when learning and knowledge, especially of the sciences, was associated with the West. Many teachers, for example, are radical in outlook, even violently so; but I found it difficult to discover how deep their political preoccupations went.

It may be thought that all the sophistication and materialism in Japan are confined to the urban areas, and that rural Japan is still primitive and backward. This was not my experience. Japan is much more 'of a piece' than most countries which have reached a high standard of economic development. Granted, Japan has still a peasantry, but it is a literate and a progressive peasantry.

It was my very good fortune to be able to travel a good deal through the remoter provinces. On several occasions my companion was Professor Miyahara, Professor of Education at the University of Tokyo. He was a man of liberal views, with an insatiable curiosity about education, especially as practised in Britain, a country which he and his wife knew

well. He had been a defender of liberal values all his life, and he had
suffered for his views during the war. Apart from that, he had a most
genial temperament, and travelling with him was as entertaining as it was
informative. Through his good offices, I was able to address audiences
and visit institutions to which I should otherwise have had little chance
of access. We had some good adventures together, in fair weather and
in foul. Above all, I was able to stay with Japanese families, and this was
not otherwise easy to arrange. As the pleasures of travel depend largely
upon one's travelling companion, I could not have had a better one than
Miyahara Seichi.

In implying that the country in Japan enjoys a measure of uniformity
with the town, I do not mean to suggest that conditions are invariably
similar. It is only natural that there should be marked differences. These
differences are most obvious in the way people lived. In most country
towns, modern architecture has established a wearisome sameness. In the
vicinity of the station there is usually a rather dull piazza containing a
variety of shops, all built of material which, though durable enough,
tends to look cheap and drab. The streets which run off this piazza are
often lacking in pavements, and in winter they can be very muddy.
Whereas many of the shops are wide open to the passerby, with packaged
goods spread out on tables or trestles encroaching on the pavement,
private houses are built on an opposite plan: they are stockaded and
hedged in with dark, weather-stained wood, concealing often a neat
little garden and usually hiding the home from view, which is the
intention. Beside the numerous bars, empty bottles are piled high, just as
beside many of the residences are piles of unsightly rubbish. If you wish
to explore an unfamiliar town, you are likely to end up with a feeling of
greater unfamiliarity, because it is easy to get lost in the maze of narrow
passages (they can hardly be called streets), especially those between
private houses. This applies as much to the suburbs of big cities, including
Tokyo, as to provincial towns. Losing yourself is the easiest thing in the
world, because the houses are arranged in *bancho* or lots, and numbers are
not consecutive; it will take years before this traditional arrangement can
be rationalized, if indeed it ever is.

In the villages, the ordinary people live frugally in small wooden
houses which are prone to rapid dilapidation; but the farmhouses of any
size are places of great charm and even comfort. Moreover, owing to the

new affluence of the Japanese people, rural living conditions have greatly improved. The traditional practice of rebuilding and extensive reparation, due to earthquake and typhoon, means that a poor house can become presentable within a very short time; and the regular replacement of the *tatami* mats can give the interior a fine 'new look'. Old or worn *tatami* lends the room a slatternly appearance. Nevertheless, there has been a great drift from the villages. During the early years of my stay (i.e. between 1960 and 1965) the agricultural population declined by as much as 20.8 per cent, which meant a drop of 4,430,000.

I first had an opportunity of seeing how countryfolk lived by visiting, in Professor Miyahara's company, Sakata city in Yamagata prefecture— I should mention that the word 'city' can be given to very small townships—and, after that, by going up to Akita, in the north of Honshu. We met at Ueno Station at 8 p.m. on 11 January 1965; and, as it was extremely cold, we drank several cups of *sake* before climbing into our sleepers. Fortunately Japanese sleeping cars are very comfortable, so I awoke refreshed, and, peeping through the curtains, I found that my eyes were momentarily blinded by the snow-covered countryside. On arrival, we put up at the house of Professor Miyahara's father-in-law, owner of a very pleasant restaurant called the Kamezaki. Here I had my first real insight into Japanese home life. Mr. Ikeda received us by the traditional hearth, or *irori*, a rectangular space in the middle of the room, over which a steaming kettle was suspended. We greeted each other in the traditional manner, which involved getting right down, planting one's palms firmly, but slightly inward, on the *tatami*, and lowering one's head to the floor. Here one paused for a second or two, and sometimes repeated the obeisance. As this amounted to little more than bowing very low from the sitting position, it was far less complicated a posture than it might seem. On regaining the upright position, we found ourselves seated round the hearth, and again I noticed how pleasant and convenient it was for the host, on such occasions, to be able to conduct conversation while stirring away at the ashes and cinders: an excellent mode of tidying over those pauses which can otherwise become a strain.

We then met Mrs. Ikeda, the eldest son and his wife and their three children. Mrs. Ikeda was a hostess of the old school. She was the soul of kindness and solicitude; and, because of being of the old school, she kept much in the background, though she always seemed to be on call. The two youngest children, who were twins, proved most endearing. Never shall I forget how, to the accompaniment of some singing and strumming on the samisen, they clapped their hands in perfect time and with looks of mounting ecstasy. During my stay, I was never aware of them causing any trouble; and although they were both doted upon by both generations, there was no sign of their being spoiled.

After I had addressed an attentive audience, which included the mayor, and shown a film at the City Centre, I was taken round the town. There was much slush, so I was provided with an enormous pair of rubber boots; I cannot imagine who had last worn them. Sakata is a centre of rice-distribution, and it was the site of a granary built in 1672, the first of its kind in the country. I was first taken to the modern granary, a huge place serving the whole Shonai plain. We also inspected an old wooden structure called the Abumiya Building, formerly the rice-market. In Old Japan, a granary and a rice-market were not to be regarded as secular buildings; they were almost as sacred as temples. Their importance was obvious, as officials were paid in rice, and the process of weighing and distribution were meticulously carried out. The poet Basho, famous for his *haikus*, paid his respects to this particular edifice, and the citizens are proud to remember the fact. Then we strolled through the Hiyoriyama Park, with its Hie shrine and enormous library. At the shrine, the villages give special Kabuki performances in February, and in May there is a grand festival in which the myth of the Sun Goddess Amaterasu is re-enacted on floats drawn by young men through the streets. From the shrine, there is a view of the harbour bar, over which great chilly waves were breaking. Beyond, the Japan Sea looked dour and forbidding.

In 1947 a local magnate had built the Homma Museum, and next day I paid a visit there. Some of the exhibits were of extraordinary interest: a set of Jomon pots, and some rare examples of *kakemono*. One of these *kakemono* was adorned with Basho's own calligraphy. Another example was that of an emperor who, being very hard up, was obliged to sell his brushmanship for a living. At certain periods this was not uncommon, and more than one emperor put his poems on the market as well as his calligraphy. The poverty of emperors was in fact so frequent during the period of their retirement that on certain occasions today, such as the New Year reception for the Diplomatic Corps, the fare is deliberately kept simple in commemoration of that time of penury.

I had always wanted to visit a genuine Japanese farmhouse, and the opportunity presented itself the next day, when we went to one of the oldest remaining houses of its kind. We were received by the owner, a toothless old woman, with an enormous sense of humour: she reminded me of the jolly crone I had met at the hotel at Mihara. She had apparently outlasted most of her family, and she gave the impression of having decided to relax from household burdens for the rest of her days, as well she might. Judging from her spirited personality, she had many days left to enjoy, and she looked a good deal more robust than her asthmatic sister.

My first impression of this venerable thatched building was its commodiousness. It might have housed not merely a large family but a little community, and in point of fact, the traditional family or *iye* did form a sort of community. Great ingenuity had been employed in constructing the house, with interlocking joists and a system of splicing which dispensed altogether with nails. A roof of abundant thatch flowed down to a point near the ground, as if a fur coat had been draped over the building.

What interested me about the reception-room, apart from its size, was the number of books carefully kept in glass cases: not just a few tattered paperbacks but good solid reading to which the old soul evidently applied herself regularly, her bright eyes needing no glasses. As we sat on the *tatami* and drank tea, my eyes wandered to the Buddhist shrine, with a shelf above for Shinto devotion. Both these shelves were well cared for, and the customary offerings were placed before the elaborate gilded altar, to be renewed daily.

Just as I felt at home in this peaceful atmosphere, so I had come to feel at home at the Ikedas, and consequently it was difficult to leave them. At the Kamezaki restaurant we had enjoyed some sumptuous meals together, and on the last evening we menfolk spent some time in one of the local bars, where we danced with the kimono-clad and somewhat buxom hostesses. Before departure we had a regular banquet at which we were joined by the mayor. On entering the public room where this was laid out, we found a local official seated on the floor and draining his last glass of *sake*. Being in a most expansive mood, he entertained us with a song. Then, suddenly glancing at his watch and deciding that it was time to go home for the night, he rose to his feet, and with due ceremony took his leave. This afforded an interesting insight into Japanese social habits.

Having had a busy day, the man was tensed up, and he had decided to unwind. By the time he joined his family, the light fumes of the *sake* would no doubt have evaporated, and he would become the benign husband and father. That was the theory and I suspect that it worked in practice, because I saw it happen more than once.

II

Owing to heavy snow, the express train to Akita had been cancelled, and we had to catch a slow one. Conforming to the traditional practice, Mr. Ikeda, cancelling his other engagements, accompanied us as far as our destination. Here the snow was piled much higher than at Sakata, and the sky glowered and shivered with the promise of more. Our resting-place was a comfortable *ryokan*; I was to notice that the more northward the traveller goes, the greater the comfort and interior warmth, until in Hokkaido it is positively luxurious.

Akita prefecture is the gateway to the north. It was here that a powerful garrison was established in A.D. 733 to repel repeated attacks by the Ainu. The inference is that the aboriginal people were still firmly lodged in the northern tip of Honshu. The title of the commander of the garrison was Shogun, which literally means 'generalissimo'; and the name came in due course to apply to the military ruler who assumed overall rule, while the Emperor reigned in seclusion in Kyoto.

A curious fact is that in Akita, the people, particularly the women, have a distinctively light complexion. We talk about the 'yellow races'; but the Japanese are on the whole more the colour of ivory which, as their skin is smooth and satiny, gives them, but especially the women, the appearance of fine porcelain. Nevertheless, the whiteness of the women of Akita is striking, and they are sufficiently proud of the fact to avoid too great exposure to the sun and weather.[1] There are old prints showing them wearing special hats with veils, and some of them did so until fairly recently. The cause of this highly prized form of complexion is unknown. Conceivably, it is due to a mixture with the Ainu themselves, because such miscegenation went on in the past as much as it does now; but this

[1] It will be recalled how, in Mishima Yukio's story, 'Death in Midsummer', the character Yasue was 'very proud of her fair north-country skin'.

explanation is one that most Japanese are disinclined to accept. Whatever the reason, a good many women I saw in the area were strikingly beautiful.

I was able to meet a number of ordinary folk at Akita city at a gathering held in a municipal building, of the local parent-teacher association. As I have pointed out, such associations exert considerable power. Here, with the aid of Professor Miyahara's interpretation, I had what was for me a most valuable two hours of exchange of ideas. After that, we paid a visit to the Mining Museum, with its fossils of plants and animals 350 million years old (some were from Britain), and then to the Aramasa *sake* factory, where I came to realize how complicated a process is involved in making this delicate wine. We climbed up vats the size of gasometers, and inhaled an atmosphere pungent and slightly nauseating, like an old-fashioned anaesthetic. The whole place was exquisitely clean and, as usual, the workers were going about their business as if in a pleasant sort of trance, which, in this case, may well have been their habitual condition.

For centuries the northern prefectures of Honshu have energetically kept up traditional festivals and practised communal arts. This was their chief means of diversion during the long winters which held them almost incommunicado from the rest of the country. Many books on Japan give the impression that the Noh drama, with its extreme refinement of gesture and speech, was cultivated only by a sophisticated upper class in the urban areas. The truth is that Noh, as well as Kabuki, has been kept up in rural areas as well, and the same applies to the traditional sacred dances or *Kagura*, which, meaning 'joys of the gods', were originally performed in shrines to appease the demons. For the children, there was the excitement of constructing snow igloos outside their houses. Here candles were lit at night and votive offerings made to the God of Water, Mizu-no-kami. I wish only that we had been able to stay in Akita for the *Bon-ten matsuri* at the Miyoshi shrine, which takes place on 17 January; for this is a very ancient purification ceremony, at which long *gohei* or Shinto prayer-wands are used to asperge the onlookers. Needless to say, these sacred wands, like much other religious apparatus, are giving place to sets of vertical wires installed on house and even shack, signifying communication on a more secular level.

III

It was the following March that we set off again for the North, where the snow still lay thick. This time Professor Miyahara's son Yoichi accompanied us, and we benefited greatly from his companionship. He was invaluable at ensuring that we were on time at the stations and ports, and that we did not leave items of luggage—and sometimes ourselves—behind; for there was one occasion when, sleeping off the effects of a late night, we all but missed a station, and, for once, the Japanese railways held up the train while we descended in great confusion. Had not Yoichi thundered on the carriage window, we should have been carried hundreds of miles further. Apart from that, he was a very able photographer.

We were bound initially for Niigata. A year before, the severest earthquake I was to experience in Japan (there an average of 1,000 tremors a year) had its epicentre thereabouts. I remember our office building in Tokyo swaying slowly from side to side for what, though it cannot have been more than a minute and perhaps less, seemed an interminable time. Slightly unnerving though this was, such lateral movement is a sign that nothing serious is likely to happen: only vertical movement is really dangerous. Many large buildings in Niigata, though considered to be earthquake proof, were tipped over at an angle; but one of the structures to sustain least damage was, interestingly enough, the mediaeval bridge.

This time we did not stay long in the city, which was well on the way to reconstruction; our destination was a place which I had always wanted to visit, Sado Island, sixty or so miles off the coast. Now at last the opportunity had arrived. We boarded the ferry, but we were only a few minutes out of port when I realized that our voyage, which was due to last two and a half hours, promised to be a rough one. So indeed it proved. There was a heavy swell and, to make matters worse, it was markedly chilly. Fortunately, good *tatami* was spread on the deck, and we were able to roll ourselves into thick blankets and drowse it out; and although some passengers were sick, our little party survived tolerably well.

Our first view of Sado, when we managed to stagger up to look at it, was of a mountainous island, dusted over with snow. Mount Kimpoku, standing 3,740 feet, looked majestic, but the island, at that distance, seemed withdrawn and uninviting; and I felt a slight dread that our days there might prove something of a trial. As soon as we landed, however, such forebodings were put to flight: for there awaiting us at the landing stage was Professor Miyahara's friend, Mr. Chikamatsu, a man of warm friendliness, whose entire life had been spent on Sado, and who knew every inch of its territory as well as every phase of its history. He told us that, owing to extremely rough weather, the previous day's ferry had been cancelled. Accompanying him were his three daughters, bonny and strapping girls, Keiko, Reiko and Atsuko, whose function on this occasion was to produce their cameras, snap us, and promptly disappear, presumably in order to hasten forward the household preparations for our stay. We then set off to drive from Ryotsu, the main port, across the 'waist' of the island. Sado is of such a shape as to suggest two halves which have been pulled apart and never again placed in true alignment. The countryside was typical of Old Japan, for thatched homesteads were numerous, including large farmhouses resembling that which I had visited at Sakata. One was now a museum, preserving traditional agricultural implements, peasant clothes, straw hats, capes, sandals, and snowshoes, all made with a kind of rough art. There were the usual Shinto and Buddhist shelves, and, to remind the visitor of another epoch, an articulated prehistorical monster, of which Mr. Chikamatsu had himself found a tooth. I noticed also a stuffed crested ibis, or *toki*, a bird of singular beauty, of which only four are said to remain on Sado, and five in Ishikawa prefecture. Great efforts are being made to preserve this lovely bird.

For many centuries, Sado had a life of its own, its territory being sufficiently distant and bleak to make it a suitable place for the deportation of criminals. We visited the old gold mines, begun in 1601, where these miserable exiles toiled. Above was a gaunt, cleft peak which had resulted from the working, and following through, of veins on the surface. In fact, gold and rice were the products for which the island was renowned. Not merely criminals but some distinguished men took refuge here, among them the Emperor Juntoku (1197–1242), exiled for trying to topple the Kamakura Shogunate. He paid for this rash attempt by a stay of twenty-two years in a little wood palace at Szumi until his death at the age of forty-six. A briefer stay was made by the fanatical religious leader Nichiren, whose exile lasted from 1271 to 1374. His followers today, members of the Soka-Gakkai sect, often make special pilgrimages to

Sado. The number of samurai of distinction who came to Sado to evade the Shogun's wrath was so great at one time that the intellectual life of the island compared favourably with that of some urban centres on the mainland. These samurai brought with them the Noh drama; and some of the most authentic Noh was until recently performed on the island. Indeed, it is said that there were at one time 100 Noh stages there.

On Sado there is a very strong feeling of local patriotism. Hitherto, there has been no flight to the mainland, still less to the capital, such as has disturbed the life of many islands, often resulting in their total evacuation. I found this spirit of sturdy independence especially among the island's potters. Here as elsewhere, these formed a proud profession. We paid calls on some of them. Mr. Shimizu, a long-haired man, invited me to inscribe two of his pots, made of red clay called *Mumyoi-yaki*. Mr. Miura, sitting like a Diogenes in a disordered office-studio, inveighed against Tokyo and its 'decadence'. Unlike most artists I met in Japan, he was restless and choleric, but at the same time amusing in a way that perhaps he did not always intend. Finally, we visited the tiny house of Mr. Miyata, who made little wax objects, popping the spare material in his mouth while he worked on a whimsical model, such as a group of frogs pulling a rickshaw.

I remember 2 March as being a specially pleasant day on the island. After we had driven round the rocky coast of Sankaku Bay, we took lunch at a little hotel by the sea. We were on the first floor, seated round a low lacquered table. The sun, of which for the first time we were getting our fill, flooded on to the *tatami* like a light syrup. It was rare to eat in these conditions in Japan, because meals on the ground floor were usually partaken in enclosed rooms, sometimes very small, access to sun and air being minimal. (Such conditions were naturally different in the case of a special 'viewing' ceremony, whether of flowers in season or of the moon: then partitions would be removed, or seats would be taken on the verandah.) Now, as we drank *sake* and beer, we might have been on board ship, with the light twinkling through the portholes; I remember the feeling of peace which was due partly to the prevailing quietness of the island, and partly to the simplicity and contentment of most of the islanders. That same evening—local hospitality being a continuous process—we had dinner with the Mayor of Sado (I had lectured at the Town Hall in the afternoon), a wealthy farmer of expansive personality, together with some local officials. One of the guests was a teacher of mathematics, who, to my great surprise began, after a few drinks, to quote Tennyson; he knew by heart long passages of *Enoch Arden*. I enjoined him to continue, because the novelty of hearing Tennyson declaimed in so remote a spot stirred my fancy, apart from the fact that the Japanese love to recite poetry. He and his companions soon burst into song; and I have to admit that towards the end of the evening, and at the insistence of the Mayor, I got to my feet and gave my guests a rendering of the only song that came to my mind, which was 'Loch Lomond'. This general mood of conviviality provided the excuse for adjourning to a bar, where there was a certain amount of mutual instruction by the hostesses and myself in Japanese and English and Scottish dances, to the great amusement of the older guests. We also performed the most attractive local ballad song-dance called 'Okesa', where the participants, originally miners, form a single line and gesture gracefully to one side and the other, regularly clapping their hands. For its proper execution, a large circular straw or cape hat must be worn, drawn down at the sides like large blinkers, and secured under the chin by a ribbon. Various theories have been put forward to explain the shape of this hat, and it would seem that it was designed to prevent the miners looking at the Emperor. Meanwhile, Professor Miyahara, from the vantage point of a seat at the bar, acted as master of ceremonies, an office which at a late hour we had some difficulty in persuading him to abandon.

When Mr. Chikamatsu felt that it was time for us to rejoin his family, we took back with us the owner of the bar itself. At least I presume she was the owner. She was very much in charge. Perhaps, however, like many women who keep bars, she had a 'patron'. Instead of being a buxom Mama-San, she was a bright, attractive, youngish woman of obvious good family and education. Here I had another insight into Japanese life. From lunchtime onwards, our party had been exclusively a male one; and at the bar, hostesses had played their customary role as entertainers. When we arrived home, we found awaiting us Mr. Chikamatsu's three daughters, and also his son (their mother was unfortunately ill in hospital); but our friend from the bar was received quite naturally as 'one of the family'. We continued the party with more *sake* and some welcome *sushi*. The girls were thoroughly emancipated, with none of the timidity sometimes characteristic of their sisters of the mainland; I do not suppose they had met many foreigners before, and certainly not an Englishman. But it has been remarked that women in distant places seem often to enjoy greater equality than in more sophisticated circles, and of Japan this is certainly true. We had a somewhat uproarious party, after which I slept soundly in my newly-*tatamied* room; for Mr. Chikamatsu, a typical Japanese host, had newly done up my quarters.

It was sad to say goodbye to this charming family. My stay under Mr. Chikamatsu's hospitable roof had had something special about it. This was due largely to his endearing personality. I fancied he was a devout Buddhist. On my last evening, at the party described, he showed me with obvious pride and reverence, a beautiful book of Sutras; and when I had returned to Tokyo, he wrote, in answer to mine, a letter which contained the following passage: 'My three daughters, Keiko, Reiko, and Atsuko, too say in unison that they have vivid memories of your stay here. . . . I am now convinced that it is fully out of divine providence that the souls of us all came together and melted into one just in the midst of the isolated island of Sado.' I had experienced the same feeling too: it is not so very common, especially across so wide a cultural gulf.

Our journey back from Sado was a good deal smoother than our way out, though we spent the voyage recumbent in order to make up for lost sleep. From Niigata we took the train along the coast, in sunny weather, to dusty Naoetsu, with its oil wells. It was here that but for Professor Miyahara's son we should have been carried further on. The train brimmed with laughing school-children, in neat dresses and shiny wellingtons, a necessity in the Snow Country. At the hotel, with which I was already familiar, I was delighted to find a practice Tea Ceremony in progress, under the supervision of a venerable and extremely strict tea-master. Having been invited to participate, I watched for the first time the several niceties of the ceremony explained by one of the old school. Here was no 'free expression' or 'creative movement'. Such things tend to *limit* the effect of a ritual or dance, and soon acquire a stereotyped pattern of their own. Having time enough to spare, I did not begrudge the long while I remained seated, more or less in orthodox fashion, at this function: which, once the bowl of tea began to circulate, turned into a genuine Tea Ceremony, leaving me in that calm of mind which is one of its reputed results.

Next day we had our first real experience of the Snow Country. The novel of that title, *Yukiguni*, by Kawabata Yasunari, awarded the Nobel Prize in 1968,[1] gives a graphic insight into a region of Japan which, being in the direct line of the Siberian winds, is dumped from December to May with more snow than anywhere else in the country. In places, it reaches a depth of fifteen feet, obliterating roads as if they had never been, and assuming fantastic shapes on hills and trees, which are plastered as with a kind of flocculent dough.

We were bound for the hills, a hard drive through a great sliced cutting, and our destination was the Takasumi Primary School in the Kuwatori district. As no foreigner had ever been to the school before, the occasion was treated as rather a special one. The parents had arrived to form part of the reception committee. Many of them were in traditional costume and had brought with them precious dolls for display. The day before had been the *Hinamatsuri*, or dolls' festival, which must be at least 1,000 years old. The change to the solar calendar meant that the festival now takes place in the cold weather, whereas it was originally a spring festival, signifying that 'the winter is past'. At one time, dolls, male and female, were made of paper and then thrown into a river, as a means of warding off evil spirits. Today, dolls are elaborately dressed, often in court costume, and displayed on shelves in department stores and in hotel lobbies. They are treasured in families and handed down from one generation to another. The display at the school was very colourful, and so were the other decorations which, to my Western mind, lent an air of Christmas to the scene, especially in such an environment.

The first-grade pupils sang in my honour a *hina* song, and I came to appreciate the importance that dolls still hold in Japanese life. As this district was one in which many old ceremonies were kept up, I had no doubt that the tradition still lingered on, here rather than elsewhere, that dolls represented gods or *kami*—a tradition presumably much older than that which held them to be charms. For it has been an immemorial custom for the dolls to be 'fed' on the occasion of the *matsuri*, and for children to drink a sweet rice-wine called *shirozake*. What was my gratification, therefore, when, at the end of the song, I was handed a glass of liquid, sweet to the taste, which I realized to be the traditional drink. The little girl who offered it me was dressed in a beautiful kimono, ablaze with colour, such as children wear at the *Shichi-go-san* festival,

[1] He committed suicide in 1972.

when those aged seven, five, and three are accorded special honour. Afterwards, she made a graceful speech to Professor Miyahara and myself in a piping voice, bowing low at every sentence.

During my visit, I was put through all kinds of ritual, one of which struck me as curious. It consisted of my being beaten, though lightly, with swords, which was evidently a form of purification. What is more, I ascertained that I was being treated as a bridegroom, though I could not identify, among the tiny tots clustered around, the one destined to be my bride, unless I were to be symbolically united to them all. What struck me was that all this activity seemed to be undertaken without a trace of self-consciousness. No doubt the children had been coached for the occasion, but the festivals were familiar to them. All that was novel, I assume, was having, as a subject for treatment, a human frame which must have seemed absurdly large and ungainly.

I ought not to give the impression that this visit was nothing but a display of local customs and folklore, though it was folklore that was still alive. I saw a good deal of the children's work, which was particularly neat: even the cursive script must be absolutely legible as well as aesthetically satisfying. I was impressed, too, with the headmaster, Mr. Hayashi, whose rule over his 147 little pupils seemed benevolent and kind; and no less with the women teachers, who had a gentle sweetness, and an attractiveness of dress, not always associated with their profession. But what was warming to the heart above all was the gaiety and cosiness of the school in its tough wooden building, crouching beneath a cowl of snow.

After I had made a short speech from the platform, and presented the headmaster with a box of sweetmeats which we had calculated would provide the children with one apiece, we took our leave, receiving a rousing send-off with many high-pitched *sayonaras* and much waving of Japanese and British flags, which momentarily scattered the falling suds.

Our next call was Nakano (not to be confused with Nagano). The train made its way through what seemed to be eternal snow, banked high on either side. When the white sheen was reflected in the compartment mirror, I was reminded of one of the scenes in Kawabata's book which had always impressed me: that in which the geisha's low mirror reflects the glare of the snow outside, so that the Snow Country penetrates within the warm *ryokan* and cannot be shut out. In fact, I know of few works, even taking into account Hardy's, in which the environment plays such an integral artistic part as in *Snow Country*.

That evening we put up at the house of another friend of Professor Miyahara's, Mr. Takeda. It was a large wooden establishment, and Mr. Takeda's parents lived there too. The older couple enjoyed obvious precedence over the younger; I have rarely seen such authority in the family exercised in a more paternalistic manner, though there was nothing rigidly formal about it. I was made to feel instantly at home. This was due partly, I think, to the prevailing sense of hierarchy, so that everyone knew his place and acted accordingly, myself included, and partly to the fact that the young Tekadas had three lovely children who, with their bright red cheeks, radiated cheerfulness whenever they were brought in.

Although we were in the heart of rural Japan, presided over by Inari, the farmer's tutelary god, there was no lack of efficiency in the organization of day-to-day affairs. There was much communication between the house and outside. At first I thought that the medium used was the telephone; but I soon discovered that it was a network of speaking-tubes which connected most of the houses of the village. A call was announced by something resembling a bleep or whistle, as with the contraptions in old London houses. Nowhere esle did I see anything of the kind.

Although we were rather tired, I was so keen to talk with the Takedas that when Professor Miyahara took to his *futon*, our hosts, Yoichi and I sat round the *funatsu*—a cauldron of wood-ash covered with a thick rug— and discussed life in Japan and Britain until quite a late hour. Finally, we touched on the subject of religion, which often preoccupies those who are still conversing at midnight. I was a little surprised to find that the elder Mr. Takeda, who did most of the talking, held no strong beliefs. He even went so far as to denounce the whole story of the Buddha as a myth, whereas I was trying to sustain at least the historicity of Sakyamuni. I realized that Mr. Takeda's youth had been spent at a time of insurgent secularism; and no doubt the disaster of 1945 had destroyed any faith he may have had in the traditional system. I asked him what had meant most to him during his long life, and he said that, for him, the welfare of his family had been his chief concern. He would die happy, he added, if he knew that he was able to leave his children and grandchildren in a condition of prosperity. As he spoke, I dimly saw the traces of ancestor-worship in his thoughts. Somehow it was difficult to reconcile oneself to life without some link between past and future. I do not believe that old Mrs. Takeda was without a deep, if simple, faith.

Next day I arose in good spirits, knowing that I had a morning free from official engagements. My hosts were extremely indulgent, and in fact we breakfasted and talked from 8 a.m. to 11 a.m. Beside the low table was a large television set; and when we were not talking, we were viewing. I remember a rather horrifying documentary on L.S.D. in America. This prompted us to talk about the influence of drugs upon Japanese youth. What emerged from this was a point that impressed me. Western drug takers were chiefly keen to obtain—at least in the case of those who were not 'hooked'—a higher consciousness, a new insight into reality. The oriental mind was, by contrast, much more meditative, more prone to a mystical approach, at a quite humble level: so much so that it is doubtful whether the word 'mystical' applied at all in such a case. If, as I had myself supposed, the Japanese, like many orientals, made little distinction between the sacred and the secular, the disparity felt by the Westerner loomed much larger. Before I went to Japan, some people had told me not to expect to find the ordinary person 'interesting', in the sense of being able to express original thoughts: I was even given the impression, by some authorities, that the normal Japanese had very little inner life at all. After six years, I came to a rather different conclusion. I do not believe that the Japanese set such store by thoughts or ideas as we do; but that does not mean that they lack inner life. I believe that they enjoy a much greater empathy with nature and objects and with one another than we do, to a degree perhaps that we are incapable of recapturing. If the word mystic may be used, they are natural mystics, rather than deliberate ones. And what is already natural does not need to be artificially stimulated. I do not believe that drugs will become the problem in Japan that it is elsewhere, even though the practice in certain circles is much older than with us.

Before I left the Takedas, I wrote a brush-inscription on a piece of white cardboard which was immediately framed and hung on the wall. Then we drove, this time in heavy rain, to Nagano. The town is renowned for its high educational standards, and I gained an insight into this when that same afternoon I lectured at the Town Hall, for there were many cogent questions at the end, framed in good, confident English. I could not leave this famous town without paying a visit to the Zenkoji temple, after which the town itself had originally been named. Founded at the beginning of the seventh century, it became the home in due course of a famous statue of the Buddha, which may have come from Korea. For centuries, it has been concealed, but a picture is shown of it annually. The temple belongs to no sect. People flock to it for an interesting reason. On the wall of a dark crypt-like tunnel hangs a heavy key, which, if located and touched, is supposed to ensure long life. Negotiating the passage is not easy, especially as there are two sharp turns to the right. Yoichi preceded me and, presumably by means of the empathy with objects animate and inanimate of which I have spoken, he succeeded in finding the key without difficulty. Groping my way along behind, I evidently was feeling too high up the wall, and Yoichi was obliged to guide my hand to the spot. I do not know whether this counts or not. The exit to the tunnel is near the entrance to the temple.

IV

There are many Buddhist temples and Shinto shrines where superstitions of this kind survive; but we can hardly condemn them when we bear in mind the relics and 'miraculous' images and statues that draw crowds to certain Christian churches, and indeed the absurdities which some political cults encourage, despite the 'materialistic' doctrines on which they are based. Nor can everything of this nature be dismissed out of hand as hocus-pocus. I am not naturally credulous; but on one occasion, and again in Professor Miyahara's company, I had an experience which was certainly out of the ordinary, and for the authenticity of which the reader will have to take my word. It was in Ina city, in Nagano Prefecture, in July 1965, and we were sleeping for a night or two in a temple. It happened that the priest there held views similar to those of the author of *Honest to God*, except that he had discarded the vocabulary of theology altogether and did not even have a jargon to put in its place. Like many other priests, he had great difficulty in maintaining his temple, and he was obliged to undertake some teaching in order to supplement his income; and so far as pastoral work was concerned, he seemed to me to be a conscientious and compassionate man, whom I could not help but like.

My bed was a thick *futon* laid out on the floor of the temple's 'chancel'. A gilded statue of the Buddha was on my left. I remember feeling a sense of awe as I glanced up at it before settling down to sleep. The silence, enhanced by the presence of immobile statues and images, was almost 'audible'. But having listened to so much secularist talk, my mind was in no mood to anticipate anything unusual: and apart from the novelty of my surroundings, there was nothing to prevent me from being as cool and collected as could be.

The fox plays an important part in Japanese religion and culture. In all the shrines dedicated to the god of rice, Inari, he figures prominently, as he is the special emissary of this god. Some shrines are dedicated to this animal; many contain representations of him. To the worshippers at such shrines he is a benevolent deity, bringer of good fortune and protector of the harvest. Some peasants believe that he inhabits the rice fields, in spirit at least, while the plant is maturing, after which he retires to the mountains to spend the winter. But the fox can prove also a malevolent deity, greatly to be feared. Assuming a variety of disguises, he can lure people to their destruction; he is particularly sinister when he adopts the role of a priest; and he is at his most dangerous when he 'possesses' a person. All this may sound like gross superstition, especially as stories about foxes (and badgers: another mischievous animal) date from the legendary records of both China and Japan. The legends seem to have first entered Japan in the eleventh century, so their Chinese origin is evidently much earlier. Allowing for the usual measure of absurdity, and the fact that one story or related experience may *induce* a similar experience in another person, the fact remains that even today many people of intelligence, including some medical practitioners, believe that possession by foxes (*kitsune-tsuki*) is a reality, and that when it occurs, recourse must be had to special measures.

Those most susceptible to fox-possession are usually women. Basil Hall Chamberlain in his *Things Japanese* quotes a high academic, Dr. Baelz, then professor at the Imperial University of Tokyo, as affirming that 'possession never occurs except in such subjects as have heard of it already and believe in the reality of its existence.' This may suggest either the 'inducement' of which we have spoken, or the assignment of a cause to a condition otherwise hysterical in origin. There are well-attested 'fox stories' today. Carmen Blacker has witnessed at least one exorcism, and Lewis Bush in his *Japanalia*[1] writes as follows:

'Not many years ago the writer was confronted with a quite handsome female at a family gathering in Shiba who suddenly began to roll on the *tatami* while uttering quite hair-raising screams. It was assumed quite seriously by my host that she had a fox in her stomach and would have to be taken to a certain shrine to beg the gods to make it depart. In the past, the priests most adept at "casting out foxes" were the famous Yamabushi, or mountain monks, and therefore the ceremonies of exorcism took place, as a rule, on high places.'

At the time when I was staying at the temple, I knew little about such fox stories; what I did know were merely old and extravagant legends. Yet the strange thing is—I use this adjective advisedly, for no similar experience has happened to me before or since—that in the small hours of that first night I was awakened from a deep sleep by a sensation, so powerful as partially to rouse me, of being nuzzled in the left side by an animal which I knew at once to be a fox. This nuzzling and chivying were so deliberate and determined as to cause me to roll over on my side and finally to slide off the *futon* altogether. At the point at which I was out of bed, I found myself wholly awake. All was quiet; nothing was lurking around. Nevertheless, the sensation of having been accosted and pushed, in a manner distinctly hostile, by a fox was compelling; and it caused me to remain awake for some hours, until towards morning I dozed off out of exhaustion. I must explain that I do not claim to have seen a fox in a physical sense; but in my mind's eye I saw one quite distinctly, and I *felt* its muzzle nosing me. Nor do I suggest that I was in a condition, even for a moment, of fox-possession. At least I trust not: my Japanese companions (to whom I did not relate the experience, since I dismissed it at the time as a nightmare) noticed, so far as I am aware, no unusual behaviour on my part. All I felt was that some power, hostile to me and resenting my presence in the temple, was operating, and that this power or influence —I do not know how to describe it—personified itself, in my semi-conscious state, as a fox. Fancifully, I wondered whether this intrusion

[1] Vol. 1 (1967), p. 92.

had something to do with the officiating priest's own sceptical views. Only later, as I say, did I come to hear of experiences similar in nature; and I now consider that I had, so to speak, skirted a reality which, in severer forms, is described as fox-possession.

Such an experience, even if not wholly 'imaginary', would seem more likely to occur in a shrine than in a temple, and in a fox shrine most of all. On the other hand, Buddhist and Shinto traditions have become so intermingled that Buddhist priests have often been called upon to 'cast out' fox demons. The role is not the prerogative of the priests of Shinto.

That was my only experience in Japan that I would describe as uncanny, though I shall relate an experience considered to be so, but not by me, in describing a visit to Mount Misen near Hiroshima. I became aware repeatedly of Japanese superstitions in everyday life: for example, the avoidance of certain days as unlucky when planning a particular function or journey, the fear of persons with facial or other blemishes, the idea that good luck comes from the south-east, and a marked interest in spiritualism. (Francis King in *The Custom House* has given a vivid account of such a preoccupation among show-girls.) Otherwise the Japanese seemed to me remarkably like ourselves in their general contempt for superstition, but also in the occasional revelation of a side to their nature which considered it best to propitiate the powers of luck or chance rather than deliberately to ignore or to thwart them. We are accustomed to precisely such furtive but deliberate concessions to the powers our forefathers believed in; and if a Japanese were to write a book on British superstition, taking as his material certain regular features of popular newspapers alone, he might well represent us as an incorrigibly superstitious people. With Japanese intellectuals such as Professor Miyahara, I felt myself in the presence of persons who were more governed by reason than were many of their Western colleagues. It was I who earnestly sought out popular beliefs about holy and venerated places, and who expressed curiosity as to the Japanese attitude to the supernatural, etc. Consequently, it was I, rather than Professor Miyahara, who had the encounter with the dream-fox, and who kept it to myself in case my friends, and above all the *Honest to God* priest, should regard me as a victim of primitive credulity. Indeed, our priestly host, presiding over his secularized temple, would, I believe, have been more shocked than anyone, though I have wondered since whether my night-time intruder, having reminded me of forces undreamt of in his philosophy, did not later choose some occasion to put him in mind of them too.

V

No visit to the Japan Sea coast would be complete without a stay at the coastal towns of Toyama and Kanazawa; and I was able to make my way there in due course and to visit them in excellent company. At Toyama, I was royally entertained by Professor Takase, Dean of the Faculty of Science and Literature, who had not long before visited India for the purpose of studying sacred mountains. Many studies of Japan, and perhaps many Japanese also, fail to take account of the great Indian heritage. Professor Takase was accompanied by several interesting colleagues, of whom I may mention Professor Shimizu (who, as well as being Professor of English, was chief librarian) and his assistant, Professor Sunuma. I met more of the staff at a *zadankai* which took place after a lecture to 650 students—certainly one of the largest concourses I was to address.

After these functions, I was presented with one of my most treasured Japanese possessions. This was a miniature temple bell, for most of the country's temple bells are cast in Toyama. At one time the sound of these bells, on festival days and not least at funerals, was a familiar feature of everyday life. Now, like so many church bells of the West, they evoke often no more than a feeling of nostalgia for an age that seems beyond recall. The bells, rich in tone, are of fine workmanship. Even my own little bronze model emits a remarkably fine tone when struck by the hammer which hangs at its side.

Also bestowed on me were a collection of little boxes and capsules which, had their contents been as efficacious as claimed, would have given me something like unrivalled virility and the longevity with which to exercise it, as well as keeping me in great psychological euphoria. These medicines have a long history. During the seventeenth century, a doctor named Moku Josan from Katayama presented the local *daimyo*, Maeda Masatoshi, with a medicament of his own preparation. It evidently worked wonders, and the *daimyo* authorized it to be sold under his auspices under the name of *Hangontan*. In a short time, it became popular not merely in Japan but beyond her borders. It and its subsidiary curatives are still popular, bringing in an annual profit of thousands of pounds. Many of the latter are now manufactured at Toyama. Whether or not they are approved by the medical profession does not seem to matter; the laity has strong views on what it considers likely to do it good, and its convictions are not easily shaken. When one considers the changes of fashion displayed in the orthodox pharmaceutical market, the continuing vogue of *Hangontan*, which has not altered substantially for three hundred years, suggests that the enthusiasm of the *daimyo* may not have been misplaced. When I showed my collection to Teiko-San, however, she examined each neat little packet with great care and many exclamations of wonder, and, as I thought, some amused scepticism. Despite their supposed efficacy, she did not recommend me to keep any by me, and I believe she may have given them to Soma-San, who probably treated them with greater respect. In view of the great reputation which Toyama still enjoys for its medicines, I should not be surprised if, a century from now, they are still available. At the same time, the Toyama product owed its initial vogue to advertising: one of the first examples of this medium being applied to curative products. It was originally sold by licensed pedlars, who visited the villages annually, leaving a bag of medicines at each house. The following year, on their rounds, the pedlars would charge the family according to the amount consumed. Finally, the whole country was divided into twenty-one districts; and the travellers or their representatives enjoyed special rights to their patch of territory.

It would be wrong to suggest that Toyama is renowned only for its ancient pharmaceutical industry. On the contrary, it is a town which has shown great progress in several spheres, not least in rice-production. In 1955, Japanese rice-production per hectare was 3.8 tons. A Toyama farmer, using electric heating, succeeded about this time in increasing his yield to as much as 9.15 tons per hectare; and his method has been widely adopted. As about 73 per cent of arable land in Japan consists of paddy fields, the national production is now enormous.

Professor Sunuma took me by car to Kanazawa, over a good road, rising all the time, amid much wooded country. Like Kyoto, but not for the same reason, Kanazawa had the good fortune to escape bombardment during the war. Consequently, it preserves many of the characteristics of an old, traditional Japanese town. The name means 'gold marsh', as gold dust was originally found there. Like Kyoto again, it is an important cultural centre. Many famous men came from there, including the philosopher Nishida and Suzuki Daisetz. James Murdoch, author of one of the best histories of Japan, taught there. At the end of the sixteenth century, the whole area came under the rule of the great Maeda clan, whose representative had sponsored *Hangontan*. The *daimyo*'s mansion stood in what is now the famous Kenrokuen Park, which remains one of the three great gardens of Japan. The other two are the Tokiwa at Mito and the Korakuen at Okayama. Here I was shown round by Professor Osawa, who called for me in the morning, and with whom I was to strike up an immediate friendship. Professor Osawa was one of those gentle Japanese who seem to embody the Buddhist way of life, even though they may not be practitioners in the strict sense. In this opinion, I was not alone: I recommended several visitors to him, and one, my friend Alan Pryce-Jones, declared him to be a saint. Professor Osawa had another distinction: that of being president of the Thomas Hardy Society of Japan, founded originally by Edmund Blunden back in the 1920s. The distinction was no mere formality: the Japanese Hardy Society was, I believe, the first to be established anywhere, antedating that of England by thirty or so years. Consequently, when the English branch was formed in 1965, Professor Osawa, with about twelve other Japanese (the largest foreign contingent), attended the meetings at Dorchester and appropriately contributed an article to the Festival programme, which was much admired.

Apart from the museum, with its magnificent scrolls, calligraphy and Chinese porcelain, part of the collection of the late Mr. Yamakawa, the park was noted for a beautiful house of two storeys called the Seisenkaku. This was one of those wooden structures which, like certain old Scandinavian houses, lend an 'ancestral' impression more effectively than many of stone or brick. But for me the chief joy of the park, apart from its spaciousness (for it is the largest of the three mentioned), was the view it afforded from an eminence called Kasumigaike of places so distant as the mountains of the Noto peninsula, which stretches out like a bent finger, and beyond which is Hekura Island, where the girls from the *ama* villages of fisher-folk engage in underwater food gathering.

Apart from lecturing, I spent some time at the University. Here I found an English library of remarkable scope, containing a number of sets of English authors, forming the best collection I had seen outside

Tenri. Among the many interesting people I met there, Professor Okubo proved to be an enduring contact, for he has since remained in touch with me by letter. He was a considerable Shakespeare scholar, and I recall that at a dinner at the Senpokaku restaurant we spent much time swapping quotations. I came to acquire a special affection for Kanazawa; and although I never succeeded in visiting it again, I kept in touch with the University there throughout my stay in Japan. Apart from its close contacts with Western learning, the city has its traditional side. A Noh theatre, representing the Kaga-Hosho school, remains one of the most famous of its kind; for its regular performances are no mere revivals, but finished works of art.

So I returned from my pilgrimage to some of the most rarely visited parts of Japan. I shall not forget the warmth and friendship of Sado Island and the Snow Country, remote places in which I saw the Japan of tradition. Here people lived the good, hard life, lent meaning by an annual round of festivals and observances. Was I wrong to suppose that Japan, despite its sophistication and its surface materialism, has kept this sense of 'meaning' better than most other countries, and that this is why her people communicate an impression of spiritual well-being, as if they were drawing silently upon a source of strength denied to others, and perhaps not always understood by themselves?

CHAPTER VIII

Shikoku and Kyushu

I

Although my visits to Kyoto were frequent, I went to Osaka and Kobe comparatively seldom. Our office in Kyoto 'serviced' them; and despite the close connection of Kobe with British residents, I had no occasion to explore these places with the same care or interest as I had less international cities. My work lay among the Japanese. Osaka reminded me much of Chicago, a city in which I had not long before spent a winter; and, admittedly, like Chicago, it has been unjustifiably denigrated. Some of the times I best remember are when I went down for the Festival of the Arts, organized each spring by the remarkable Miss Murayama Michi. One of Japan's most distinguished women, Miss Murayama came from the powerful family associated with the *Asahi Shimbun*, an influential newspaper with a well-edited English version. In a 'man's country', she had built up the Osaka Festival almost single-handed. The Festivals were always great social, as well as artistic, occasions. At the opening night, a fanfare of trumpets would inaugurate the proceedings, after which a chorus of young girls in white (not, alas, in kimonos, which would to my mind have been more suitable), rising on a platform, would sing the Japanese anthem, 'Kimigayo', which signifies 'The Reign of our Emperor'. This is a solemn piece somehow embodying the very spirit of Japan. (It has just a hint of the parody-anthem in *The Mikado*, but I do not believe that any connection between them has been established.) After speeches, the concert would begin. I have heard some of the world's best orchestras, conductors and soloists in the Osaka Festival Hall. After the opening concert there would be a sumptuous buffet. Deservedly, this

Festival has become one of the most famous in the world. Osaka was the centre of the great International Festival of 1970.

It was at the Osaka Festival of 1962 that I met Mr. Matsushita (pronounced Mat-sush-ta), the great industrialist whose career was similar in many respects to that of Lord Nuffield. He was a quiet, unassuming man whom one would not have picked out in a crowd; but, judging from the enormous sum in income tax he was reputed to pay, he must have been the richest man in Japan. More important, he was also something of a philosopher: a philosopher, that is to say, in the Japanese (and Indian) sense of a person who reflects about life and endeavours to understand its meaning, not one who enquires about the meaning of everything except the meaning of life. And he sought to realize his ideals in practice. We were introduced in the interval and, after a brief conversation, he invited me to visit his Osaka factory. And so the following October I was shown over the great Matsushita Electric Company works.

First, I was ushered into a luxurious lounge in order to see a film of the company's activities, and then I was taken round the Transistor Department, where, as I was to notice in other factories, the employees were going about their work like somnambulists. My impression was that they were happy, though I was told that the Labour Unions were proving difficult. I was taken through several other departments, where the atmosphere was no less quiet and even decorous, perhaps because more than half of the total of 38,000 employees were women. From these great hushed halls of industry, Japan's economic success was derived; for the workers were toiling away in a spirit of service, both to their company and to Japan, which they expressed in the rousing hymn sung each morning. And even if the paternalistic system, so evident here, was beginning to change, as some observers assured us that it was, the Matsushita company would, I felt certain, be one of the last to dispense with it.

Meanwhile, my guide explained to me all the technical details of the various processes; but since information about these is readily available, and since they do not vary substantially from company to company, I am not concerned with them here. I was interested above all to see the welfare services, for this would bring me into contact with the people as people rather than as mere labour-producing units. There was a recreation centre, where employees could stay for a trifling sum per day; there was a room for weddings and receptions, as in most big concerns of this kind; and, above all, there was something which went by the name of the Psychological Clinic. It was this last which proved unexpectedly interesting, as it was a place the like of which I had never seen before.

In view of the up-to-date industrial methods employed in the factory, I had expected to find a highly sophisticated centre of treatment, with consulting rooms, an array of equipment, men and women milling about in white coats, and an atmosphere of antisepsis. Nothing of the kind. One of the rooms was bare of furniture save for two large distorting mirrors, much like those found in fairgrounds. Those employees who were getting 'above themselves' were required to stand on a white line in front of the mirror which reduced them in size, and those who had complained that the work was getting 'on top of them', or who had developed a feeling of inferiority, were put in front of the enlarging mirror. Treatment was as prolonged as the supervisor deemed necessary. In another room hung a large punch-ball, decorated with a face that looked to me very much like that of the boss, which the employee with a grudge against the company could belabour until his aggressive feelings left him. In the same room were various effigies, the identity of which I was uncertain; these could be beaten with poles, with the same intended effect. My guide hinted that this was also a means of self-punition.

I confess that, at first, I thought that all this paraphernalia was some sort of a joke, or that I had been taken in error into the Sports Department; but I soon realized that I was mistaken, and that here was the place of treatment for 'psychological troubles' in one of Japan's most advanced factories. I understood that about thirty persons, mostly women, were brought here for treatment per week. I enquired how many came back. 'They don't come back,' said my guide. I saw no reason to disbelieve him.

II

Apart from my annual attendance at the Festival, and a few visits of the kind I have just described, my acquaintance with Osaka was as a bird of passage; for from there I would set out on journeys to the two southern islands, Shikoku and Kyushu. One of the most consistently bumpy air passages was that from Tokyo to Osaka, but I never felt anything but

confidence in Japan Air Lines and All Nippon Airlines, and their standard
of service was invariably high. Thus, when I set out to leave the island
of Honshu at Osaka, it was always with a sense of a great adventure
before me.

I first touched Shikoku, the smallest of the four islands, at the port of
Takamatsu on 1 October 1962. I had business to do at Kagawa University;
but my hosts, as always, ensured that I should see as much as possible of
the neighbourhood. I was taken first by Professor Masuda and Professor
Mitani to the Yashima plateau, a volcanic land-mass which, once an
island, now forms a peninsula. Here, as we scanned the horizon, heavy
rain gave way most obligingly to warm sun, and we had a magnificent
view of the Seto Sea and its numerous islands. On this strip of land, in
A.D. 1185, the great battle was fought between the Taira and the Minamoto, the two rival families, in which the Taira clansmen suffered defeat at
the hand of Yoshitsune, a warrior who became a mythical figure and
who was later deified by the Ainu. We then visited the temple, renowned
for its statue of Kannon, with its dozens of arms, though it is at present
concealed. Nearby there are numerous little vendors' stalls, as so often
outside temples. At one of these, thin earthenware 'biscuits' could be
purchased, the object being to make them glide through the air, rather
like a flat stone over water; and I was forthwith put to work to try my
skill, though I was a duffer to begin with. At another stall, some remarkable stones were on sale, which, when struck with a hammer, made
melodiously ringing sounds. There were pines everywhere; and, indeed,
the name Takamatsu means 'tall pine trees'. Finally, I was taken to the
Ritsurin Park, once the site of a villa owned by the Matsudaira clan,
which amassed great wealth in Shikoku. This park again owes its design to
the pine tree, as it is intended to provide a foreground to the great mass
of pines and rocks behind. It dates from the eighteenth century, and took
nearly 100 years to make. In October, despite its six lakes, I found the
place a trifle dusty and past its prime; but the local people claim that it
rivals in layout the Korakuen Park at Okayama. I shall not forget the
local lacquer-ware in one of the villas, some of the best I was to see in
Japan.

Shikoku is a place of pilgrimage from all over the country. It is associated with Kobo Daishi, with whom at least eighty-eight temples are
linked, many having been personally founded by him. He was a native of

Shikoku, and the Zentsuji temple outside Takamatsu is said to mark his birthplace. Whereas there was merit in visiting each of the temples in turn and on foot, the pilgrims, though still coming in considerable numbers, are less pious and thorough than their forerunners, though the cult is still very much alive. The Zentsuji temple is appropriately the local headquarters of the Shingon Sect.

When the time came for me to leave Takamatsu, I was escorted to the station, and put on the train by Professor Shimida and Professor Mitani; and at Tokushima, a town devastated during the last war, I was met by President Kodama, a doctor, whom I had already entertained in my house in Tokyo on the occasion of an important conference on Spectroscopy. Owing to examinations, my engagements at Tokushima University had to be adapted to the availability of the students, and I found myself on the platform giving a lecture within a few minutes of my arrival. After this engagement and a very good discussion with staff and students, there came the moment for relaxation; and again there are no people, and no academic personnel, who can compare with the Japanese for dropping formality for a time and for letting themselves go. Our rendezvous was a restaurant where we were waited on by some lively geisha; and half-way through the evening we were all performing, as best as we could, the famous local dance, the *Awa-odori* (Awa being the name of the province). Strictly, the proper time for this dance is August; and on such occasions it is performed in public to the sound of drums, flutes and samisen, and it usually reaches a frenzied climax. Although it was October, we did not fail to generate something of the required enthusiasm; and our geisha attendants simulated the public performances by letting loose a tremendous racket, using gongs as well as samisen. Nor shall I forget how Professor Kodama, who must have been well over seventy, participated with as much verve as anyone else, until out of prudence he decided to join the orchestra. It was an occasion of rare enjoyment.

How good it was, too, that on this as on many other occasions in Japan the function ended at an early hour, 8.30 as I recall: at which time cars were standing by to take me to Naruto, where I was due to spend the night. Putting up at the Mizuno hotel, I had a most relaxing Japanese bath to the sound of lashing waves outside: for this was the famous 'Roaring Gateway' separating the Pacific Ocean from the Japan Sea. Between tides all is quiet; but at other times gigantic whirlpools are formed in the channel and the great ugly teeth of rock are awash with spume. The sight in the grey light next morning was awe-inspiring. A special seaweed grows hereabouts, once called 'the maiden of Naruto', and it was so prized that it was sent up regularly to the capital.[1]

My friends of the previous night, including the indefatigable President Kodama, called for me at 10 a.m. First, they wanted to show me the Oceanarium. I was fascinated to watch a variety of luminous fish, and some astonishingly flat sting-ray, which lazily flapped their way across the tank like outsize autumn leaves. This glimpse of marine life prompted us at lunch to discuss the nature of life in general; and the presence of Professor Fujino, a biochemist, as well as President Kodama himself, made this an occasion for more than vague 'uplifting' theorizing. In this case our conversation took a practical turn; for, observing my keen interest, Professor Kodama suggested that we should repair forthwith to the University hospital. Here for the first time, looking through a microscope, I examined a cancer cell. Next I watched a heart operation in progress. So far as I could judge, both the organization and the equipment were excellent. One of the doctors had made some important discoveries concerning blood corpuscles. According to him, they moved at different angles depending on the state of health. He had also come to some novel conclusions about gum-pigmentation in young people. I do not know to what extent these observations have become common medical knowledge, but I was struck by the fact that at a university of which I had previously heard nothing, these interesting conclusions should have been reached.

Still with these matters in mind, we took the cable-car to the summit of what was called Eyebrow Mountain, which forms part of the Bizan Highland Park. From here we obtained a magnificent view of Tokushima, with the long Yoshino River cutting through it, and of the swirling, turbulent Naruto straits with the maelstrom in action. On this eminence stands a pagoda, built in 1958, dedicated to 30,000 Japanese war dead in Burma, whose ashes are buried underneath. Like many war memorials in modern Japan, it is also a peace memorial. In reflecting on the Pacific and South-East Asian war, we tend to remember the losses on

[1] It is mentioned in the thirteenth-century tale 'The Captain of Naruto' (*vide*, Donald Keene, *Anthology of Japanese Literature*, 1962, p. 215).

our side, together with the appalling conditions under which Allied prisoners were obliged to live: we think less about the losses sustained by the Japanese forces, which, given the comparatively small size of their invading armies, were considerable and, from the most realistic view, futile. In the pagoda stands an altar containing a casket of ashes reputed to be those of the Buddha himself: that is to say, a pinch of them. My companions, to a man, regarded this claim to be thoroughly suspect; and I wondered how many people coming here were duly impressed. According to tradition, the Buddha died of a surfeit of truffles. There is no evidence that his ashes were distributed after his death, or that the casket which may well contain his remains, and which is to be seen in the Peshawar Museum,[1] has ever been opened.

That evening, we had another convivial meal, this time at a *tempura* restaurant, where, instead of kneeling on the floor, the patrons sit up at a counter and dangle their legs in a deep trough. I had become a devotee of *tempura*, a dish, supposedly introduced to Japan by the Portuguese, which consists of fried fish, or onion or egg-plant, or all three, cooked in butter and aniseed oil. With *sake* or beer and preferably with both, it is delicious. Here our party was joined by Professor Ogata, Professor of Pathology who, though born in Peru and Spanish-speaking, had an excellent command of English; Professor Shimida, who had taught for thirteen years in the United States at U.C.L.A.; Professor Uino, of the English Department; and Professor Mitsui of the Department of Ophthalmology. Again, it struck me what a body of talent was concentrated at this University, and how closely-knit and enthusiastic the academic group seemed to be. At the end of the day I felt as if I had been initiated, if only momentarily, into the friendly circle, and I should have slept that night peacefully but for the attentions of mosquitoes, on whom I was obliged to wage war with the flit-gun until the small hours, occasioning great slaughter.

III

Although it was necessary to get up at 6 a.m. next morning, my hosts, with typical courtesy and solicitude, were round early to say farewell,

[1] A replica is on show: the real container is locked up in the Director's office.

and to put me on to the ferry for the next port of call. This was Waka-yama, for I was due to return briefly to Honshu for an engagement. With the sky overcast and the sea rather rough, there was little to observe, so I spent the two-hour crossing lying on a bunk in a little cabin, watching a pattern moving across the low ceiling. Needless to say, just as I had been seen off by old friends, so I was greeted by new ones on the quay at Wakayama. These were Professor Tadakoro and Professor Deguchi, both of the Faculty of Education. The hotel to which I was taken, the Todoroso, had recently been honoured by the presence of the Emperor and the Empress, and I was proudly shown the suite which they had occupied. The bedroom was decorated in what I may call Japanese-Balmoral style, and the *tatami* was covered by heavy green carpets, which were delightfully soft to the tread. The two beds were again Western in style, with bed-clothes of finest silk, and the pillows were stuffed with buckwheat husk, which the Emperor had specially requested for its coolness. I gathered that the room was to remain unchanged in per-petuity.

My first day in Wakayama was marred by a heavy squall, which turned the view from my window into a dirty smudge, perpetually renewed and doodled over by the pelting rain. This partly ruined my visit to the famous Kimiidera temple, which is situated in surroundings even more beautiful than those of most religious houses, and famous for its cherry blossoms; but I would not have missed the sight of the eleven-headed Kannon, a wooden statue still accorded particular devotion. The temple is in fact one of those to be visited in due order by pilgrims, like those in Shikoku. The castle, like so many others, was destroyed in the war and reconstructed in 1958. Built originally in 1585, at the command of Hideyoshi, it formed one of a great chain of fortresses which included those of Osaka and Himeji.

Fortunately, the next day turned out to be as serenely beautiful as the previous one had been foul. When I awoke, I found women in *yukata* strolling along the beach, a pleasant and reposeful sight which I remem-bered so well from my visit to Amano-Hashidate. My two professors called, and invited me to a drive along the coast. The little coves, one seeming to unfold from another, were crowded with dipping fishing-boats; I was reminded of Cornwall. We passed one village where the inhabitants consisted exclusively of members of the same family. The region was wholly unspoiled; and knowing what had happened to much of Japan's coastline, I trusted that it would remain so. Here was the Japan which lived by and for the sea; so far as the countryside is concerned, this edge of Honshu was very similar to the parts of Shikoku I had just visited.

I was back in Shikoku some few months later, when I visited Matsuyama, a town lying on the western side of the island. Largest of the island's cities, with some Portuguese influence, it had received a terrific battering from the American Air Force during the war. Two officials from Ehime University met me, Professor Oue, Dean of the Faculty of Science and Literature, and Mr. Souto, Chief of the General Affairs Section. We drove through some beautiful rural areas, almost uncannily quiet, to take lunch at the Eyoteksu restaurant, after which I delivered a lecture at the University, and participated in a *zadankai* of the staff in Professor Oue's room. Here we were joined by, among others, Professor Igata and Professor Inoue, of the Faculty of English Literature, and Professor Iwazu, of the Faculty of Agriculture. I used always to admire the way in which the Japanese, though often timid about their accomplishments, expressed themselves in English; but there were inevitably some malapropisms, and at the end of this *zadankai* I was thanked (not by one of those mentioned) for my 'expiring' lecture. After further talks at the Bansui restaurant, I retired to my hotel, the Funaya, where the maid, sizing me up a trifle nervously, produced the first *yukata* that really fitted me. Fresh from a hot-spring bath, I sat on a balcony which looked on to a wood of very tall trees, and breathed the still balmy air. The phone rang. Professor Inoue had arrived at the hotel, accompanied by his wife. They brought me a present of pottery. We talked for an hour, and I was glad of their company.

Next morning, Professor Murakami, a geography expert, called on me. He too was accompanied by his wife. Husband and wife do not often pay such calls together; but I noticed that in Matsuyama the women seemed to assert themselves rather more than in other provincial towns. This pleasant couple brought with them an Englishman, Major Monkman, who had set up in the town as a freelance teacher and was making a great success of it. In his case, there was no question of 'going native', or of making ludicrous attempts to behave exactly like the Japanese. He was very English, of military bearing, and forthright in opinion. I believe that the Japanese preferred it that way. He had certainly won their respect and affection.

Together we went to see the Ishiteji temple, dating originally from the fourteenth century, but damaged by fire and partially rebuilt in the seventeenth century. Of the eighty-eight temples to be visited by pilgrims, it is the fifty-first. Guarded by wooden carved 'devils' at the entrance, designed to ward off evil, it had a fine gate, bell-tower and pagoda, and the museum contained some Buddhist pictures showing very much the Indian influence. What for me was perhaps most interesting of all was a long panoramic picture of the district in the thirteenth century. This was a typical 'map' of its kind, of which I had seen many examples; but to be able to study the exact layout of a mediaeval town, down to the smallest detail, was a source of particular fascination such as Western engraved 'prospects', however well executed, fail to provide. Although I could not read the annotations (and nor could anyone but the highly trained scholar), I was able to get something of the 'feel' of the place, which would seem to have resembled a well-ordered garden suburb. Alas, the hastily reconstructed modern town possessed nothing of this character.

We then visited the Shojuji temple, where the priest who spoke quite good English, showed us the house (it is in fact a replica) of Masaoka Shiki, a poet born in Matsuyama in 1867. He died in 1902 and composed a great number of *haiku*. Some of his hair is buried here, and the priest told us that another poet's beard reposes nearby. To the foreigner, such practices seem trivial and even absurd, though it is not so long since Westerners were adopting the same attitude to relics, and many people still have a particular tendency to venerate hair. Masaoka's *haiku* are like wisps of hair, looped into simple designs, but none of them, I suspect, have been correctly rendered into English, nor can be genuinely appreciated by anyone but the Japanese scholar. He was a reformer of the *haiku*; and in the case of a form which has been so much exploited, genuine originality must betoken a kind of genius.

Having inspected the two chief temples, we drove over wooded hills and through mist almost numinous in quality, to the well-known Ume-No-Take-No-Suke pottery. Perhaps because of this rather awesome approach, I found myself impressed by the 'elected silence' in which the potters were going about their work, as if they were mesmerized by the concentration needed to bring it to perfection. We were invited to sign our names on some *sake* jars and cups, which were then fired and later sent to us by post. These remain some of the most delicate ware I possess. As I contemplated this quiet but industrious scene, I felt refreshed, though that June the weather was getting both hot and oppressive. In the neighbourhood there are twenty or so potteries, all intensely proud of their local traditions.

That evening I had dinner at Major Monkman's house in Tobe. This is another pottery centre and also famous for its persimmons, which are said to be the best remedy for the after-effects of *sake*. Although Monkman had remained very English, he lived in a beautiful Japanese villa, waited on by a maid of twenty-one who had the creamiest complexion I had seen outside Akita. She also, despite her youth, seemed to wear an independent air. What could be a more arcadian existence, I thought, than to live thus free and independent among a friendly people! At least Monkman realized his good fortune. I saw him several times after that, and he proved very helpful to us, especially with visitors. More than once he hinted that he must one day return home, but he remained in Japan during the six years of my own residence, and I should not be surprised if he were still there.

Before leaving Matsuyama, I paid a call on the President of the University, Professor Kagawa. He was a plant-breeding expert, and he spoke very good English. I told him how much I had enjoyed my stay in Shikoku, at which, forsaking language, he laid bare one of the most expansive smiles I can recall, even for a Japanese. There are two kinds of Japanese smile: the sometimes too prolonged and artificial one, which is displayed for the sake of politeness, and the more rare transfiguration of the whole countenance, such as the President had just exhibited. Sometimes when I had been rather startled to be greeted by a deadpan look, which scarcely modified itself, I discovered that this was a mask deliberately assumed in order apparently to spare embarrassment to the foreigner. Nevertheless, I came to be accustomed to the polite baring of the teeth, which in women was often exceedingly beautiful, perhaps because they had not so much gold-stopping as the men; but a spontaneous and effulgent expression of pure pleasure such as President Kagawa vouchsafed to me, and which remained my last memory of Shikoku, was worth all the formality in the world. So much for the idea that the Japanese never reveal their true feelings. I believe that they do so, both in person and on paper, more than we, who often pride ourselves on our forthrightness.

IV

My first visit to Hiroshima was undertaken from Matsuyama. This, together with the fact that Hiroshima forms a transition-stage to Kyushu, the furthermost island, is my reason for speaking of it here, though it is situated in Honshu. I confess that I went there with some feeling of apprehension. Here a new epoch had begun; but unlike most other epochs, it was easily determinable in time, having been initiated in a few seconds. Moreover, the whole world was made aware of it almost simultaneously. Nothing comparable had happened before.

If you were to arrive at Hiroshima unaware of your destination, you would notice that it was a typical modern Westernized town, with as much or as little character as any other. If, however, you were to survey the layout from one of the upper floors of a hotel or public building, you would observe, though only if you looked carefully, a kind of boundary line within which, but for one forlorn building (the old Industry-Promotion Hall, now the Atomic Bomb Memorial Dome), *everything* was new. This was the area devastated on 6 August 1945, at approximately 8.15 a.m., Japanese time.

What is the truth about the Bomb? Did it cause the super-destruction popularly attributed to it? Did it kill the enormous number of people— 270,000 according to some Japanese sources—at first reported? Was there such a thing as radiation sickness, and are people still dying or likely to die from it? Did the Americans set up their research institution genuinely to relieve possible suffering, or in order to study the effects of the bomb as a means to devising better defences against more potent forms of destruction? Finally, did it really have the *psychological* effect which in my first chapter I have maintained?

I think the answer to the first two questions is that the destruction and the loss of life were enormous. As to the exact number killed, however, as many if not more died in the great fire-raids on Tokyo. Indeed, Hiroshima represented only 3 per cent of the war-destruction in Japan. Perhaps as *few* as 70,000 died in Hiroshima, though that is bad enough. It was the immediate and almost automatic slaughter from one single weapon that marked out the Hiroshima and Nagasaki attacks from any others. As to radiation sickness, experts differ as to whether or not to count this as a new kind of disease. There are, I believe, unlikely to be further deaths as a direct result of the attack. Nor are there any known 'genetic freaks' attributable to the bomb. The suggestion that the Atom Bomb Casualty Commission is primarily intended for America's own military preparedness in case of atomic war misinterprets America's intentions, which are primarily humanitarian, though an English novelist wrote an article in the *Daily Telegraph* asserting that America's motives were utterly hypocritical. Of the psychological effects of the bomb, I have no doubt at all. To the Japanese psyche, it introduced a new *pollution*, and the Japanese find this as abhorrent as any material destruction and physical maiming it may have caused.

I arrived in Hiroshima on 13 June 1962. Three people met me: Miss Morita, daughter of the President of the University, Professor Masui and Mr. Yuasa, both of the English Department. (Mr. Yuasa later became one of our scholars in England and produced a delightful book in the Penguin Classics series on Basho, perhaps Japan's greatest poet.) As President Morita was then a widower, his daughter acted as his hostess, and a very capable one she proved. Professor Masui, a world authority on Chaucer, had been on the outskirts of the town when the atom bomb exploded: Mr. Yuasa was in a village not far away. The political scientist Maruyama Masao was two miles away. Naturally, no one knew that the terrible flash and explosion were due to an *atomic* weapon. Mr. Yuasa told me that, in his district, there was a flash but no apparent sound; the only indication that something unusual had occurred was when, after a day's disruption of the railway system, trains began to arrive full of maimed and hurt people. Miss Morita was too young to remember the bomb; but its impact had told upon her, as upon all her generation. On that subject, I think that Karl Bruckner's book, *The Day of the Bomb*, though written primarily for children, gives an authentic account of the effect on young people.

I was taken to the Grand Hotel, where Professor Robert Lifton was awaiting me. He had been undertaking an intensive investigation into the effects of the bomb, and had interviewed hundreds of survivors.[1] He

[1] His study, entitled *Death in Life* (1968), is the only thorough investigation of the subject. The survivors in Hiroshima, called *hibakusha*, numbered about 90,000.

struck me as a balanced and humane man, and his published results have been received with respect both in Japan and elsewhere. Even so, I was told that his interest in the humanitarian aspect of the problem had caused some of his fellow-Americans to accuse him of 'communism'. Lifton tended to the view that the number of casualties was a good deal less than many Japanese believed; but he was fully persuaded that the impact of the attack had been different in kind from any other. 'Nuclear weapons left a powerful imprint on the Japanese which continues to be imprinted, historically and psychologically, through the generations.'[1] I found talking to him very rewarding, and I enjoyed his company and that of his attractive wife, a writer of children's stories. Lifton later wrote a remarkable book about modern China.

On the day following my arrival, Miss Morita took me to see the Mayor of Hiroshima. He struck me a most intelligent though quite unassuming man. His life was a busy one, because in addition to his official activities he was much in demand as a delegate and speaker at international conferences. The next day he was due to leave for Ghana. His assistant, Mr. Ogori, had undertaken an investigation into the effects of the bomb, and had collaborated with Robert Juncke. I was anxious to see for myself what the results had been, in so far as these could now be appraised, and accordingly I asked Miss Morita if I could obtain permission to visit the Atom Bomb Hospital. This was speedily arranged: in fact, we were obliged to go there at once, as a delegation of Soviet surgeons was shortly expected. In outward aspect, the hospital is much like any other; I was impressed, as elsewhere in Hiroshima, by the total lack of 'histrionics', or any attempt to wring the hearts of the visitors. Indeed, the facts spoke for themselves.

Dr. Shigeto, Director of the Hiroshima Red Cross Hospital and Atom Bomb Hospital, who showed me round, was a quiet, matter-of-fact man, who spoke excellent English. He confirmed that the alteration visible in X-ray plates was the first evidence he had had of the precise nature of the attack. At the time of my visit there were about 120 inpatients, some old and some very young. One girl, suffering from anaemia, had been two years old at the time of the attack. Anaemia was common, though I suppose that this could not necessarily be traced to the nuclear explosion. Radiation-burns, and evidence of 'subcutaneous

---

[1] Op.cit., p. 10.

haemorrhage', could be inspected. The incidence of leukaemia had increased and decreased without apparent reason: it rose steeply in the 1950s and had since decreased.

There were 150 regular out-patients, who carry special green cards entitling them to free treatment. It was common for anyone, even then, who had some unusual complaint, to hurry to the hospital for examination and reassurance. The fear of 'contamination' is still so ingrained that young people from Hiroshima often conceal the fact, as their chances of marrying might otherwise be reduced. It is said that 76 per cent of women surviving the bomb remained single.

Moving round the wards was a somewhat harrowing experience, and I sought to analyze my feelings. It might have been easier had some obvious resentment been shown; but although such a feeling was very strong for some years after the war, and must still linger subconsciously in many people, the inmates of the hospital, like the doctors and nurses I met, showed nothing but kindness and a warm spirit of welcome. What induced a mood of chastened melancholy was the prevailing atmosphere of quietness, as if we were in some religious institution. There were no bright smiles or 'cheerful' patients. As we passed their beds, they bowed gravely. The prevailing mood seemed to be one of resignation.

I should mention that I saw no 'idiot' children, and, as stated, no evidence of genetic mutation, though it is not beyond the bounds of possibility that this may yet occur. If so, it will be the most horrible of all the results of the atomic attacks on Japan.

At the moment of departure, I felt that I wanted to do something more than simply to murmur my thanks and sympathy. It seemed so trite. As a former blood-donor, I asked if I could give some blood; but the blood-bank was very well stocked, and the offer was declined, though Miss Morita seemed touched. Finally, I brought some flowers, which were placed in one of the smaller wards. Although we walked out into brilliant sunshine, my mood was so sombre that I asked Miss Morita if she would remain in my company for lunch. I found her presence reassuring, for she was one of those Japanese who, like the girls in my office and in many ways like Teiko-San, seemed to emanate serenity and calm. Her father later remarried, and his new wife, whom I was to meet, had a similar quiet beauty and serene bearing.

I met President Morita that same afternoon, after which Professor Masui took me to the English Department, where I delivered a lecture. Somewhat to my surprise, this proved an exhilarating experience. The audience was alert, ready for a good laugh, and extremely friendly: in fact, I still remember Hiroshima audiences as among the most amicable in Japan. It was as if the younger generation were determined to turn its back upon the horrors of the past, and to seek to construct a more neighbourly world. I was not alone, as I discovered, in detecting this mood among the younger generation in Hiroshima: some of my colleagues had a similar experience.

The atmosphere necessarily changed when I visited the Atom Bomb Museum. This was a large collection of photographs and objects, the latter being curiously twisted, melted and disfigured by the intense heat. With a few exceptions, such objects did not reveal much of the nature of atomic attack, and we are still accustomed to the sight of war-damage; but the photographs were heart-rending. Particularly poignant were the pictures of the temporary hospitals and casualty stations set up in schools, and of the little groups of tattered people huddled together after the attack. The bomb fell in the hot season at the outset of a particularly torrid day; and that, together with the general food shortage, made the misery greater.

There is much controversy as to whether any warning was given of the attack. I noticed some framed leaflets, representing a picture of Uncle Sam unleashing hordes of planes, and the wording made it clear that more than usually violent raids were to be expected, and that the people would do well to take to the countryside. According to some experts, these leaflets fell after the raid itself, but I am inclined to believe the contrary. To pick up and read enemy leaflets was a serious offence; consequently, the number of people who received the warning and could obey it, was probably small. Nevertheless, it struck me as commendably objective that these leaflets should have been included in the display.

I noticed that those visiting the museum were mostly apathetic, though this apparent lack of emotion was perhaps not to be taken at its face value. One or two women shed tears, particularly at the sight of the string of paper-folded cranes made by a young girl who died ten years after the raid. It was believed that any ailing person who succeeded in making 1,000 paper cranes would recover: this young girl made well over 900.[1]

I cannot help feeling that in some countries an attempt would have been made to dramatize the whole episode and its aftermath. There was no attempt to do so. Outside the museum it is another matter. There are several memorials, including one to the children who died in Hiroshima.

On my last evening, I wandered round the new Hiroshima. Although it was not so vulgar as I had been given to understand, I experienced a strange sensation in finding a 'bar life' quite as flourishing as that of any other big city. I had not the heart to go drinking. Instead, I went early to bed in the up-to-date hotel, wondering whether the 'realists' were right to say that the bombs dropped on Hiroshima and Nagasaki must have saved thousands of lives, both Allied and Japanese, since an invasion of Japan would have been made at enormous cost.[2] Could not the Hiroshima bomb have been exploded higher in the air (it was in fact dropped by parachute and detonated just above the city), so that something of its tremendous power could have been demonstrated, and an explanation *then* have been given of its exact nature and potential destructiveness? The war would presumably have come to an end just the same; and the bomb, never used save at Los Alamos, would have remained as effective a threat as the 1,000-times more powerful hydrogen bomb today, without the expense of developing the latter monstrous invention. The world would have been a happier place; and the present international lunacy, with five nations stockpiling weapons capable of destroying life several times over, would have been prevented. Whenever I came back to Hiroshima—and in 1965 I brought my sister and son there, and I was there again in May 1967—I felt this argument to be the more cogent. But the position is that we have to live as sanely as we can in conditions which are in certain respects out of control; for even if the nuclear powers came to wish to disarm altogether, the disposal of the present stockpile of bombs would present insurmountable difficulties. Meanwhile, Japan remains the one country to have experienced the

[1] Her story is retailed in Bruckner's book.
[2] In his book *The Night of the New Moon* (1970), Laurens van der Post maintains that had the bomb not been dropped all the Allied prisoners in Japan would have been massacred. The Japanese commander in Java, Field Marshal Terauchi, laid it down that the date of the massacre was to be co-ordinated with the day on which the Allied invasion began in the South-East Asian theatre. There is some dispute about this.

trauma of atomic attack. There is reason to believe that, despite all the protests and demonstrations and the publicity given to C.N.D., the actual awareness of what happened at Hiroshima and Nagasaki is still rudimentary. To leave the last word with Lifton: 'We need new myths to grasp our relationship to the cool, ahuman *completely* technological deity which began its destructive reign with Hiroshima'.[1]

V

The next morning Mr. Yuasa took me to Iwakuni. We drove past oyster-beds, which stank abominably, and had in view the placid Inland Sea which, alas, for all its beauty, was becoming seriously polluted. We crossed the Kintai Bridge, made of wood with five huge stone bastions, and constructed in a series of up and down curves so that people appear and reappear as they cross. For this reason, it is called the 'Abacus Bridge'. On the hill above was the *daimyo*'s fortress, built in 1603 but partly modelled, so far as the donjon is concerned, on a European castle. By the bridge, a huge teenage crowd was awaiting the arrival of a film star, and music blared raucously from a loudspeaker. Such manifestations are the same the world over, so we were glad to move on. After a Japanese lunch, we took the ferry to one of the most beautiful and, indeed, most tradi-tionally sacred, spots in Japan. This was Itsukushima or, as it is better known, Miyajima, or Shrine Island. Here stands an enormous Shinto shrine, dedicated to the three daughters of Susa-no-o Mikoto, the brother of Amaterasu. The camphor wood *torii*, constructed at some distance, is submerged partially at high tide, when the whole edifice appears to be afloat. I have seen Miyajima in the morning and at dusk, from near and from afar, and as the setting of a performance of Noh: I do not think that, apart from Ise, there is a shrine to compare with it in beauty. It is of very ancient foundation, having been built originally by the Heike clan, though it has been reconstructed several times, and in fact the impressive *torii*, the largest in Japan, was set up in 1875: but, as we know from Ise, mere antiquity of structure is not so important as the fact that tradition has venerated a certain spot. At one time it was taboo for births or deaths to occur on the island.

[1] Op.cit., p. 20.

After wandering round the various halls designed for oblations, for worship, for purification, and for the display of sacred utensils, Mr. Yuasa and I climbed to the maple park. From thence we obtained one of the loveliest of sights—the gleaming shrine spread out below and, to our right, a delicate pagoda of five storeys emerging through the trees. In order to survey this delectable scene, we felt the need to go higher, so we took the rope-way to the top of Mount Misen. As a rule, heights or depths do not greatly disturb me, but I found riding in the tiny car, suspended over the plunging valley, a little unnerving. My companion preferred going up to the return journey, when the valley yawned even more capaciously. There was just room enough in the box for us both and I wondered what it would be like to stay up there, even briefly, if the mechanism should fail. On arriving at the first station, we changed to a larger car for the summit. Here a trim little lady in uniform was in charge; and when we were seated and locked securely in, she began her commentary (for there is always a commentary on such occasions) with the proud words 'Thank you for riding in our cable-car,' as if there were at that juncture any alternative to our doing so.

Mount Misen, which commands a fine view of the Inland Sea is, like Mount Hiei and Mount Koya, a popular place of pilgrimage, though it possesses a primitiveness which those other sacred mountains lack. True, there is a temple called Gumonjido, just below the summit, which Kobo Daishi, on his return from China with the Shingon teaching, caused to be built; but the rest of the area is associated with apparently more ancient cults.

It so happened that on 15 April 1967, having flown once more to Hiroshima, I paid my last visit to Miyajima, this time putting up at the Iwaso Inn. My librarian, Ann Gegg, an inveterate traveller, who had also climbed Mount Fuji with me, was in the district at the same time. Together we took the two-stage rope-way to the summit, or near it, as there is a twenty-minute walk to the top. We were anxious to be present at the fire-walking ceremony to be held on that day. This ancient ritual was under the supervision of the *Yamabushi*. As we approached, we heard the thud of drums, and we soon found ourselves in a piazza or clearing where an enormous fire of cypress branches was burning, tended by the monks and nuns, all dressed in white. Despite rain, a large crowd had assembled. Into the fire the monks were casting all kinds of objects, and blessing others, each action being preceded by a ritualistic rubbing of sticks, which was intended to ward off evil spirits. When the branches had been consumed, the embers, glowing and spluttering, were beaten down so as to form a flattish surface, upon which salt was cast, another mode of purification, as in *Sumo*. Then, after saying a prayer at each of the four corners of the 'hearth', the barefooted chief priest, his hands held aloft, padded firmly across the hot ashes. He was followed by his colleagues, and then by a whole concourse of people, mostly elderly men and women, but with some young ones too, all having removed their shoes and stockings. It was a somewhat awe-inspiring spectacle. As for me, I felt that I could not stand by while such a demonstration of faith was in progress, so, baring my feet, I joined the line of devotees. I believed that if I had sufficient confidence, I should not be burnt; but as I did not particularly want to get wet, I held aloft my umbrella. This, I soon discovered, was not *de rigueur*. Folding it and hanging it on my arm, I moved forward. Before me was a man with a crutch, who behaved with great fortitude. Walking across the winking embers involved about six paces, which, remembering the instructions I had been given, I took firmly, planting my feet down as flat as I could. A priest grasped my arm as I crossed the threshold. I had an impression of heat, but no pain; and, as I verified in the bath afterwards, I sustained not the smallest injury. Nor, so far as I could see, did anyone else, though it is not uncommon to do so, and this indicates lack of faith.

After many more people had stepped across the testing-ground, the surface was sufficiently worn down to form a path on which there was little danger of being scorched; but at the time I went across there was, as I took care to verify, a good layer of glowing ash. The secret is undoubtedly to avoid tripping along too gingerly. I will not say that firm resolution does not play a part in avoiding injury; I think it does; without resolution, the crossing would not be made firmly or adroitly enough. When the chief priest went over, the chances of being severely burnt were considerable; but of course a *Yamabushi*, like any other Japanese monk, has exceptionally tough feet. I observed also that no one, in my view at least, examined his feet immediately after the so-called 'firewalking'; and if anyone had felt pain, he would not, if a Japanese of the old school, have admitted to it.

Both Ann Gegg and Mr. Yuasa were witnesses to this ceremony; they were looking on from the balustrade of a temple called the Long-Nosed Goblin, where the more pious were praying. After the fire had died down, some people received the 'laying on of hands' by the priests for the relief of various ailments. I noticed that many of the patients took this in a somewhat perfunctory and lighthearted fashion, whereas the fire-walking had been conducted in all seriousness.

The fire ceremonial, though probably of much greater antiquity, dates at least from the time of Kobo Daishi, as he is said to have come here to light a sacred fire similar to one on Mount Koya. Indeed, opposite the temple of the Long-Nosed Goblin stood another building with a large hearth. Over this a cauldron was suspended, from which tea was being made. This is the perpetual fire which has been burning, so it is said, ever since Kobo Daishi's visit.

At one time, a professional witch lived near by; but, though we were anxious to meet her, we could not find her coven. She was evidently a 'wise woman' and told fortunes. Someone informed us, however, that, although she was no longer in business, she had been present at the fire-walking. In wandering about, I happened to look into a hut where some women had gathered, but I was obliged to beat a hasty retreat, as one woman, a fine strapping creature and perhaps the witch herself, was changing and already stripped to the waist. Japanese do not mind appearing in the nude on certain occasions, but there is a taboo on being seen undressing, and a naked witch is a sight for initiates only.

To reach the bottom of the mountain again was no easy task. So great was the press of people that additional cars had to be shunted on to the rope-way, and we were obliged to wait our turn. Fortunately, we were down in time to witness some *Bugaku* dances in the Miyajima Shrine, its lamps now glowing. Performed in a railed-off square in front of the shrine altar, these religious dances were slow and hieratic and immensely satisfying to watch. The dancers, all priests, wore Chinese-style costumes. *Bugaku*, which dates from the Nara period, and is still associated with the imperial family, is accompanied by special *Gagaku* music, unique to Japan, though showing Chinese influence, which I was able to hear on two other occasions in the precincts of the Imperial Palace. At Miyajima, however, the setting for both dances and music was all but perfect; for this was no 'folklore' performance, but an integral part of the Shinto liturgy, like the performances at Ise. No wonder that the priests expressed indignation when a TV team, filming for N.H.K., all shirt-sleeves and cables, temporarily obstructed the view of the altar.

VI

On Sunday 16 April, our third day at Miyajima, special Noh performances were given in the theatre in the shrine, one of the best-preserved and perhaps the oldest in the country. The festival began with a curious and unique ritual. This ritual, no doubt much modified, has been handed down in the form of the play called *Okina*, which is really only half-way to drama. It was a memorable experience, especially as many Noh devotees have never seen it.

First, the mask-carrier or *Senzai*[1] gravely entered, bearing a large lacquer box. He was followed, at the same slow pace, by the chief actor, an old ascetic-looking man, who moved over to stage-left, and there remained in statuesque pose. The singers then entered, lining up facing the audience, while the members of the orchestra seated themselves along the oblique *hashi-gakari*, with the Kyogen player taking precedence.

Standing with his back half-turned from the audiences, the mask-carrier slowly opened his box and offered it to the chief actor. This was a kind of signal for both singers and orchestra to move over to assume their customary places on the stage, the orchestra at the back and the singers ranged down stage-left. All was now set for the main action. The flute-player, producing the familiar 'breathy' skirl, initiated a vigorous dance by *Senzai*, and only then did the chief actor, Okina himself, don his mask, thereby symbolizing his assumption of god-like status. Intoning his words, he wished prosperity to all present and to the land. He then stamped on the ground in three different places, representing heaven, earth and man. This is a dance called *Manzai* (literally 'ten thousand years').[2] The dance completed, he knelt down, removed his mask, deposited it carefully in the lacquer box, and took his leave.

To the accompaniment of vigorous beating on the drums, the character Sambaso, played by the Kyogen actor, now took over. He executed three bounds into the air and stamped hard in order to awaken the God of Nature below. After this invocation, he put on a strange and rather

[1] *Senzai* means 'a thousand years'.   [2] This, like *Senzai*, signifies 'long life'.

forbidding black mask, and, holding a *suzu*, or bunch of bells, performed a seed-sowing dance. The black mask and the dance are believed to symbolize that rice-planting and possibly the Japanese people (or one branch of it) came from the South.[1] At the conclusion, he removed the mask, and returned it to *Senzai* who, at that point, assumed the role of a delegate of the audience.

Okina, which is common to all five Noh schools but performed with some modification by the Kanze and Hosho schools on the one hand and the Komparu, Kongo and Kita schools on the other, is basically a religious drama. This is to assume that religious drama is basically not so much an allegorical or didactic charade, as a symbolic representation of the link between gods and men. Special ceremonies of purification always precede the performances of *Okina*, and for this reason it is given only on occasions of special importance.

Observing this moving ritual, I was prompted to reflection. Never having experienced until recently that division between the sacred and the secular which has for so long split the psychic life of Western man, the Japanese, and this audience in particular, were in tune with what was taking place in a manner impossible to a modern Western audience of a Miracle or Mystery play. And throughout the day, when *Takasugo, Ebira, Kakitsubata, Kagetsu* and *Nomari* were performed, interspersed by the Kyogen *Irumagawa* and *Suo Otoshi*, this impression of participation or spiritual empathy was intensified. For although the Kyoken plays were 'secular' in one sense, their significance depended upon the sacred background against which they were performed. The most diverting Kyogen we saw, *Hana-go* was a satire on hypocritical practitioners of Zen meditation. Even the most knockabout Kyogen, such as *Boshi-bashari*, with its uproarious *sake*-drinking act, cannot be appreciated save as reflecting or refracting Shintoist or Buddhist traditions. I have seen Noh plays in Buddhist temples, such as Mibu temple in Kyoto, followed by Kyogen which would certainly seem inappropriate to such precincts in the West;[2] but the transition was in no way violent or offensive. The

[1] So far as rice-cultivation is concerned, this is historically correct. *Vide* Creel, *The Birth of China* (1957), p. 51. *Dengaku*, the precursor of Noh, seems to have begun as a dance celebrating the rice harvest.

[2] One was the famous *Mibu-Kyogen*, or medieval pantomime, consisting of twenty pieces, including the *Horoku-wari* or 'plate-breaking'. The fragments, pitched over the railing of the stage, are seized upon by members of the audience as a protection against disease.

reason is that Kyogen, though possibly older than Noh, remains parasitic upon it, and has an underlying moral purpose. Admittedly, there was much boisterous humour in some of the Miracle plays, from which traditional Western comedy is derived; but it could not be said of most modern Western entertainment that it is dependent upon, or even remotely related to, the Christian liturgy.

The Western enthusiast for the Noh can easily be carried away by his fascination with a form so different from anything in his own tradition; and it is important likewise not to exaggerate the hold which the Noh has upon modern Japanese youth. Noh performances still cater for the minority; they cannot hope to compete with commercial entertainment. Yet whereas I have rarely attended a good Noh performance which was not crowded out, the audiences for *Shingeki*, or modern drama, are usually limited and always a trifle self-conscious. But if the Noh is not thronged by the masses of young people who haunt the cinemas, we must remember that a pure art form has never attracted a mass audience, and that the Noh demands as extreme an effort of concentration as the cinema invites the reverse. The wonder is that the Noh receives today as much attention as it does.

The foreigner cannot hope to appreciate all the finer points of Noh unless he is a scholar of the subject (and that means one of twenty or so experts throughout the world); but even so, he is not quite so cut off from its subtleties as might be supposed. Although the language of Noh is archaic, and the delivery, especially when the actor is masked, strikes the ear as muffled, most devotees equip themselves with an annotated text of the *Yokyoku*, or Noh ballads, and the foreigner can follow a number of the plays in English translation. To attend a Noh performance with a knowledgeable Japanese can be a rewarding experience, and the knowledgeable Japanese are not all academics. Noh experts are found in every walk of life; one of the most dedicated I knew was a member of the Foreign Service. Finally, the Noh has a strong appeal to women, who study the singing; and at Miyajima I was greatly impressed by the rapt attention of the peasant women, many of whom were expounding the text to their families.

When Ann and I finally took our leave of Miyajima, we experienced, by way of contrast to so much calm, one of the worst air-flights we had known. As the weather at Hiroshima was very bad, we were driven on to

Iwakuni, where there was an American base. We started off reasonably well, but the plane soon ran into severe turbulence, bucking, rolling and heaving in the most alarming manner. Only on a short flight from Delhi to Agra, caught in a dust storm, and once over the Sudan desert, have I experienced such prolonged turbulence. Several passengers were sick, and I shall not forget the poor man in front of me, doubled up with nausea, whose wife massaged his back while with the other hand she soothed her baby. Ann and I managed to bear up, and I diverted myself by reading *Twelfth Night*, in which I was shortly due to appear. The plane finally groped its way unsteadily down to Haneda airport, and made a surprisingly good landing. Out of solicitude, All Nippon Airlines gave us a free taxi ride home. I arrived back, four hours late, just as it was starting, of all things, to *snow*.

VII

Compared with Honshu and Shikoku, Kyushu is a world of its own. A rich and prosperous island with a proud tradition of independence, it was ruled over for many centuries by the Satsuma clan. The original name for Kyushu is thought to be of Ainu origin; and indeed there is good reason to believe that the Ainu occupied this southernmost tip of Japan as its original inhabitants. Today, its people are sometimes called the Latins of Japan. Certainly the atmosphere is at once relaxed and hospitable.

At the head of the island, where it all but touches the extended finger of Honshu, five cities are grouped together—Moji, Kokura, Tobata, Yahata and Wakamatsu—which, since 1963, have formed the immense conurbation of Kitakyushu. This is now the seventh biggest town in Japan. It was here that in October 1967, I made acquaintance with its heavy industrial complex; my visit to the great Yawata Iron and Steel Works at Tobata complemented my visit to the Matsushita factory. One morning, the public relations officer of Yawata, Mr. Kimura, called at my hotel to take me on a tour of the works. They consisted of a mass of sheds, connected by enormous tubular corridors, as if an entire drainage system had erupted out of the ground. Once again, I do not intend to enter into the technical details of what I saw, though I was admirably briefed by Mr. Kimura and by Mr. Imai, senior assistant to the General Manager; and I learnt more in an hour about Japan's steel industry than I should have done from a month's study of documents. I was shown the pig-iron being converted into molten rivulets, flashing with gold, sending out showers of sparks, and finally dropping into huge containers; then the rolling-shed or hangar, where incandescent ingots lumbered along on rollers and were compressed, then slung on their sides, and reduced to long, flat strips, which in a third shed (we omitted the intermediate one) reappeared as rolls of thin sheeting. All these processes were controlled from small cabins, swinging high up in the hangars, and managed by one or two men. Although the plant contained thousands of employees (about 35,000 all told), what struck me was the apparent *absence* of personnel, and the economy with which it was used. Established in 1901, Yawata is now the biggest steel works in the East, and the fourth largest in the world.

There seems little doubt about the quality and toughness of Yawata's products. When the *Torrey Canyon* was heavily bombed by the R.A.F., its resistance to breaking up was remarked upon at the time. Mr. Imai pointed out that it was made of Yawata steel.

I was able to survey the extent of the Yawata works when I crossed the Wakato Ohashi suspension bridge, the biggest in the Orient, which links Tobata and Wakamatsu, and drove up Mount Takato to Takatoyama Park. The view thence of the huge plant, and the wharf built largely on reclaimed land, the largest in Asia, capable of berthing shipping of up to 80,000 tons, was grimly impressive. By contrast, I was standing on a verdant patch near a temple with a statue of Jizo, the guardian of children and farmers. This statue was supposed to act as a defence against a monster. The story of this creature was written about by a local novelist, Tino. Here were two Japans indeed, in violent confrontation.

Just as a new bridge has to be consecrated by a Shinto priest, so there is a religious festival, *Kigo-sai*, to commemorate the opening of the Yawata Iron and Steel Works. It lasts for three days, 17 to 19 November. The people greatly enjoy this *matsuri*, but they live increasingly in a 'charged' atmosphere, and the smell of gaseous exhalations is everywhere. I remember feeling that if I were to strike a match, the whole place would be blown sky-high. Yet from the window of the Ninkatsu hotel, the scene was like that of another age, with the castle (restored) looking like a batch of stacked fans, and young people rehearsing a traditional dance in the parking space below.

I was taken to Kitakyushu University by the Dean of the Foreign Languages Department, Professor Ishihara, who introduced me to the President, Professor Imanaka (an unusually huge man), a political scientist. I delivered a lecture on 'The New Scientific Outlook' to 500 students. It was one of those rewarding occasions when the audience and speaker get on well together, and I felt that lightening of spirit which comes of having said with moderate clarity what I intended, instead of having to fight the audience in a desperate battle for comprehension. Afterwards I talked with the University President, and with Professor Matsunobe, a most intelligent man, familiar with Whitehead. They were much worried about the Marxism of so many Japanese students: and they had cause to be, as the great university upheaval was not long in coming. We went to dinner at the Nikkatsu, the other guests being Professor Ishihara and a younger man, Mr. Kato. It is not often that a group of this kind should be found to talk familiarly about subjects so diverse as the Noh, Marx, and T. E. Hulme. Afterwards, I was all for bed; but Professor Ishihara and Mr. Kato, after taking some evening classes, insisted on calling for me and taking me to a night spot, the Metro Cabaret, one of those places where coloured lights travel ceaselessly round the room, dappling everything with polka dots. Here I made friends with and, after *sake* and beer, swore eternal fealty to, an exceptionally sweet hostess, whose card I placed among the others I had accumulated on this trip. These moments belong to the 'floating world' of Japan, which no other country, save perhaps Korea, can match. Merging gently with the dream-world which succeeds them, they are forgotten by morning; but how different—it will bear repeating—is this night life, even in places so flashy as the Metro Cabaret, from that of Europe and America, where the girls, especially in America, make no bones about being there to fleece the customer! Naturally, the Japanese hostess is out to make money too, but she does so more subtly, and she makes herself agreeable in the process. Better to be drained of cash by a frail Japanese butterfly than by a bumptious Anglo-Saxon Bunny. If the pocket is lighter, so is the heart.

From Kitakyushu I went on to Fukuoka. I had first visited that dynamic city in 1962 when I made acquaintance with the President of the University, Dr. Enjoji, a paediatrician and, in respect of his speciality, Japan's Dr. Spock. He was a strong, hearty man, probably much older than he looked, and he spoke excellent English. We had sent him on a visit to Britain. I was to spend many pleasant hours in his company.

Fukuoka, Japan's ninth city, was almost totally destroyed in the war; but although it has been re-designed according to the latest town-planning standards, it is not a beautiful city, though it remains a proud one. It was extremely hot that June, and I had to sleep against the hissing of the air-conditioner. My room, six floors up, looked over a desert of melancholy roofs. The hotel roof had little shelters, where some of the waiters slept, and these, together with the top of the lift-shaft and the water-tank, gave the effect of a somewhat forlorn township of its own. Steel rods, running through the concrete and gripping it, protruded at each end like rusty crochet-hooks, giving an oddly unfinished and neglected appearance. Modern buildings such as this seem to throw up their débris, whereas traditional roofs are sometimes the most beautiful and elegant parts of the entire structure.

I was glad to escape from such oppressive urbanism to the great Shinto shrine of Dazaifu, whither I was taken by Professor Matsunami and Mr. Wellings, our lecturer at the University, and his attractive wife. The shrine is dedicated to Michizane who, according to the little pamphlet published in England, 'has been enrolled among the gods in the name of Tenjin ("heavenly god") or Kanko'. Poet, historian and statesman, Michizane was exiled by the Fujiwaras to Kyushu, but was 'rehabilitated' after his death with the consolatory title of Prime Minister. The chief of the shrine, Mr. Nishitakatsuji, had studied at the Harvard Divinity School. I had a long talk with him about Shinto, and I was made to realize once again that this fascinating faith was far from being a refuge for the credulous. On the other hand, I was shocked to see a row of slot-machines in front of the shrine, from which, on payment of ten yen, one could obtain one's fortune written on a piece of cardboard, like a railway ticket. Although the Chief Priest admitted that this was the extreme of superstition, he said that the ordinary people implicitly believed in it, and and that he did not propose to have the machines removed. I duly put in my ten yen, receiving a card indicating that I was in for a spell of good fortune. My companions did likewise, with the same result; I had the impression that most of the cards conveyed this opitimistic message, so that everyone must have felt at least that he had got his money's worth. I was reflecting on the stupidity of it all when I found myself suddenly stepping to one side, as if moved by a powerful instinct: I had nearly walked under a ladder leaning against the wall. No one, I think, noticed this little detour, but it was a lesson in humility for me.

We went on to the Treasure House, which was full of scrolls (some of great antiquity), pictures and swords. By the iris garden, where the plants grew from submerged pots, we ate beancakes, the taste of which never fails to bring back memories of Japan. We moved on to the lovely Zen temple, where we had ceremonial tea. All around were apricot, plum, camphor and cherry trees; and, talking of superstition, there is a famous apricot tree in front of the shrine which is reputed to have grown from a spray which flew in one day from Kyoto—a perfect theme for a Noh play, for it followed Michizane into exile here.

Finally, we visited the Kanzeonji Tendai temple—needless to say, shrines and temples are often found in the same compound—with its red, black and green lacquer and its many Buddhist images of enormous size, made of wood but covered with gold-leaf, some being housed in a separate building. In its own kiosk hangs the temple-bell, cast in the early Nara period. By means of a log suspended from two chains, and acting like a battering-ram, this can be made to give out low, rich tones, followed by a wang-wang-wang of echoes. We each gave a heave at the log, with the most pleasing results.

Mr. Nashitakatsuji told me that his father had been Chief Priest of the shrine, and that he hoped his son, then studying at an American school, would succeed him. In running the shrine and its annexes, he was assisted by forty helpers, including dancing girls. The latter give special performances at the Shrine Festival, which takes place on 23 to 25 September.

I was back in Fukuoka on 1 May 1965 to take part in the opening ceremony of the Fukuoka Japan-British Society and on 9 July in the following year I flew to Fukuoka again, as guest speaker at another meeting of the now flourishing Society. But for an interesting experience, I should hardly think this brief visit worthy of recall. As I was entering the plane at Haneda, I began to feel distinctly unwell: my pulse quickened and I had a peculiar numb feeling in the head. On arrival, I was met by the kind Mr. Iwaynami, who, observing that I was ill, took my temperature at the *ryokan*. Despite fever, I duly attended the meeting and made a speech, though not a particularly good one. Afterwards we adjourned to the Nakayanagi restaurant. This has a carp pool, from which the guests

can select their fish. Whereas I was off colour, Dr. Enjoji (President of the
Society) and Commander Banks, honorary Consul at Moji, were in
excellent spirits and kept the party going. Among the guests was another
doctor, Professor Emeritus Onadera, who offered to examine me. There
was no need to move my place—we were sitting on the floor in Japanese
style—for this method was to prod me gently, to scrutinize the sides of
my fingers by the nails, and to observe my head from all angles. To my
relief, he said that I was in good shape, but that I had a kind of proto-
diabetes, which later proved to be correct. (This ailment is not serious, but
it requires abstention from too much carbohydrate intake, due to a low
threshold for sugar.) I discovered afterwards that Professor Onadera had
won a prize at the Japanese Academy for his remarkable diagnostic
talents. That night I sweated profusely and by morning I was myself
again. I have never heard of anyone who had practised the professor's
techniques; I think he was one of those gifted men whose skill is difficult
to transmit.

My last visit to Fukuoka took place in October 1967, when I came to
lecture and to say farewell. Professor Ebihara, an ex-British Council
scholar, was the interpreter at my lecture. He was the best type of young
Japanese academic, with a brilliant mind and a dignified grace of manner.
He told me that he was about to get married, and I felt what an excellent
husband he would make. Afterwards, President Enjoji took us to the
Shinmiura restaurant, where we had the special local dish, *mizutaki*,
composed of chicken, leeks, and bamboo shoots and cooked at the table.
During the meal, President Enjoji rose and made the following speech:

> 'Mr. Tomlin, it is a great pleasure for us to welcome you to
> Fukuoka again. Let me take this opportunity of thanking you for the
> kindness and assistance which you have been extending to Kyushu
> University for so long. I hope you will come back to Japan again and
> continue with your efforts to promote friendly relations between
> Britain and Japan. Today I would like us to talk together over the
> dishes of *Mizutaki*, the special meal of Hakata. I do hope you will now
> relax and enjoy yourself.'

This brief discourse was both typical of the man and of Japanese
academic hospitality. There was the usual combination of formality and
of childlike warm-heartedness, with special emphasis on the conviviality

to be derived from consuming the local product, and not least on physical and mental relaxation. It is this capacity to relax and enjoy oneself unaffectedly that permits the Japanese to take to his work again with such enthusiasm and efficiency.

VIII

It was from Fukuoka that I took a train to the rather remote town of Saga, once the headquarters of the Nabeshima clan. We had a long connection with the University there, and an old friend, Professor Midzunoe, met me. He was one of those rather solemn looking Japanese who have a warm heart and much humour. He it was who told me that, fearing to annoy the Westerner with perpetual smiling, he assumed a deliberately reserved air. He drove me straight to Arita, picking up another Professor of English, Nakajima, on the way. By contrast to Saga—a rather sleepy, dusty town—Arita was spick and span, as if it had taken on some of the qualities of the porcelain for which it is famous. It is surrounded by thick woods. We began by having lunch together and good talk went with it. Professor Midzunoe had a special interest in the Victorians, above all the Brontës, and Professor Nakajima was an expert on Spenser. Afterwards I went round the town to buy some plates at Koronsha, and at the oldest of the porcelain makers, Kakiemon. These firms take great pride in their traditions. The potteries began in 1592, as a result of the visit of a Korean potter, and Kakiemon has been in the same hands for twelve generations. The work is beautifully pure and delicately designed. We went to see the quarry from which the clay had been obtained for centuries. There, too, was the persimmon tree, or rather its first offshoot, from which the enamel colour came: this was first used about 1650. It was the Dutch, operating from their little factory on the man-made island of Dejima (Deshima) near Nagasaki, who first discovered the beauties of Arita pottery, and began exporting it.

We drove back to Saga through farmland, where much rice was being harvested. Saga was once a great rice-producing centre; but while the farmers are still rich, the prefecture as a whole is poor. At the *ryokan*, my friends left me, and I found myself installed in a comfortable room with a view of the frothy river and a great sweep of hills. Along the river bank, little hot-spring hotels clung, similar to my own. Soon a strong wind arose, and I was obliged to seal myself in. The little inn heaved and winced as the tempest churned about it. I could not help contrasting the old wooden shack with the gleaming Hitachi refrigerator in my room. Here was a stock of drinks, from which I selected a bottle of excellent Japanese beer. Fearing that I might have difficulty in sleeping in the general hubbub, I went down to the big bath and had a good soak. It worked: I slept long and well.

Next day, when the storm had lifted, Professor Midzunoe called for me, and took me to the University to meet the President, Professor Tanaka, a specialist in agricultural economics. He was a shrewd, balanced man, who had had a student strike on his hands for the past five months. A *zadankai* was arranged, and I talked to the staff, including two teachers from the Junior High School attached to the University. We discussed the nature of language, and, a subject that I had always found fascinating, the early history of Japan. Then President Tanaka took me to a very attractive Japanese restaurant, the Yoryutei, accompanied by Professor Nagese, Dean of the Faculty of Letters and Science. We were attended by two pleasant girls, and I was interested to see how they kept up, while serving, a rattle of conversation with my hosts, with a good many references to myself, only some of which I understood. These references were made with such grace and deference that, even though they might be construed as 'personal remarks', these were in no sense rude, and I enjoyed this 'democratic' atmosphere. This I mention, because the President, who had been called away from the *zadankai* and again from the lunch, had spoken of his fears for Japanese democracy in the larger sense. His absences were due to the strike; but we were all the more delighted when, on his re-appearance at the board, he told us that the troubles were at last settled. The country was to see worse convulsions in the months to follow; but Japanese democracy has survived and may even have been strengthened. The rest of the meal was especially carefree, and the sun-filled room reminded me of the gay atmosphere of Sado Island. In fact, the President and Professor Nagese had to take their leave before the end, in order to begin to get the University back into running order; and so Professor Midzunoe and I were left with the girls to finish a liberal amount of food and drink. On the spur of the moment, one of the girls produced a book of local songs, and we formed an improvised

chorus, afterwards signing our names in the album. I left Saga with happy
voices and much laughter in my ears, and a parting remark by Professor
Midzunoe that he had had his fill of *sake*.

IX

I visited Nagasaki first on 9 June 1962, a few days before my visit to
Hiroshima; but I deliberately describe my visits slightly out of chrono-
logical order, first, because my description of Kyushu is more logical by
following the island round the coast, beginning with Kitakyushu and
concluding with Beppu—an anti-clockwise sweep—and secondly,
because Nagasaki, being the second town to suffer atomic bombardment,
comes better after Hiroshima.

As I was to find at Hiroshima, the people at Nagasaki were unusually
friendly. In fact, no sooner had I set out on a stroll round the town by
myself than I was approached by two demure schoolgirls who asked if I
would be good enough to talk English with them. Pointing out that the
lesson might break off prematurely if we did not forthwith gain the pavement, and deciding that the crowds would make conditions difficult even
there, I suggested that we should repair to a nearby restaurant. Here I
gave them a snack, while they plied me with questions about life in
Britain with almost febrile excitement. My little companions had never
used a knife or fork before, so this novelty afforded them instruction as
well as amusement.

We had a good conversation, as both knew a surprising amount of
English. I did not want to prolong our discourse, and I half hinted, no
doubt quite unnecessarily, that it might not be advisable for them to go
up to every foreigner whom they happened to spy in their walks. I do not
believe that they had any knowledge of 'the world' in the sense in which
I was trying, however clumsily, to depict it. We said goodbye with the
utmost friendliness. But that was not the end of the story. Japanese always
want to know precisely who one is, where one comes from, one's age,
and other necessary information. So I left them my card. Some months
later, one of them dropped in at my office in Tokyo, and left me (I was
out) a box of handkerchiefs. My receptionist was rather puzzled.

The official from the University who met me was a woman, Professor

Masaoka Fujii. In all my journeys outside Tokyo it was rarely that I met a woman teacher. After my lecture on 9 June I went sightseeing with her and Professor Takesue, though it was pouring: I had hit the rainy season. We visited the Sofukuji or Chinese (Zen) temple, built by the Chinese community in the seventeenth century, and exhibiting architectural features from the Ming period. Like some other temples, it was built as a challenge to Christianity. As Nagasaki was for years the gateway to Japan to foreign merchants, and as the Chinese, with the Dutch, were the only people allowed to remain after the Spaniards (the Portuguese and the British had been banished by the Tokugawas), Chinese influence was very strong. It seemed to me that this was still revealed in many of the faces I saw: they were wide Chinese types in contrast to the long Japanese physiognomy.

Nagasaki has many other shrines and temples, including the Kodaiji and the Kofukuji, both Zen temples, and the Suwa, a shrine but also known as the Bronze Horse Temple, because there is a statue of that animal in the front. For me, however, the structures most poignant to visit were the Oura and Urakami Catholic churches. Built in 1865 by a French missionary, the first church was a memorial to the Christian martyrs who were crucified nearby in 1597. This and the Urakami church, now a ferro-concrete cathedral, symbolized the tenacity with which Christianity was practised among the Japanese in Nagasaki throughout the years of persecution; for when the ban was lifted, thousands of 'secret' Christians came out of hiding, the faith having been preserved. It was therefore ironic that on this city, with these churches at its centre, the second atomic bomb should have been dropped on 9 August 1945. One could somehow have wished that so-called Christian nations had avoided such a deliberate act, if symbols are to mean anything at all. And just as I have suggested that the Hiroshima bomb might have been exploded well above the city, so the fact that it was purposely detonated to cause the maximum devastation might have been a reason for refraining from repeating the act elsewhere. There is the usual argument as to how many people were killed, and comparisons are again made with the fire-raids on Tokyo. I still feel that the difference in *kind* between the nuclear weapon and any other was enough to condemn its use, at least for the second time.

I was told by my companions that, although many tourists visited

Nagasaki, few expressed a wish to visit the churches. 'They are not interested,' said one of my companions. But overlooking the port is the house of Dr. Glover, an English merchant. This is sometimes mistakenly held to be the house of Madame Butterfly and tourists flock there.

The 'atomic bomb' museum is part of the International Cultural Hall, another ferro-concrete building which is not beautiful, though it has a fine garden. Although, as at Hiroshima, I did not find that the exhibits brought home the horror of the attack, the same absence of histrionics was to be commended. Twisted bottles, Catholic images tarnished and out-of-shape, and other *disjecta membra*: these might have been caused by any violent explosion. A few photographs of forlorn people, or of hands inextricably mingled with melted glass: these were more telling. One photograph, of a hospital temporarily set up in a primary school, showed two boys grinning happily: that was no doubt how it was, and there was courage in showing it. The truth is that horror cannot be sustained at full pitch in retrospect, and most of those who experienced the real horror are dead. I found the statue in the Cultural Park of a man pointing skywards more impressive than anything of the kind in Hiroshima, even though this bronze muscular figure was a typical 'exhibition park' statue. But Hiroshima, perhaps because of my more frequent visits and because I saw more living evidence of what had happened, affected me on the whole more deeply than Nagasaki. On the other hand, the fact that Nagasaki had such a long history of heroism made the place poignant for me.

I was driven to the spa of Unzen in a University car. We passed through terraced hills, with rice fields of livid green—it was the season of irrigation —and along a beautiful coast, with a placid sea beyond. Mist like muslin scarves frequently descended on us, but its lifting enhanced the sparkling verdure. Having reached Unzen at 11 a.m., however, I experienced a 'post-arrival' feeling, which is most oppressive in the mornings, when the only sound in the hotel is the Hoover roaring away, the sterile hour. To retrieve my equilibrium, I went for a stroll among the hot springs. Out of the ground, out of vents in rocks, and out of large pipes, the water issued in great bubbles. There was a prevailing acrid, sulphurous smell, as from a laundry in which very dirty clothes were being washed. Clouds of steam hovered everywhere, and even from the gutters there arose little puffs of it. Up the hilly paths, tourists proceeded with cameras, taking pleasure in photographing each other against a shifting background of steam. At rickety stalls, old women sold eggs, which, placed in the spring water, boiled in an instant. With its white, friable soil, Unzen is locked in a valley between a series of extinct volcanoes, some 4,500 feet high. The Shimabara peninsula, which also perspires from great ugly pores, was the site of the peasant Christian rebellion of 1638, which the Shogun put down with great difficulty. Before being massacred to the last man, woman and child, the defenders made their last stand by using pots and skuttles as weapons. It was the last open Christian resistance.

In August 1965, we held a Summer School in Unzen; and it was surprising how, after a few days, we became accustomed to the sulphurous atmosphere. Besides, the nights were fresh. The School proved a great success. Alan Baker was Director, Verner Bickley, Director of Studies, David Short, General Entertainer, and Miss Kosugi Miyoko, who later became Mrs. Adrian Thorpe, Secretary. I had to return to Tokyo in the middle of it, but I was in Unzen for the great typhoon which hit the area as far as Hiroshima on the night of 6 August. Some rooms had to be evacuated: I understand that Miss Kosugi rode out of hers triumphantly on her suitcase. The light failed, and when I went down to an early bath, the servants were scurrying about as if we were on board ship in a storm. Not until mid morning did the electricity come on again, and we were able to resume our programme. It later appeared that there had been some deaths in the Hiroshima region.

X

I had first visited Kumamoto in June 1962, the month of my visit to Nagasaki. I was greeted there by President Honda, formerly Secretary of the Japanese Science Council; Professor Sato, a medical man and an ex-British Council scholar; and Professor Kawarabata, of the Faculty of Law and Literature. In the soft, warm and slightly humid evening, we had dinner together at the Castle Hotel, where there was an iris garden with flowers the size of fancy silk handkerchiefs. After the meal I wandered round the town, which had been much damaged in the war, visiting a few bars and, feeling uncomfortably sticky, paying my first visit to a public bath. Here I was pommelled unmercifully by a middle-aged lady in bright blue shorts, with the result that I retired to bed flat out and slept heavily. Kumamoto can be one of the hottest places in Japan in summer.

I spent the next morning at the University, which had a large campus, including a red-brick building which was originally the High School, an up-to-date Medical Faculty, and a good library with some Lafcadio Hearn relics. Hearn spent some time here after his stay in Matsue, and the two towns compete to honour his memory.

By way of diversion in the afternoon, Professor Sato and Professor Kawarabata took me to Mount Aso, which has the greatest crater—in reality formed of five craters—of any volcano in the world. The road thither from Kumamoto, constructed by the Tokugawas, was cut deep in the hills, so that troop movements could be concealed. It took us two hours to reach the cable-car, which, once swung into action, brought us to the crater in two minutes. There had been a long wait for our turn, on account of the usual crowds of school-children. Professor Sato remarked, that, in travelling in England and America, he had come to the conclusion that there were no children in those countries. We were able to walk to the top of the crater, which displayed a 'moon' landscape, with smoke billowing out. There was a violent wind. Spaced at intervals were concrete shelters, which are needed for refuge when the volcano releases, as it often does, a mass of fiery ash. Previously a number of people had been killed up there. The jet-black smoke and the sound of inner rumbling were rather sinister. This restive mountain is responsible for much turbulence in the atmosphere, as I experienced when I flew over the area.

Next morning I awoke to a clearer sky. The view from my window was of an expanse of green valley with, beyond, ranges of bluish hills. I was called for by car and driven down to Kumamoto at speed. I noticed cows with their owner's names painted on them, the Chinese characters being ideal for such neat labelling. The corn was surprisingly short, about half the size of that in Europe or the United States. On arrival, we went to the Suizenji gardens, which once belonged to the Hosokawa clan and where the family has its shrine, the Izumi. There are a number of Buddhist tombs of members of the clan, whose living representatives I had met. The tombs consisted of stone spheroids, balanced on square bases: a somewhat odd sight in this serene garden, where there were two delicate teahouses. We then visited the castle, a colossal pagoda-like structure on a very subtly curved stone base. It contains many relics of General Saigo, about whom I was to hear so much in Kagoshima.

In a back street we came across a restaurant called The Tiger, and here I had a *tempura* lunch with Professor Sato. I found myself on excellent terms with him. He and Professor Kawarabata were a thoughtful, interesting couple who were most kind to me, and also to Alan Baker who came here later. Professor Sato told me of his loneliness during the beginning of his stay in England, which was relieved by the arrival of his wife. I sometimes think that we underestimate the adjustment needed to be made by foreigners in a new and unfamiliar country, which is so different from what they are led to expect by their reading, and by our 'propaganda'—the 'old England' image put out by our publicity organs. Yet once the adjustment is made, I believe that the Japanese derive more profit from their stay among us than many of those from nearer countries. Somehow there is a common psychological link. For my part, whenever I see Japanese abroad, my heart instinctively warms to them, though it is obvious that many of my generation cannot bring themselves to share this enthusiasm.

Finally, we visited the house of Lafcadio Hearn. Although it lacks the attractiveness of the Matsue residence, it is admirably kept by a devoted couple. Among the relics is the manuscript of *Japan: an Interpretation*, a neat pile of paper covered with exquisite handwriting. Hearn seems to have written effortlessly; the fact that he had one eye did not impede him from keeping to even, flowing lines.

XI

No less enjoyable was my later visit to Kagoshima, situated on the inner right-hand claw of the southern part of Kyushu. I had returned to Tokyo and, arising at 5.30 a.m., I had intended to go first to Miyazaki; but as the weather was bad, we put down at Kagoshima instead. There was much telephoning as my programme at Miyazaki was hastily rearranged. To this I was indebted to President Fukuda, a retired medical man, and to Mr. Hiraoka, chief of the Student Affairs Department. We had lunch at the Kakumishin hotel, and then took the ferry to Sakurajima, one of the most beautiful as well as most active volcanoes in Japan. That day its summit was clouded over, but the smoke was belching through the active one of the three craters. All around were huge, gaunt lava-beds: the most recent large-scale eruption was in 1914, which transformed the island into a peninsula. In gusty wind we climbed to a look-out tower, and inspected the *torii* of the Shinto shrine sunk right into the lava, and the monument to Hiyashi Kumiko, the woman novelist.

Sakurajima is a spectacle of great majesty. Poems have been written about it, and it is perhaps, next to Fuji-San, the best situated mountain in the country. President Fukuda took me for dinner to the Shigetomiso restaurant, with its garden overlooking the bay. The view from there was magnificent, for the clouds round the volcano had cleared. Couples were strolling about in *yukata*; it was the marriage season. We left our *sake* to watch a performance of Satsuma dances. Associated mostly with General Saigo, these were performed with great spirit, and included complicated sword-play. The dancers were waitresses from the restaurant, dressed from head to foot in white, and during the display a poem about Saigo was chanted. The powerful Satsuma clan ruled Kagoshima for more than 500 years until the Meiji Restoration, and a strong spirit of independence still informs this part of Kyushu. Indeed, it is the only area of Japan in which a rebellion was staged against the central government. Here, too, there was a skirmish with the British Fleet, which shelled Kagoshima in 1863, in revenge for the 'Namamugi Incident', in which an Englishman, Charles Richardson, a visitor from Shanghai, was killed by samurai retainers. You can still see places where the shells fell. Interestingly enough, this incident led to friendship between the Satsuma clan and the British.

Next day, one of our ex-British Council scholars, Professor Matsuoka, a mathematician, took me on a tour of the town. The statue of Admiral Togo faces the sea, and that of Saigo stands at the place of his suicide in 1877. This is near a cave whither he had retreated with his followers after his rebellion had failed. His tomb is in the Jokamyoji temple. Then we went to see the church of St. Francis Xavier, built to mark the fourth centenary of his landing in Kagoshima from Malacca in 1549.

Xavier, the great Spanish Jesuit missionary and indeed one of the greatest of all missionaries, was the first to introduce Christianity into Japan. Although he stayed in Kagoshima (which he called Cangoxima) for only ten months, his influence was enormous, and he was encouraged to proceed to Kyoto, for many Japanese, or at least their overlords, at first welcomed the new faith. There is something touching about Xavier's view of the people he had come among. In a letter addressed to the Jesuits of Goa, and dated from Kagoshima on 5 November 1549, he wrote:

'By the experience which we have had of this land of Japan, I can inform you thereof as follows: Firstly, the people whom we have met so far, are the best who have yet been discovered, and it seems to me that we should never find among heathens another race to equal the Japanese. It is a people of very good manners, good in general and not malicious; they are men of honour to marvel, and prize honour above all else in the world. They have a quality which I cannot recall among any people of Christendom; this is that their gentry, howsoever poor they may be, render as much honour to a poor gentleman as if he were passing rich.'

The letter is a long one, but a few other extracts are worth reproducing:

'They are small eaters albeit somewhat heavy drinkers, and they drink rice wine since there are no ordinary wines in these parts. . . . There are many people who can read and write, which is a great help to their learning quickly prayers and religious matters. . . . They abhor beyond measure [the] vice of theft. . . . They are people of very goodwill, very sociable and very desirous of knowledge. . . . They like to hear things propounded according to reason. . . . Now we have to be like little children learning the language; God grant that we may likewise imitate them in true simplicity and purity of soul, striving by all means to become like them, both as regards learning the language as in showing the simplicity of children devoid of malice. . . . This people live wonderfully healthy lives and there are many aged. . . .'

Admittedly, the letter is not all in praise of the Japanese; but the striking thing is that, in the extracts given, we cannot but recognize many of the qualities of the people today. There is the same respect for others, rich or poor, the same general high-mindedness, the same honesty, the same literacy, the same wholesomeness of living, the same sociability, the same thirst for knowledge, the same thirst for *sake*. In a short time St.

Francis succeeded in grasping the basic qualities of the people. He also learned about the country—about Miaco (Kyoto) where 'the king' lived,[1] about Mount Koya and other religious centres, and about the flourishing universities. It was an astonishing achievement, and for a time it had astonishing results. For this was the beginning of Japan's Christian century.

Xavier was to become disillusioned not with the people but with the rigid structure of Japanese society. He ended up by taking the view that, before Japan could be Christianized, China would have to be. In Japan, whereas one *daimyo* would be willing to allow missionary activity, another would refuse. Moreover, loyalty to the secluded 'king' in Kyoto was stronger than he had supposed. Finally, the rivalry between Jesuit and Franciscan friars aroused the suspicions of the Shogun, who came to the conclusion that the missionaries were nothing but a cover for economic and political infiltration. In this he was not so far wrong. There were Europeans who did not scruple to kindle such suspicions in his mind: Richard Cocks, and even Will Adams, both Englishmen, were willing to denounce competitors, and to imply that Christianity was a cloak for imperialism. Nevertheless, when persecution came, there were true martyrs to the cause; and just as it had been thought by some that a Christian Japan would compensate for an apostate England, so the 'palm of Christian fortitude' won by the martyred Japanese Catholics—and they numbered thousands, despite many recantations—was held up as an exampled by exiled Catholics at Douai to their persecuted co-religionists of England.[2]

Professor Matsuoka took me to call on the priest of the church. He was a genial man, who had spent many years in Rome. He was immensely proud of his church, as were the people of Kagoshima. I have already said that the Japanese reverence foreign religious practice, so long as it is not given to bigoted proselytizing. Nor must it be forgotten that Christianity, though embraced by no more than 1 per cent of the population, has played an important part in Japanese history.

After the appalling persecutions towards the end of 'the Christian Century', Christianity went, as I have said, underground, to re-emerge after the Meiji Restoration, especially in Kyushu, where it had made its

[1] Miyako was another name for Kyoto at the time.
[2] C. R. Boxer, *The Christian Century in Japan, 1549–1650* (1967), Chapter VII.

first converts. Many persons in key positions in Japanese society today are Christian. The late adviser to the Crown Prince, Mr. Koizumi, was one. He was a remarkable man, with a face which, though severely burnt in one of the raids on Tokyo (he was saved by someone pouring a pail of water over him), retained its nobility. Sometimes, however, missionizing inculcates a strange brand of Western cultural veneer, so that the result is an erosion of the gentle Shinto and Buddhist qualities and their replacement by a brash sort of 'heartiness'.

Attached to the church was a kindergarten, where the atmosphere was merry in the best sense. It is interesting to record that St. Francis Xavier found children's education in Japan especially well organized; and indeed the present-day system of infant and primary education seems to me to be among the best in the world. However poker-faced Japanese adults may be, above all the men, Japanese children, wearing their yellow hats, are invariably a cheerful sight.

After wandering round the precincts, so quiet in the sunny weather as to make it difficult to realize what enormous spiritual energy was commemorated there, I was taken to see the University hospital. This is of interest by reason of another link with the West; for it was founded by an extraordinary Irishman, Dr. William Willis. Dr. Sato, whom I met there, told me his story, which is part of the history of his epoch.

Born in County Fermanagh, Ireland, in 1837, Willis received his medical training in Edinburgh. In 1861, he went to Japan to join the British Diplomatic Mission as medical adviser. He worked not merely among the foreign residents of the capital but among the Japanese; and in due course he was called upon to treat the wounded in the struggle between the government, namely that of the Shogun, and the 'rebel' forces, who supported the Emperor.

All the work which Willis undertook among the Japanese was entirely voluntary. When, therefore, the victorious Emperor moved in 1868 from Kyoto to Edo, as Tokyo was then called, Willis, though still a young man, had acquired a considerable reputation not merely as a doctor but as a pioneer of British medicine. For this reason, the British Mission was not altogether surprised to receive a request from the new government that Willis should establish the first Western hospital and medical school in Tokyo. A period of secondment was arranged; but in due course Willis became so absorbed in his new activities, and inspired such confidence and enthusiasm among his Japanese colleagues, that he decided to resign his position with the Foreign Service and to devote his career to medical work in Japan.

With all his personal success, however, Willis had to contend with growing difficulties, chiefly of a political nature. It was a time of rivalry among the great powers to win the favour of the new government; for once it had become clear that the Emperor, still young and remarkably intelligent, was bent upon a policy of rapid Westernization, the European nations sought to outbid one another in offering their services to speed this transformation. Above all, attempts were made to gain the attention of the officials concerned with public education. Thus it came about that, through the powerful advocacy of an influential group, German medical methods came to be preferred.

Willis was placed in a dilemma. Although he was devoted to his work in Tokyo, and although his hospital and medical school were flourishing, he found for the first time that his path, as well as his methods, was obstructed. In fact, this apparent check was to lead to the most rewarding part of his career. This came about as follows:

Among the Emperor's most ardent supporters, many came from the South, especially from members of the Satsuma clan. The remarkable General Saigo was perhaps the most versatile and enlightened of these men. He had a passion for education, and he it was who invited Willis to Kagoshima. To Willis, the change was something of an upheaval. From the busy new capital, Kagoshima seemed a remote and unimportant city. Nevertheless, the Satsuma clan had always been one of the most enterprising in the country; and despite the quarrel that had followed the Richardson incident, Saigo, with his two colleagues Admiral Aoyama and the local feudal lord, Shamazu, remained great admirers of Britain. So Willis set about founding a medical school in Kagoshima, conducted on British lines.

From the very beginning, the project, like that at Tokyo, proved a success. Assembling about him an able Japanese staff, Willis acted not merely as dean of the school but, in due course, as director of the hospital which was built under his guidance. He devoted his mornings to the school, and the afternoon to his patients. Soon the school boasted both a microscope and a plaster replica of the human body. Students were attracted from remote areas. Several of those whom he taught were to become famous doctors: one of them ended up as Surgeon-General to the Japanese Navy.

Notwithstanding all his labours in the field of medicine, surgery and also public sanitation, Willis found time to enjoy Japan. Like Lafcadio Hearn, Neil Gordon Munro (the Ainu expert) and James Murdoch (the historian of Japan), he found his soul-mate in a Japanese woman. They had one child, a boy; and this boy, Albert, though he visited Britain and worked in business in Australia, decided finally to return to Japan and take Japanese nationality. His descendants live in Osaka.

Willis was in due course honoured by the Emperor; and the British Ambassador, Sir Harry Parkes, wrote of him: 'I consider it only due to him to state that the cause of humanity and the progress of scientific medicine in Japan have been helped materially by his able and long sustained exertions.'

In the very year in which Sir Harry Parkes wrote, however, Willis's Kagoshima idyll came abruptly and sadly to a close. In 1876, the strong-minded but tempestuous-natured Saigo found himself in violent conflict with the Emperor's government over Japan's policy towards Korea. The upshot of this crisis was that Saigo, true to his sense of honour and independence as a Satsuma clansman, and commanding the passionate loyalty of his followers, ordered a march on the capital. Willis, for his part, had become so devoted to his friend and patron that he expressed willingness, despite the fact that Saigo had been proclaimed a rebel against the Emperor, to join his army as a medical officer. Fortunately, perhaps, this decision was changed as a result of urgent representations from Tokyo; but when Saigo's rebellion collapsed and he took his own life, Willis was obliged to leave Kyushu in a British battleship. He never returned.

The people of Kagoshima did not forget Willis. As a result of public subscriptions, a monument which can still be seen in front of the hospital was erected in 1893. He had a long career outside Japan, partly at home and partly in Bangkok, where he spent seven years. But Kagoshima was the place where he sank his deepest roots, where he made his greatest innovations and where he is best remembered.

Nor have the people of Kagoshima forgotten Saigo. Partly because he was a local patriot, and partly because he died what many Japanese still consider an honourable death, that of *seppuku*, he remains a hero in the area, and much has been written about him. He is a legend, like the 47 Ronin. One of the great Japanese experts on his life is Professor Sakamoto of Kagoshima University, whom I used to know. In the room at the hospital occupied by Willis, there is a picture of the Emperor Meiji entering Kagoshima. Saigo, then a loyal subject, is on foot. He had elephantiasis, so he could not ride. Dr. Sato told me that the disease is still common in those parts.

On the advice of my new-found friends at the University, I took 'time off' to go along the coast to Ibusuki. Here, amid date palms and much semi-tropical greenery, is an enormous open-air bath, or rather a series of baths, patronized by both sexes. My friends had telephoned there concerning my arrival, and the proprietor had somehow got it into his head that I was the British Ambassador. I tried to make the position clear and to strip down my rank, but nothing, not even my stripping altogether, would disillusion him. The only person who knew my real identity was Donald Ritchie, the American film critic and film-maker, whom I unexpectedly ran into. He too was escaping from the gaseous capital in order to do some writing.

I do not know how long the natural aspect of Ibusuki will last. Plans were afoot for a gigantic tourist centre, with a heliport. I could only hope that the superb views of Satsuma-Fuji and the Kinki Bay would not be ruined.

XII

I went on by plane to Miyazaki. This journey should have taken twenty minutes, but owing to bad weather it took fifty. It was a most uncomfortable flight. My neighbour, an English-speaking girl, had her handkerchief to her mouth most of the time. To emerge from the lowering, scurrying clouds, and to be met by a friendly face, was therefore a great relief. The face belonged to a young man, Professor Takasu, who turned out to have attended a lecture of mine in Matsuyama five years before. He had been converted to Catholicism by Father Roggendorf of Sophia University, and he had written a thesis on Cardinal Newman. He took me to the Kanko hotel, which had a lovely view of the Oyodo river.

That evening I was the guest of Judge Motoyoshi, another of our

ex-scholars. We are accustomed to venerable judges: my host looked a
very young man, and he was besides a gracious host. The restaurant, the
Yamabuki, provided another charming companion: a girl called Yazuko,
one of a category of entertainers who are more than waitresses or hostesses
and less than geisha. She diverted us with songs, some of which I could
follow in the book she provided. The words and gestures were on
occasion a trifle 'broad', or what would have been considered so in the
days before our new fashion in entertainment; but it was harmless
enough, and Yazuko's exuberant spirits were catching. Judge Motoyoshi
relaxed when he saw that I was not averse to enjoying myself, and
between us, which included Yazuko-San, we got through a large
quantity of *sake*. I have chronicled many hilarious evenings in Japan: all I
can say is that these festive occasions are part of the life of the country.

Like Kagoshima, Miyazaki, the surroundings of which are of great
beauty, is a world apart from the rest of Japan, and even of Kyushu.
With its palms, hibiscus flowers, and phoenix trees, it reflects the southern
origin of at least part of the Japanese people. It is here that the first
Emperor, Jimmu, was supposed to have had his palace, just as he is
reputedly buried in the great Miyazaki shrine. To commemorate the
events of 2,600 years ago, when the Japanese state was reputedly founded,
a *Heiwadai* or 'peace' tower has been built. The Japanese love towers.
This one is reached by a great flight of steps and somewhat resembles a
ziggurat. In point of fact, its association with peace is of recent date, for it
was built originally in 1940 and dedicated to the War God, Hachiman.
Inside is a *mikoshi*, or portable shrine. Nearby is a lovely garden, laid out
on the instructions of a remarkable man, on whom I paid a call, Mr.
Iwakiri, chairman of a local transport company, Miyazaki Kotsu, and a
public benefactor. Despite his seventy-four years, he looked barely
middle-aged; he had, he told me proudly, eleven grandchildren. I recall
that he gave me a box of cactus pickles, the first I had tasted. Part of the
garden consisted of a *haniwa* park. Found in some of the oldest tombs,
haniwa are small figurines, usually of rather squat men in armour, with
'flair' skirts and very thick legs. The sight of so many at a time, all life-size
models, was rather grotesque, like an assembly of immobile dwarfs.

At the Miyazaki shrine, which resembles in part that at Ise and where
there is an 800-year-old wisteria, we met the priest, one of a family of
priests. He received us in a room with comfortable armchairs and white

antimacassars. He told us about the history of the shrine, and of its activities. Apart from two services every day, there were many marriages, from which he obtained most of his fees. Some couples, he said, expressed the wish to have a Christian wedding, even though they were not believers, and he would then perform it. It was as though an English couple were to insist on the local vicar conducting a Shinto ceremony.

I had a *zadankai* with members of the University, and then a lunch at the so-called Columban restaurant, presided over by President Hiroka, a physicist, and finally we went on a tour of Aoshima, or Blue Island. This was approached by a bridge and lengthy causeway, against which a typhoon-lashed sea was breaking, wetting groups of schoolgirls who, at each fresh inundation, squealed delightedly in chorus. Crowded with sub-tropical betel palms, the island rests on an enormous grid of rocks, called locally the Ogre's Washboard. You can walk all round it, taking in a fine view of the Pacific, which is disturbed here by the so-called Black Current, edging the 'washboard' with foam. On one corner of the Island there is a hothouse, where tropical plants of amazing and bizarre luxuriance grow. On our walk we were fanned by hot winds, like the breath of strange animals; it was like skirting the edge of Japan. We speculated how those first men, the proto Japanese, came across the southern sea, to help establish the island empire. Tokyo seemed infinitely remote, and I breathed the charged air of another continent. Not far away, at Saitobaru, were as many as 380 huge mounds, perhaps the burial places of the chieftains of the 'new people'. The old chronicles, the *Kojiki* and the *Nihon Shoki*, though compounded of myth and legend, describe a region which is still recognizable in the Miyazaki of today.

Indeed, the region hereabouts fades away into an almost primitive state. On Kojima Island, with its papaya and bananas, there are wild monkeys, and at the Cape of Toi, wild horses. The great Kirishima National Park, the first area in Japan to be so designated, contains more volcanoes than any other area in the world. There are twenty-two of them; seismologists fear that there may at any time be large-scale eruptions. Whereas the country here has a moonscape quality, the Horikiri Pass, part of what the Japanese like to call the National Park of Nichinan, is a fine built-up road, lined with phoenix trees, and affording a view of a great expanse of the Pacific. We gazed thereon for a long time, like 'stout Cortez' (except that it was Balboa).

Yet Miyazaki is famous for its personalities who helped to civilize the area: Yasui Sokken, the great Confucian scholar was born there, and it was from there that Mansho Ito, a thirteen-year-old convert to Christianity in the sixteenth century, set out on the long journey to see the Pope, as a member of a children's delegation. I visited Sokken's house, a thatched building now converted into a museum.

With its avenues lined with pampas, oleander and canna, and its fantastic local dances, Miyazaki is not simply a tropical paradise. Industries are growing up, and at Hyuga there is an 'industrial belt' with its own harbour, which seemed to me likely to grow into a dark, gas-filled complex like that at Kitakyushu. Having seen so many parts of Japan suffer from this creeping industrialization, I hoped that Miyazaki might not be spoilt in the same way. Men like old (or young) Mr. Iwakiri are needed to insist that gardens are laid out in these grim zones.

The last lap of this sweep round Kyushu was Beppu. I first came here in 1962. Then it was very much a gay spa, or rather the centre of a complex of spas, with sand-baths and curative springs of every kind, and not a few young ladies apparently ready to provide what in *Figaro* is called *un certo balsamo*. When I arrived there, in the hot summer evening, men and women were walking the streets in *yukata* and *geta*, and life seemed to go on until the small hours. I put up at the Kamikoi hotel, where a very sweet-looking maid in a kimono prepared my bed on the floor, to reappear the next morning in smart Western clothes.

I was keen to try the famous sand-baths; but when I drove out to Kamegawa, I found that the tide was in. As the caretaker was showing me round the public baths nearby, I found myself looking into the women's section, which seemed to surprise the occupants less than it did me.

Beppu is surrounded by tree-covered hills that rear up steeply, dominated by Mount Tsurami. All over the town, steam rose in columns. On stretches of hillside were rice paddies, with peasants toiling away, wearing straw conical hats. School-children wound their way home up the sides of the valleys, the girls in their neat white blouses, the boys in their Germanic uniforms. A light-hearted feeling seemed to prevail.

I returned to Beppu some years later, bound for another Summer School. What a change had taken place! The relaxed, carefree town had become brossy and noisy, and ugly new buildings had shot up. I had seen this happening over so much of Japan, and I could not but regret it. Nevertheless, the Japanese know when to call a halt; and just as they have tackled the pollution problem, so, I feel sure, they will arrest the ugliness which is spreading like a blight over their country. If they cannot do it, nobody can.

CHAPTER IX

Farewell to Japan

My last weeks were hectic, and I was glad that they were so. It prevented me from fretting at the separation from so many kind friends, and from a country I had come to love as no other.

On the day of my arrival back from a journey in the North, I took part in a performance of Dryden's *Marriage à la Mode*, produced by Verner Bickley, now head of the East-West Centre in Hawaii. We performed it, appropriately in view of its gentle satire of English aping French manners, at the Maison Franco-Japonaise. This was a moment when Anglo-French relations were not at their best; but I recall making a short but impassioned introductory speech in French, to an audience of about 100, on the existence of a Common Market in European culture. I also recall nearly falling off the stage as I walked into the wings, whether from emotion or from fatigue I do not know. I had admittedly done the same thing on another occasion, when I came down heavily along with a pair of steps during a performance of *Everyman*, producing a reverberation which the audience seemed to regard as a necessary and even effective part of that moral drama. I should here like to record gratitude to both Alan Baker and Verner Bickley, and to all those who worked with us, for the pleasure which these performances, usually costumed-readings, afforded me. We acted a series of plays, from *Twelfth Night* to *Abraham Lincoln*, in many parts of Japan; and our little group, which depended so much on the costumes made by Peter Mann, never seemed to be ridden with the tensions and jealousies which plague so much amateur dramatic activity. This particular performance was, I think, one of our most successful, despite one false entrance on my part, which again the audience did not seem to resent. It had been a busy day, as our dress-rehearsal was at 11 a.m., and the public performance at 4 p.m., and I had been obliged to read through and answer a great deal of correspondence in the earlier part of the morning.

The next day, 30 October, I took part in the ceremony in which our new Ambassador, Sir John Pilcher, presented his credentials to the Emperor. I had bowed before the Emperor before, at the New Year. On these occasions we would assemble at the Palace, the Shogun's old castle, along with other members of the Diplomatic Corps. We formed in line according to protocol and, either singly or in couples, we walked across the room, bowed twice to the Emperor, the Empress and the other members of the imperial family, and moved out by a door on the opposite side. The ceremony, simple but impressive, was followed by a brief meal in another room. This consisted of *sake* and special Japanese food which, having been sampled, was neatly wrapped up by the waiters and carried away by the guests, together with the *sake* cup, adorned with the Emperor's insignia of the chrysanthemum, which was of a different colour each year. Of the simplicity of the food I have already spoken.

On the present occasion, which took place in the afternoon, we were seen off from the Embassy by other members of the staff and greeted by disciplined groups of watchers in the Palace grounds. First, there was a short rehearsal; and then we formed up behind a screen, while the Ambassador advanced towards the Emperor's 'throne', which was quite an unpretentious piece of furniture. Then one by one we walked forward, turned to face the Emperor, bowed, walked to a point about six feet away (having been announced by the Ambassador), bowed again, whereupon the Emperor held out his hand, which we advanced to shake, went back to the same spot, made another bow, took three paces back facing the Emperor, turned to the original spot, made a final bow, and retreated behind the screen. In a buoyant mood, Sir John spoke eloquently; and in reply to a polite enquiry about the Queen's health, he described it as 'robust'. The credentials were duly handed over, and the ceremony brought to an end. On returning to the Embassy we drank champagne. To go back to the office afterwards was not easy; but I had much to do there, and more was to come—a party to celebrate the Turkish National Day, and work on my *Tokyo Essays* proofs at home. I refer to this book, not because of any merits it may possess, but because its production was something of a publishing feat. Composed by men who knew no English, it was issued, with very few printing errors, within two weeks of the delivery of the page proofs. I do not know of many publishers who could emulate the Hokuseido Press in this respect.

Another memorable occasion for me was a dinner party given by Prince and Princess Mikasa. This took place on 31 October at the Crescent restaurant in Akasaka, where the *cuisine* was French. I was touched by their invitation, a gesture on my impending departure. There were also present their son who was soon to go to Oxford—a nice, bearded young man with a twinkle in his eye, whose resemblance to the Emperor Meiji had often been remarked upon; their daughter and her husband, Mr. Konoye; and Mr. Kuroda of the Imperial household. We talked about Oxford, my *alma mater*, and about travelling in Japan, some of which I have done in the Prince's company.[1] He said that when he and his wife were climbing Mount Daisen, they had encountered two bears, which had fortunately made off in the opposite direction. The Prince really knew his Japan. When he had a moment free in Tokyo, which was not often, he enjoyed going ice-skating, when he was able to feel anonymous. This particular evening passed delightfully not least because we had a delicious *bouillabaisse* to begin with and exquisite *crêpes suzettes* to finish up. It happened to be the day of the funeral of the great statesman, Yoshida, and, as the afternoon was a holiday, enormous crowds had assembled. I had once visited Yoshida's house near Hakone, with its photographs of Churchill, whom he greatly admired, and its Shinto shrine in the garden. To everyone's surprise, except perhaps to his intimate family, Yoshida was received into the Catholic Church on his death-bed.

I will not detail all the calls that were made and all the farewell parties I attended. When I think of those occasions—at the P.E.N. Club, at the *Mombusho* (Ministry of Education), at many universities, at many restaurants and at many more private homes, I feel a touch of sadness; for these warm functions were sandwiched in between the arduous business of packing up. This I did with Teiko-San, ever resourceful and tireless (which was more than I was), if a little subdued. I could not recall leaving any other country with such a pang. And the presents! I scarcely had time to unpack them before they vanished into crates. Some of them, I confess, I have never unpacked since. There will be time, when I am feeling in the

---

[1] This belongs to the account of my travels in Hokkaido.

mood. But they are all labelled; I know from whom they came; and I will never part with them.

On Thursday 9 November, I got up at 5.15 a.m. to go with John Hill, my colleague, to meet Arnold and Veronica Toynbee, who had arrived in Yokohama on the *President Cleveland*. Toynbee, at seventy-eight, was in excellent form. We sat on the sun deck and talked. He said, or rather his wife did and he agreed, that his *Reconsiderations* was a better book than the last three volumes of *A Study of History*. His mind was eager in a manner quite astounding, and his affection for Japan was evident. He had come as a guest of the Kyoto Industrial University, and President Araki had arrived in Tokyo to meet him. We saw him back to the Imperial Hotel. It was some years later, reading his *Cities on the Move*, that I realized how much he had managed to absorb about modern Tokyo in the course of that brief stay.

The next day I attended the imperial garden party in the Akasaka Palace Gardens. Unfortunately, the weather had turned very cold; and, despite the warm *sake*, we felt shivery. The Emperor and members of his family walked along the prescribed route, and I thought that the Emperor in particular was looking well. I could not help reflecting how much history lay behind that somewhat frail but undaunted figure: for it was to him, more than to anyone else, that Japan owed its 'salvation'. Powerless to stop the war from starting, he had exercised his authority to bring it to an end. Here he was, more than twenty years later, at the head of a recovered country, its self-respect restored. Not merely Japan, but the world, owed much to him. I was to see him again during his visit to London in October 1971.

That evening I gave the Toynbees dinner at the Zakuro restaurant, Akasaka, where we had a Japanese meal. A rowdy table next to ours made conversation difficult at first, but fortunately the group of young men soon got up to go, and we had the usual stimulating talk. The Arakis, Professor Kobayashi, Professor Kawai, a British Council scholar, Professor Ishizu from Sendai and Professor Kimura were the other guests. Again, I was amazed at Toynbee's vivacity. Although he wore a hearing aid he caught most things, and he never failed to make an apt comment and to seize on any point that was new to him. I had noticed that, before we left the Imperial Hotel, he had posted several—perhaps half a dozen—letters, all written by hand. He had shown the same alertness at a press conference in the Imperial Suite the day before.

Toynbee's arrival was the occasion for my last visit to Kyoto. I was in many ways glad to escape from packing and the strain of a prolonged period of farewell. On Tuesday 14 November I took the Hikari Express, and was met by Mrs. Araki and taken to the Kyo-Yamato restaurant near the Kodaiji temple. In an outside kiosk, I found the Toynbees engaged in painting designs on pottery. Whereas I set about making some conventional and rather crude designs, Toynbee, with his steady hand, did a *Yin* and *Yang* crest, and also one in Greek. Then, with President Araki as host, we had a sumptuous meal, seated on the *tatami*. Peter and Joan Martin were there, and a concourse of professors. I sat next to Professor Iwamura, an expert on Mongolia from Kyodai, and Professor Izui, a linguistic expert from the same university. Toynbee was again in excellent spirits. He made a speech, delivered in his rapid conversational style, full of felicitous references to Kyoto's past history, his head ducking as he emphasized a word. There followed some beautiful Kyoto dances by geisha, who wore superb trailing *obis*. When I said goodbye to the Toynbees at the end, I expressed the hope that he would not 'overdo' things, as guests in Japan are liable to be overwhelmed with hospitality. Toynbee seemed to be not in the least worried, but his wife shook her head in mock resignation; she knew from experience that there was no holding him back. A year or two later a book was published on Toynbee's visit, and Professor Kobayashi sent me a copy to Paris. I had to return to Tokyo the next day, when I plunged again into a whirl of activity.

While I was busy clearing up my things at home, I had half hoped that I might come to solve a mystery which had been haunting me for more than a year. On 11 December 1966, I had opened the cupboard in my little upstairs study with the object of doing some work on the book, *The Concept of Life*, on which I had been working for eleven years. In Tokyo, there was little enough time for private writing; but at week-ends and on holidays I could sometimes manage to draft a page or two. On that occasion I had a shock. The space where I invariably kept the bulky manuscript was empty. I searched everywhere; but, knowing that I never kept the papers anywhere else, I realized that something was wrong. My other papers and notes were in place: the manuscript which I had worked over repeatedly and nearly completed had clearly been stolen. I consulted Sir Francis Rundall, who was as usual most sympathetic and on whose advice I summoned the police. I also published an appeal in the press. It was all to no avail. To this day I have no idea what could have happened. This was the one shadow cast over my time in Japan. All I can say is that my friends, and many with whom I could claim only acquaintance, such as the Yugoslav Ambassador and his wife, were most consoling. As for Teiko-San, she was at first almost as distraught as I was, and she puzzled her brain to know what could have happened. In her brave way, she said at last: 'Master must write a better book.' Whether I did so I do not know; but the British Council was most understanding in allowing me a period of leave in order to start the writing over again, and later in supporting my application for a Leverhulme Fellowship, whereby I was able to rewrite the entire work. But this incident, which others have experienced in different forms, was of the kind which inevitably leaves a scar, chiefly because it is painful and baffling to be in a position never to know, and with difficulty to surmise, what really happened.

It was on the morrow of this loss that I paid, at the advice of friends, my first visit to Atami, which I had so often passed in the train. A finely situated coastal town about fifty miles from Tokyo, Atami is supposed to be a bachelor's paradise, in the sense that, as the 'unofficial' guide-books put it, single men are unlikely to remain alone for longer than they wish. I was in no mood for company, however charming. I spent one night there, reading desperately for my book; but the pull of home was too great, and I was back in Tokyo earlier than my friends had expected. One haunts the scene of misfortune and, in my case, my little household had become dear to me; I crept back sad but relieved to be among my books, my *bonsai* trees, with my dog, and, above all, my trusted servants.

The case was closed, so to speak, when the last of my books and papers were stored and labelled in large cardboard containers by Teiko-San, and stowed into crates by the removal men. The last days in the house were strange in such a gaunt atmosphere, though there were so many social engagements that the place had become merely a dormitory. Yet it was sad, too, to see Teiko-San packing up her own belongings, including her remarkable range of kimonos, and Soma-San, whose health was begin-ning to fail, removing his. There was an occasional mix-up: Teiko-San's miniature umbrella turned up months later among my things in

Cornwall, and there it remains, along with the staff I purchased on the summit of Mount Fuji.

On 17 November I called the staff together at the office, and we had a farewell session. I made a speech which was answered by my deputy Paul Hardwick, a man of few words but who chose them well. I had conducted so many ceremonies of this kind for others about to leave us that this, to me, was something of an anticlimax; but at least I did not become maudlin, as I feared that I might. That same evening there was a farewell party at the Toshi centre, where we had given so many official receptions. Despite a bout of very bad weather, a large crowd assembled, and afterwards I felt that, even if I saw few of them again, they were friends of a special kind such as one makes only in Japan.

On the next day, a Sunday, I paid my last visit to St. Alban's, reading both the Lessons, as I had done so often in the past. There were friends of mine, especially some of the young British lecturers, who could make neither head nor tail of my fidelity to the little Anglican church, seeing that I was particularly interested in the sciences, which they deemed to be incompatible with any but 'humanist' beliefs. But to me, humanism was as incredible a philosophy as they found my own affiliations, and I cared very much for the liturgy, which many people, it seemed to me, found wanting in their lives, without always knowing what it was that they lacked. I must here record my gratitude to three incumbents of St. Alban's, the Revd. Bennett Sims, the Revd. R. M. (Bob) Smith, who was there for the greater part of my stay and with whom I was on terms of close friendship, and Father Peter Webber. In the evening the Hardwicks gave a dinner-party at their house. I was by this time very tired, but I danced a pretty vigorous monkey-dance with Miss Honda, our expert translator.

When, on Monday, 20 November, I opened my eyes at 8 a.m., I could not believe that it was my last morning in Japan. I had Teiko-San and Soma-San up to my study, where I gave them in addition to a bonus on salary, a present each—Soma-San a transistor, and Teiko-San a sort of table work-basket from the Mitsukoshi department store. Despite his limited English, Soma-San delivered quite an eloquent speech, while Teiko-San stood by looking unusually pale. So I said goodbye to the best of servants, who had time and again sustained my morale. To Luke I also said goodbye: the previous evening he had nuzzled up to me as if he knew that I was going. Teiko-San remarked that he could do everything except speak. Then they bowed me off from the gate. At that point we all displayed a becoming stoicism.

After I had called in at the office to say farewell to the staff who were to remain behind, a group of us set off in three cars for the airport. Here we were given the *kiku*, or chrysanthemum room, where, in company with a number of Japanese, including the Miyaharas, the Kurodas and Embassy staff, we drank champagne. Then we were led through the Customs and I said a final goodbye. When I walked out onto the tarmac, a shout went up from the staff, who had ascended post-haste to the balcony, and I waved a last greeting from the door of the plane. The flight to Osaka was, as so often, bumpy; but I sent the office a radio-telegram of greetings from there, and consoled myself with a whisky. Then, streaking across Shikoku and Kyushu, we touched down at Okinawa, where we remained at Naha for half an hour. I was glad to catch a glimpse of the island, now restored to the homeland. The weather was hot and sticky, but it was still for me Japan. As darkness fell, we headed for Taiwan, the first step on my long tour through South-East Asia and Communist China.

I do not know how to sum up my six years in Japan. All I can say is that they added a new life, a new dimension, to an existence that could hardly be called uneventful. Basil Hall Chamberlain, author of the still valid *Things Japanese* and a masterpiece on the Japanese written character, once said that Japan would be a wonderful country but for the people. I cannot see it. For all their baffling characteristics, the people were to me the essential Japan, which is why I have recorded so many names. Although I preserve happy memories of other oriental people, especially the Thais and the Vietnamese, I know no people like those of the four islands I had traversed with such enthusiasm. I am glad that I saw them at the moment when they had recovered their morale, just as I am glad that I saw the country, and especially the remoter areas, before it was made uniform by the urbanization which may one day reduce to nothing the difference between one nation and another.

When I look back, however, there is one little group to which I shall always remain deeply attached. This was my local Japanese staff. It was to them that I dedicated my *Tokyo Essays*, 'with respect and with affection'. It was true. In my mind's eye, I still see their sweet, eager faces—at our office parties, where they would dance the Scottish dances I, as Sassenach, taught them, play musical chairs with the delight of children, sing our folk-songs and theirs with beautiful modulated voices, but also at their desks, typing with straight backs the letters which they took such pride to do neatly and accurately, thumbing through their dictionaries to check an unfamiliar word or phrase. And there would be the one who meant most to me, always looking serene, her inner quietness being the language she spoke best. Somehow, I am glad we are separated. I am glad that I saw the Last Country at its best, while its magic, despite disaster, still clung to it, and while I, credulous no doubt but perhaps not altogether deluded, was alive to its spell. As for the one of whom I have spoken, I recall the words of Landor:

> *There is delight in singing tho' none hear*
> *Beside the singer: and there is delight*
> *In praising, though the praiser sit alone.*

Historical Outline

3,000 B.C. – 200 B.C.   Jomon Culture, named after 'corded pattern' pottery of which five types have been identified. The Jomon have sometimes been regarded as the ancestors of the Ainu aboriginal people.

200 B.C. – A.D. 300 *c*.   Yayoi Culture, named after a site in the University of Tokyo where pottery of this type was first found.

A.D. 300 *c*.   Beginning of Tomb Culture, named after the presumed burial place of early Emperors.
Rise of the Yamato clan.
Present Imperial dynasty established, with shrine to Sun Goddess at Ise, and Shinto as the 'national' religion.

534 (or 552)   Introduction of Buddhism, and its spread under the influence of Prince Umayado, or Shotoku Taishi (754–622).

710–794   Nara Period. Building of the great temples, beginning with the Todaiji.

794–1185   Heian Period, with Imperial capital at Heian-kyo (Kyoto). *The Tale of Genji* (Murasaki Shikibu) and *The Pillow Book* (Sei Shonagon), written in Hiragana syllabary (see Glossary).

1185–1333	Kamakura Period, so-called because the Shogun ('generalissimo') established his Court or *Bakufu* at that town, while the Emperor lived in retirement in Kyoto.
	Rise of powerful families, the Minamoto and the Taira (Genji and Heike), and their rivalry. Establishment of feudal system.
	Rise of popular forms of Buddhism, including Jodo, or Pure Land Buddhism, Nichiren Buddhism, and Zen.
1266	First ultimatum sent to Japan by the great Khan, Kubilai.
1274	Mongul Armada attacks Kyushu. Failure of invasion.
1281	Second Mongul invasion repelled with heavy losses after violent storm (*kamikaze*).
	Prestige of warrior class, and development of samurai code. Rise of feudal lords (*daimyo*).
1338–1573	Ashikaga Shogunate. The 'warring states'. Apogee of Zen Buddhism. Rise of the Noh drama and Tea Ceremony (*cha-no-yu*).
1542 *c.*	First Portuguese ship wrecked off Kyushu.
1549	Landing of Francis Xavier, Jesuit missionary in Kagoshima (Kyushu). Rapid spread of Christianity.
1573	Nobunaga Oda (born 1534) in supreme power, though loyal to Imperial Court at Kyoto.
1582	Death of Nobunaga by assassination, and rise of Hideyoshi, Japan's greatest general.
1587	Hideyoshi turns against the Christians.
1598	Death of Hideyoshi, after invasion of China.
1600	Battle of Sekigahara, and rise of Tokugawa Ieyasu.

1600	Establishment of Ieyasu at Edo and consolidation of power of Tokugawa family, which ruled Japan until 1868. Arrival in Japan of the Englishman, Will Adams.
1616	Hidetada becomes Shogun. Bitter persecution of Christians.
1637	Christian rebellion at Shimabara, Kyushu. Christian 'underground' formed at Nagasaki.
1639	Closure of Japan to foreigners.
Edo Period – 1868	Renaissance of Confucian doctrine, and spread of education, especially among samurai class. Rise of Kabuki drama, *haiku* (poems of 17 syllables: see Glossary), and *ukiyo-e* (woodblock prints depicting the 'Floating World': see Glossary).
1651	Abortive rebellion of *Ronin*, or 'masterless men'.
1853 (7 July)	Commodore Perry arrives off Japan. 'Opening up' of the country.
1868	Meiji Restoration. Emperor returns to power and sets up Court in Edo (Tokyo).
1872	Introduction of conscription.
1877	Saigo Takamori, *daimyo* from Satsuma, Kyushu, stages rebellion. He commits *seppuku* (*hara-kiri*) after being driven back to Kagoshima.
1894	China-Japan War, in which China is decisively defeated.
1900	Boxer Rebellion in China, and intervention of Japanese troops to protect foreign embassies.

1902	Anglo-Japanese Alliance. Russo-Japanese War, in which Russia is decisively defeated.
1914 (August)	Japan declares war on Germany.
1921	Four-Power Alliance between Britain, America, France, and Japan. Joint Naval Treaty, leaving Japan supreme naval power in Western Pacific.
1925	Law forbidding agitation to overthrow state system or to abolish private property.
1930	London Naval Treaty, limiting Japan's naval growth.
1931	Manchuria 'incident'. Kwantung Army occupies Mukden, etc.
1932	Establishment of the puppet state of Manchukuo.
1933	Japan leaves the League of Nations.
1936	Japan joins the Anti-Comintern Pact.
1937	China 'incident'. Japan occupies Nanking. Establishment of Greater East Asia Co-Prosperity Sphere.
1940	Tripartite Pact between Germany, Italy, and Japan.
1941 (7 Dec.)	Japanese surprise attack on Pearl Harbour. Occupation of Pacific Islands, Philippines, Hong Kong, Singapore, Dutch East Indies, and Burma.
1942	Battles of the Coral Sea and Midway Island, reversing Japan's advance.
1943	American successful resistance at Guadalcanal.

1944	Beginning of Allied counterattack in Pacific. Bombing of Japanese mainland.
1945 (6 August) (9 August)	Atomic attack on Hiroshima. Atomic attack on Nagasaki. Surrender of Japan, and American Occupation.
1946–47	Purge of Japanese administration. Revival of Party System. Introduction of 'American' Constitution. Reorganization of educational system.
1952	Ratification of San Francisco Peace Treaty. End of Occupation of Japan. Signature of Japan-U.S. Security Treaty.
1955	Establishment of Liberal Democratic Party (still in office, 1974). Japan joins the United Nations.
1964	Olympic Games held in Tokyo.
1970	Osaka International Exhibition.
1971	*Seppuku* (see Glossary) of Mishima Yukio. The Emperor pays a visit overseas.

Glossary

AMA	fisherfolk, especially girls employed in underwater food-gathering (edible seaweed and shell-fish). The island of Hekura off the Japan Sea coast is notable for them.
AWARE	delicate sensibility, combined with the idea of the ephemeral nature of things, as found in *The Tale of Genji* Modern meaning: grief. Pronounced *awaré*
BUGAKU	a form of dance-drama, Chinese in origin and dating from the seventh century, performed to *gagaku* (q.v.) music, and witnessed now chiefly at the Imperial Court
CHANOYU	Tea Ceremony
CHAWAN	bowl, such as that used in Tea Ceremony
DAIMYO	Feudal Lord
ETA	Outcasts, thought by some to be descendants of Korean prisoners
O-FURO	Japanese bath
FUTON	thick quilt for bedding
GAGAKU	ancient Chinese music accompanying *bugaku* (q.v.)
GAIJIN	foreigner
GEISHA	trained hostesses or professional entertainers
GENRO	elder statesmen, who in the nineteenth century selected the prime minister
GETA	wooden clogs or sandals, with strap fastening round the big toe
HAIKU	17-syllable poem, usually concerned with the passing of the seasons. Greatest practitioner, Basho (1644–94)

HAKAMA	thick divided skirt for men, often worn with *haori*, a cloak fastened in front, the two usually worn for formal occasions, if Western dress is not used
HANGONTAN	patent medicines manufactured at Toyama since the seventeenth century
HASHIGAKARI	Bridge-form passageway in a Noh stage, serving as part of the stage as well as the means of entry and exit
KAGAMI-BIRAKI	ceremony involving the cutting of New Year rice-cakes
KAGURA	sacred dances performed in shrines by young women, and supposedly modelled on the dance performed before the cave in which the Sun Goddess had taken refuge
KAKEMONO	picture or scroll, hanging in *tokunoma* (q.v.)
KAMI	Lit: 'superior ones'. Shinto gods
KANA	Japanese phonetic syllabary
KANJI	Chinese character (ideograph)
KANNAZUKI	October. Lit: 'the month without gods', referring to the myth that all the gods go to Izumo in that month
KOAN	Zen riddle or conundrum
KOTO	horizontal harp or zither of 13 strings, originally brought over from China, which may have derived it from the West
KYOGEN	comic Noh drama
O-MATSURI	festival
MIKOSHI	portable shrine
NE-SAN	Lit: 'elder sister'. Waitress in café
OBI	sash made of silk material for binding kimono
ONSEN	hot spring or spa
RYOKAN	Japanese inn
SAKE	rice wine, the traditional sacred drink of Japan. Pronounced *saké*
SAKYAMUNI	one of the names of the Buddha, as member of the Sakya clan
SAMISEN	musical instrument resembling a guitar.
SAMURAI	warrior with strict code of conduct (*bushido*). Name for warrior class in general
SATORI	condition of mystical enlightenment obtained through

Zen meditation

SAYONARA	'Goodbye'
O-SEMBEI	biscuit or cracker, often with a thin band of seaweed round it
SEPPUKU	suicide by ritual disembowellment (*hara-kiri*)
SHIMAI	ritual dance in a Noh drama
SHINTO	the primordial faith of Japan, involving belief in *kami* (q.v.)
SHIRATAKI	food resembling macaroni or noodles
SHOJI	paper screens or windows, operated by sliding
SUKIYAKI	beef, pork or chicken cut into thin slices and cooked with vegetables, *shirataki* (q.v), bean curd, and sugar, in soy sauce
SUSHI	rice patties covered with strips of raw fish (*sashimi*), etc.
SUTRA	verse or verses of Hindu or Buddhist scriptures (a Sanskrit word)
TATAMI	straw matting measuring six feet by three, bound with cloth and used as units for covering floor of Japanese rooms
TEMPURA	fish etc. dipped in batter and fried in sesame oil (probably a Portuguese word by origin)
TOFU	bean curd
TOKONOMA	alcove in room where picture or scroll (*kakemono*, q.v) is hung, and where flower arrangement may be displayed The seat of honour is back to the *tokunoma*
TORII	traditional high gate at entrance to shrine, consisting of two columns leaning slightly inwards and surmounted by a curved crossbeam
UKIYO	the 'Floating World', usually regarded as symbolizing the life of actors, courtesans, etc. *Ukiyo-e*: woodblock prints depicting that world
YAMABUSHI	mountain monks
YUKATA	kimono worn in house, padded in winter, or worn outdoors in summer heat.
ZADANKAI	round table conference.
ZAZEN	the posture or act of Zen meditation See *koan* and *satori*

Index

Abdication, 113
Actors, 42
Adam, 121
Adams, Will, 241, 261
Agriculture, 179
Ainu, 92, 182, 204, 225, 259
Air France, 132
Akasaka, 67, 74, 75, 76, 252, 253
Aki-kawakita, 175
Akiko, Empress, 127, 128
Akita, 179, 182
Akiyoshi cave, 170
A la recherche du temps perdu (Proust), 126
All Nippon Airlines, 204, 225
Ama, 199
Amano-Hashidate, 82, 152, 208
Amaterasu, 144, 147, 149, 150, 151, 180, 218, 259
'Ambre' café, 74
Americans, 96, 146, 212, 214
Amida Buddha, 124, 125, 128, 129
Ancestor-worship, 15, 29, 47, 192
Anghor Wat, 105
Anglo-Japanese Alliance, 262
Animals, 61
Animism, 164
Anthology of Japanese Literature (Keene), 206
Anti-Comintern Pact, 262
Aoshima, 247
Aoyama, 243
Araki, President, 253, 254
Archery, 105

Arita, 231
Art, 49, 109, 119, 122, 137, 138
Artisans, 29
Asahi beer, 37
Asahi Shimbun, 201
Asama, 95
Ashikaga Shogunate, 260
Asia, 42, 174
Aso, Mount, 237
Assignations, 73
Aston, William, 165
Atami, 255
Athos, Mount, 118, 123
Atom bomb, 20, 212–18, 263
Atrocities, 20
Attlee, Earl, 113
Austen, Jane, 161
Australia, 244
Awa-odori, 205
Aware, 126
Ayabe, 152
Azabu, 54, 70

Bachelor's Japan (De Mente), 77
Badgers, 194
Baelz, Dr., 194
Baker, W. A. C., 236, 238, 250
Bakufu, 260
Bancho, 178
Bangkok, 244
Banks, Commander, 230
Bar-girls, 74, 75, 78, 98
Bars, 38, 74, 75, 78, 178, 187

Basho, 180, 213
Basosennin, 106
Bath-houses, 76
Bean-curd, 119, 229
de Beauvoir, Simone, 45
Beggars, 90
Benjo (water-closet), 20
Bennett, J. G., 112
Bento, 93
Beppu, 233, 248–9
Bickley, Dr. Verner, 236, 250
Bikini Atoll, 21
Binyon, Lawrence, 115
Birth of China, The (Creel), 223
Biwa, Lake, 116, 127
Bizan Highland Park, 206
Bizen pottery, 172
Blacker, Carmen, 132, 195
'Blood debt', 19
Blunden, Edmund, 133, 199
Bodh Gaya, 109
Bodhisattvas, 121, 138
Bolivia, 87
Bonsai trees, 255
Bottrall, Ronald, 54
Bowing, 179
Boxer Rebellion, 261
Britain, 183, 191, 230, 233, 262
B.B.C., 42
British, the, 167, 234, 239
British Council, 22, 34, 39, 67, 132, 184, 230, 236, 239, 245, 255
British Embassy, 66, 83, 84, 118, 251, 257
Britt, Mother, 171
Bruckner, Karl, 213, 217
Buddha, the (*see also* Gautama *and* Sakyamuni), 109, 123, 134, 136, 139, 191, 193, 207
Buddhism, 49, 61, 103, 104, 109, 110, 115, 117, 119, 121, 123, 124, 129, 133, 134, 139, 146, 151, 154, 157, 158, 172, 181, 188, 193, 196, 210, 223, 237, 242, 259, 260
Buddhism, Mahayana, 106, 110
Buddhism, Nichiren, 260
Buddhism, Pure Land (Jodo), 124, 125, 260

Buddhism, Zen (*see* Zen)
Bugaku, 141, 221
Bundy, William P., 18
Burke, Edmund, 103
Burlesque shows, 76
Burma, 19, 206, 262
Bush, Lewis, 195
Byodoin (temple), 125, 139

Cafés, 73
California, 106, 164
Calligraphy, 29, 49, 121, 180, 199
Cambodia, 105
Cambridge, 133
Canterbury, 151
Cape Toi, 247
Carlyle, 157
Carthew, Anthony, 156
Catholic Cathedral (Tokyo), 27
Cha'an (Zen), 106
Chamberlain, Basil Hall, 21, 194
Chanoyu, 108
de Chardin, Teilhard, 71
Chaucer, 213
Chawan, 108
Chen-yen (*see* Shingon sect)
Cherry blossom, 109, 113, 118, 152, 208
Chicago, 201
Chikamatsu, Mr., 185, 187, 188
China, 32, 83, 110, 114, 119, 121, 129, 134, 135, 137, 138, 148, 194, 214, 219, 221, 234, 257, 260, 261
China-Japan War, 261
Chinese classics, 129
Chinese-Russian border, 114
Chionji (temple), 124, 125
Chishakuin (temple), 123, 124
Chogen, 135
Christian Century in Japan, The (Boxer), 241
Christianity, 19, 20, 48, 61, 121, 139, 154, 169, 172, 193, 224, 234, 236, 239, 240–2, 247, 248, 260, 261
Christmas, 38, 39, 57, 69, 189
Chuguji nunnery, 136–7, 138
Churchill, Winston, 252
Cities on the Move (Toynbee), 253

Civic architecture, 26
Civil service, 35
Cloistered Emperors, the, 113
Cocks, Richard, 241
Collcutt, Martin, 129–31
Common Market, 250
Commonwealth, the, 85
Communists, 85, 214
Commuters, 27
Concept of Life, The (Tomlin), 254
Confessions of a Mask (Mishima), 88
Confucius, 30, 47, 248, 261
Cookery, 50, 55
Cornwall, 208, 256
Corruption, 35
Cotopaxi, 92
Courtesans, 42
Crown Prince, 242
Crown Princess, 172
Cultural relations, 21, 83, 114, 172
Culture, 117, 127, 199, 242, 250
Custom House, The (King), 101, 196

Daibutsu (Great Buddha), 134, 135, 139
Daigoji (temple), 125
Daijoji (temple), 153
Daikakuji (temple), 112, 113
Daimonji Festival, 132
Daimyo, 53, 197, 198, 218, 241, 260
Daisen range, 154, 252
Daisenin, 112
Daishuin (temple), 129
Daitokuji (temple), 112
Day of the Bomb, The (Bruckner), 213, 217
Dazaifu (shrine), 228
Death, attitudes to, 20
Death in Life (Lifton), 213
Deguchi, Professor, 208
Dejima (Deshima), 231
De Mente, Boye, 77
Democracy, 46, 232
Dengaku, 223
Department stores, 25
Diplomacy, 33, 53
Diplomatic Corps, 180, 251
Disraeli, 52
Doi (Morinaga), Miss, Akiko, 129–31

Dolls, 67, 189
Dore, Professor Ronald, 29
Douai, 241
Draeger, Don, 71
Dramatic Universe (Bennett), 112
Drugs, 106
Dryden, 250
Dufourq, Madame, 132
Dumoulin, Father, 165
Dutch, the, 231, 234

Earthquakes, 68, 179, 184
East Asia, The Great Tradition (Reischauer and Fairbank), 19
Ebihara, Professor, 230
Ecuador, 92
Edo (*see also* Tokyo), 42, 169, 242, 261
Edo Period, 261
Education in Tokugawa Japan (Dore), 29
Eguchi, Miss Shizuko, 34
Ehime University (Matsuyama), 209
Eisai, 110
Eland, Cyril, 54
Elephantiasis, 245
Eliot, Sir Charles, 121
Eliot, T. S., 57, 80
Ellingworth, R. W., 84
Emperor, the, 26, 30, 44, 60, 85, 114, 143, 145–6, 150, 162, 164, 182, 187, 208, 242, 251, 253, 263
England, 17, 166, 237, 238, 241
English language, 34, 35, 55, 90, 100, 151, 159, 193, 210, 233
Enjoji, President, 227, 230
Enlightenment, 109
Enoch Arden (Tennyson), 187
Enright, D. J., 78
Enryakuji (temple), 117
Erotic, the, 89, 119
Eta, the, 20, 51
Etiquette, 57
'Examination hell', 43
Exorcism, 195
Expense accounts, 35

Fairbank, J. K., 19
Family, the, 15, 16
Far East, the, 82, 226

Farmers, 150
Farmhouses, 178, 181
Fascism, 46
Fenollosa, Ernest, 115–17
Feudal system, 260
Figaro Littéraire, 88
Figgess, Sir John, 52
Fine Arts Museum, Boston, 101
Fire, 67
Fire-walking, 219–21
Floating World (*see Ukiyo*)
Flower-arrangement (Ikebana), 20, 50
Footwear, 170
Forbidden Colours (Mishima), 88
Foreigners, 98
Foxes, 90, 194–6
France, 250, 252, 262
Franciscans, 241
Freud, 167
Fudenge, Mount, 175
Fuji, Mount, 68, 92–6, 104, 152, 154, 219, 239, 256
Fujino, Professor, 206
Fujiwara family, 114, 136
Fujiwara, Mr., 172, 174
Fukuda, President, 238
Fukuoka, 227–8, 229–31
Fukuzawa Yukichi, 169
Funatsu, 191
o-furo, 50, 122, 168, 175, 205
furoshiki, 97
futon, 81, 191, 194, 195

Gagaku, 221
Gaijin, 60
Gaimusho (Foreign Office), 36
Games, 39, 257
Gangsters, 76, 77
Gautama (the Buddha), 134, 138
Gegg, Miss Ann, 219, 220, 225
Geisha, 37, 38, 67, 76, 78, 79, 80, 82, 90, 131–2, 205, 246
Geisha-houses, 79, 80, 131–2, 133
Gembudo, 153
Genetic mutation, 215
Genji (*see* Minamoto), 260
Genji Monogatari (*see Tale of Genji, The*)
Genji, Prince, 126

Genro, 34
Germany, 262
Gessoji (temple), 160
Geta, 131, 248
Ghana, 214
Ginkakuji (temple), 112
Ginza, the, 25, 73, 74
Gion corner, 81, 101, 131
Glover, Dr., 235
Goh, Professor, 172
Gohei, 183
Gold, 185, 198
Gordon, Mrs., 121
Great Wisdom Sutra, 128
Greater East Asia Co-Prosperity Sphere, 262
Gumonjido (temple), 219
Gurdjieff, 112

Hachiman (War God), 246
Hagi, 165–7
Hagi-yaki, 167
Haiku, 180, 210, 261
Hakama, 141
Hakata, 230
Hakodate, 166
Hakone, 252
Hamada, 165
Hamada, Mr. (famous potter), 174
Hamasaka, 153
Haneda airport (Tokyo), 47, 83, 225, 229
Hangontan, 197–8, 199
Hani, Miss, 172
Haniwa, 246
Hanson-Lowe, John, 70, 71
Happiness, 46
Hardwick, Paul, 256
Hardy, Thomas, 108, 191, 199
Harris, Townsend, 168
Haruko, Empress, 169
Hashi-gakari, 222
Hata tribe, 114
Hattori, President, 172
Hayashi, Mr., 190
Hearn, Lafcadio, 16, 17, 115, 155–9, 237, 238, 244
Heiankyo, 102, 114, 122, 126, 127, 259

Heian Period, 102–4, 110, 113, 114, 117, 127, 259
Heijo (*see* Nara)
Heike clan (*see also* Taira clan), 135, 218, 260
Hekura Island, 199
Hellenism, 138
Herrigel, Eugen, 105
Hibakusha, 213
Hidetada (Shogun), 261
Hideyoshi, 112, 125, 208, 260
Hie shrine, 180
Hiei, Mount, 117, 122, 219
Hierarchical equality, 52, 64
Hierarchy, 27, 29, 33, 39, 191
Hikari Express, 254
Hill, John, 253
Himalayas, 106
Himeji castle, 208
Himiko (or Pimiko), 145
Hinamatsuri, 189
Hinduism, 109
Hiragana, 120, 259
Hiraoka, Mr., 238
Hiro, 175
Hiroka, President, 247
Hiroshima, 20, 21, 170, 196, 212–18, 219, 224, 233, 234, 235, 236, 262
Hitachi, 232
Hiyashi Kumiko, 239
Hiyoriyama Park (Sakata), 180
Hokkaido, 18, 81, 166, 182
Hokkeji (nunnery), 136, 138
Hokuseido Press, 252
Homecoming (Osaragi), 31
Homma Museum, 180
Homosexuality, 88, 89
Homyoin, 115–16
Honda, Miss, 256
Honda, President, 236
Honest to God (Robinson), 193, 196
Hong Kong, 168, 262
Honorifics, 51
Honshu, 165, 183, 209, 212, 225
Horikiri Pass, 247
Horyuji (temple), 137
Hosokawa clan, 237
Hosokawa Katsumoto, 111

Hosokawa, Marquis, 132
Hosso sect, 136
Housewives' League (*Shufuren*), 44
Housing, 23
Hulme, T. E., 227
Humanism, 49
Hydrogen bomb, 217

Ibusuki, 245
Ichijo, Emperor, 126
'Ideal Japanese', 30, 45, 46
Idemitsu Sukezo, 30
Ieyasu (Tokugawa), 154, 260, 261
Igata, Professor, 209
Ikao, 107
Ikebana (*see* Flower-arrangement)
Ikeda, Mr., 179, 181, 182
Ikigami, Professor, 172
Imai, Mr., 225
Imanaka, Professor, 227
Imperial Hotel, Tokyo, 253, 254
Imperial Household Agency, 136, 145, 252
Ina city, 193
Inari, 191, 194
India, 89, 109, 110, 119, 120, 123, 134, 210
Industrial Revolution, 102
Industry, 16, 52, 248
Inland Sea, 144, 154, 174, 218
Inoue, Professor, 209
International House (Tokyo), 27
Ireland, 242
Ise, 103, 124, 143–52, 154, 159, 171, 218, 221, 259
Ise Associations, 150
Ishihara, Professor, 227
Ishikawa Prefecture, 185
Ishiteji (temple), 210
Ishiyama, 127, 128, 152
Ishizu, Professor, 253
Italy, 262
Itsukushima (*see* Miyajima)
Iwakiri, Mr., 246, 248
Iwakuni, 218, 225
Iwami, 153
Iwami-Masuda, 166
Iwamura, Professor, 254

Iwaynami, Mr., 229
Iwazu, Professor, 209
Iye, 181
Izanagi, 143, 144
Izanami, 143, 144
Izui, Professor, 254
Izumi shrine, Kumamoto, 237
Izumo, 103, 143, 144, 145, 159, 162–5, 171
Izu peninsula, 168
Izuzu River, 151

James, Patrick, 133, 136, 139
Japanalia (Bush), 195
Japan Academy, 44, 230
Japan Air Lines, 204
Japan, an Interpretation (Hearn), 157, 238
Japan before Buddhism (Kidder), 165
Japanese, the, 28, 29, 83, 86, 98, 167, 175, 182, 192, 223, 233, 238, 240, 241
Japanese Buddhism (Eliot)
'Japanese English', 84
Japanese food, 35, 36, 37, 38, 55, 97, 101
Japanese language, 33, 35, 51, 60, 71, 86
Japanese Literature (Keene), 126
Japanese, mentality of, 31, 134
Japan Folk Craft Museum, 173
Japan, Occupation of, 25, 31
Japanophily, 37
Japan Science Council, 236
Japan Sea, 152, 161, 175, 180, 197, 205
Java, 217
Jesuits, 241, 260
Jidai Matsuri, 132
Jimmu, Emperor, 144, 246
Jingoji (temple), 132
Jiyu Gakuen School (Tokyo), 172
Jizo, 226
Jokamyoji (temple), 239
Jomon culture, 154, 180, 259
Journal from Japan (Stopes), 48
Judo, 70, 71, 72
Judoji, 71
Juncke, Robert, 214
Jung, C. G., 29
Juntoku, Emperor, 185

Kabuki, 41, 127, 180, 183, 261
Kagami-Biraki, 71, 72
Kagawa, President, 211
Kagawa University, 204
Kagoshima, 238–42, 246, 260, 261
Kagura, 183
Kakemono, 36, 80, 123, 180
Kakiemon porcelain, 231
Kakitsubata (Noh play), 116
Kamakura, 134
Kamakura Shogunate, 185, 260
Kamatari clan, 114
Kami, 95
Kamiarizuki, 164
Kamikaze, 260
Kammu, Emperor, 114
Kamo River, 133
Kamo shrine, 127, 128
Kamosu shrine, 159, 164
Kamui Fuchi, 92
Kan (intuition), 55
Kana, 120
Kanazawa, 197, 198–200
Kanda, 84
Kanji (Chinese character), 49, 66, 92, 120
Kannazuki, 163
Kannon (Goddess of Mercy), 49, 105, 135, 204, 208
Kano, 112, 125
Kano Jigoro, 71
Kansai, the, 82, 100
Kanto region, 145
Kanzeonji (temple), 229
Kasuga shrine, 141–2
Kasumi, 153
Katayama, 197
Kato, Mr., 227
Katsumo, Professor, 172
Katsura Detached Palace, 112, 172
Kawabata Yasunari, 189, 190
Kawai, Professor, 253
Kawarabata, Professor, 236, 237, 238
Kawasaki Ichiro, 52
Keene, Donald, 126, 206
Kegon Falls (Chuzenji), 41
Kegon Sect (Nara), 134
Keio University, 169

Kenkyusha Dictionary, 56
Kenrokuen Park (Kanazawa), 199
Kidder, Edward, 165
Kii mountains, 118
'Kimigayo', 201
Kimiidera (temple), 208
Kimono, 39, 44, 58, 63, 65, 131, 157, 248, 255
Kimpoku, Mount, 184
Kimura, Mr., 225
Kimura, Professor, 253
King, Francis, 82, 100, 101, 104, 152, 196
Kinkakuji (Temple of the Golden Pavilion), 104
Kinki region, 144, 145
Kinokuniya, 77
Kirin beer, 37
Kirishima National Park, 247
Kitakyushu, 225, 226, 227, 233, 248
Kitashirakawa, Mrs., Sachiko, 146
Kitchingham, Mrs. Leah, 22
Kitsoeng, 78
Kitsune-tsuki, 194
Koan, 108
Kobayashi, Professor, 154, 157, 162
Kobayashi, Professor (Kyoto), 253, 254
Kobe, 201
Kobo Daishi, 120, 121, 170, 204–5, 219, 221
Kodaiji (temple), Kyoto, 254
Kodaiji (temple), Nagasaki, 234
Kodama, President, 205–6
Kodokan, 70, 71
Koestler, Arthur, 106, 173
Kofukuji (temple), Nagasaki, 234
Kofukuji (temple), Nara, 136, 142
Kohnan University, 100
Koizumi, Mr., 242
Koizumi Yakumo (*see* Hearn, Lafcadio)
Kojiki, 134, 145, 247
Kojima Island, 247
Koken, Empress, 135
Kokura, 225
Kokoro (Hearn), 157
Kongo Noh school, 116
Konoye, Mr., 252

Korakuen Football Ground, 84–5
Korakuen Park (Okayama), 172, 199, 204
Korea, 78, 105, 140, 144, 145, 154, 193, 244
Koreans, 152
Koryuji (temple), 114
Koshigayama, 167
Kosugi, Miss Miyoko (Mrs. Adrian Thorpe), 236
Koto, 38
Koya, Mount, 117–23, 170, 219, 221, 241
Koyama, Lake, 154
Kubilai Khan, 260
Kukai (*see* Kobo Daishi)
Kumamoto, 16, 236–8
Kumano, Mr., 168
Kunaicho (*see* Imperial Household Agency)
Kurashiki, 173
Kuroda, Mr., 252, 257
Kusakabe, 166
Kutani, 153
Kuwatori district, 189
Kyogen, 222, 223, 224
Kyoto, 48, 79, 81, 97–117, 125, 127, 129–33, 138, 139, 182, 198, 201, 229, 239, 241, 254, 260
Kyoto Industrial University, 253
Kyoto University, 32, 254
Kyushu, 81, 144, 145, 201, 212, 225–49, 257, 260, 261

Labour relations, 52, 202
Labour Unions, 202
Landor, W. S., 258
Leach, Bernard, 173, 174
League of Nations, 262
LeMay, General Curtis, 23
Les Femmes Japonaises (Dufourq), 132
Leukaemia, 215
Lewis, Wyndham, 140
Liberal Democratic Party, 46, 263
Lifton, Professor Robert, 213, 218
Literacy, 66
Liturgy, 16, 221, 224, 256

Lloyds, 132
London, 22, 23, 73, 91
London Naval Treaty, 262
Los Alamos, 217
Lotus and the Robot, The (Koestler), 106, 173
'Lotus seat', 37, 108–9
Lotus Sutra, 102, 126
Louis XIV, 103
Love, 46, 88
Love for Whom? (Sono), 45
Loyalty, 35, 36, 52
Luke, 62, 63, 64, 69, 256, 257

Madame Butterfly, 42, 235
Mann, Peter, 250
Maeda clan, 199
Maeda Masatoshi, 197
Maiko, 131
Maitreya, 121
Maizuru, 152
Malacca, 239
Mampukuji (temple), 129
Manchukuo, 262
Mandala, 123
Manila, 87
Mansho Ito, 248
Manyoshu, 134
Maraini, Fosco, 111, 152
Marayama, 153
Marriage, 50, 51, 215, 239, 247
Martial arts, 71, 72
Martin, Peter, 101, 115, 117, 118, 124, 127, 132, 254
Marunouchi, 26
Maruyama, Professor Masao, 213
Marxism, 30, 31, 227
Masaoka Fujii, 234
Masaoka Shiki, 210
Masuada, Professor, 204
Masui, Professor, 213, 216
Materialism, 200
Matsudaira family, 160, 204
Matsue, 154–8, 161, 237
Matsunami, Professor, 228
Matsunobe, Professor, 227
Matsuoka, Professor, 239, 241
o-*matsuri*, 91, 189, 226

Matsushita Electric Company, 202, 225
Matsushita Konosuke, 31, 202
Matsuyama, 209–11, 245
Mayor of the Night (Tanabe), 77
Medicine, 66
Meditation, 108, 109
Meiji, Emperor, 169, 170, 243, 244, 245, 252, 261
Meiji era, 113
Meiji Restoration, 21, 27, 30, 34, 42, 50, 92, 151, 156, 169, 239, 241, 261
Meiji shrine, 104
Mémoires (Saint-Simon), 103
Memoirs of a Dutiful Daughter (de Beauvoir), 45
Mendoza, Y. Amor, 87
Merchants, 29
Mibu (temple), 223
Michizane, 228, 229
Middle East, 98
Midzunoe, Professor, 231–3
Mihara, 174, 176, 181
Miidera (temple), 115–16
Mikado, The, 201
Mikasa, Prince, 132, 252
Mikimoto, Mr., 151
Mikoshi, 246
Minamoto (*see also* Genji), 204, 260
Ming period, 234
Ministry of Education, 30
Miroku-Bosatsu, 115
Misen, Mount, 196, 219
Mishima, 166
Mishima Yukio, 87–8, 124, 182, 263
Missionaries, 48, 88, 242
Mitani, Professor, 204
Mitchell, John, 67
Mitsui, Professor, 207
Miura, Mr., 186
Miwa, Mr., 167
Miyahara, Professor, 177–8, 179, 183, 184, 185, 187, 190, 191, 193, 196, 257
Miyahara, Yoichi, 184, 188, 193
Miyajima, 218–24
Miyamoto, Mr., 166, 167
Miyako (*see* Kyoto)
Miyata, Mr., 186
Miyazaki, 238, 245–8

Miyazu, 152
Miyoshi, Mr., 168
Miyoshi shrine, 183
Mizutaki, 230
Moji, 225
Moku Josan, 197
Mombusho, 252
Mongols, 260
Monkman, Major, 209, 211
Monorail, 83
Mori family, 169
Mori, Viscount, 149
Morita, Miss, 213, 214, 215
Morita, President, 213, 215, 216
Morris, Ivan, 103, 110, 126
Moss Garden, 112
Mother, 43, 44
Mother and Son (Hatano, Isoko and Ichiro), 43
Motoyoshi, Judge, 245
Mukden, 262
Mumyoi-yaki, 186
Munro, Neil Gordon, 244
Murakami, Professor, 209
Murasaki, Lady (Murasaki Shikibu), 102, 110, 126-9, 133, 152, 259
Murayama, Miss Michi, 201
Murdoch, James, 199, 244
Music, 73, 74, 205
Mysticism, 106, 110, 192
Mythology, 143-6, 164

Nabeshima clan, 231
Nagano, 52, 190, 192, 193
Nagasaki, 20, 21, 171, 213, 217, 218, 231, 233-5, 261, 262
Nagese, Professor, 232
Naha, 257
Nakajima, Professor, 231
Naka-Meguro, 57, 67
Nakamura, Mr., 133
Nakano, 190
Nakasato, Mr., 66
Nakayama Miki, 139-40
Nakayama Shozen, 140
'Namamugi Incident', 239
Nanaumi-San, 95
Nango Spa, 129

Nanking, 262
Naotsu, 188
Nara, 97, 133-42, 221
Nara Period, 134, 229, 259
Naruto, 205-6
National Museum, 84
Natural order, 16
Nature, 109
Nepal, 123
Nestorianism, 121
Newman, Cardinal, 245-6
Newton, Eric, 174
New Year, 35, 38, 71, 104, 180
New York, 23, 73, 91
N.H.K., 222
Nichinan National Park, 247
Nichiren, 185
Night of the New Moon (van der Post), 217
Nihon Shoki, 134, 145, 247
Niigata, 184
Nikko, 41
Ninigi, 144
Ninnaji (temple), 113, 114, 118
Nischino Burtara, 150
Nishida, 199
Nishitakatsuji, Mr., 228
Nobinaga Oda, 112, 117, 260
Noh drama, 50, 115, 117, 125, 127, 142, 183, 186, 200, 218, 222-4, 227
Noh, or Accomplishment (Fenollosa and Pound), 116
Nohara, Komakichi, 17
Noro, Mount, 175
Noto peninsula, 199
Notre Dame Seishin University (Okayama), 171-2
Nuclear test, 21
Nuffield, Lord, 202
Nyokobu, 131

Obi, 44, 65, 131
Ochi, Professor, 154
Ochidani shrine, 153
Ogata, Professor, 207
Ogori, Mr., 214
Ogre's Washboard (Miyazaki), 247
Ohara Art Museum, 173, 174

Oi River, 152
Okayama, 152, 170, 171–2, 199, 204
Okayama University, 171
Okesa dance, 187
Oki islands, 154
Okina, 222–3
Okinawa, 257
Okouchi, Professor, 30
Okubo, Professor, 200
Okunoin, 120
Okutango Peninsula, 153
Old age, 52
Olympic Games, 18, 20, 27, 71, 72, 74, 75, 83–6, 263
Onadera, Professor Emeritus, 230
Orient, the, 18
Original sin, 61
Osaka, 16, 82, 118, 147, 201, 208, 244
Osaka City University, 161
Osaka Festival, 201
Osaka International Festival, 202, 203, 263
Osaragi Jiro, 31
Osawa, Professor, 199
Otsu, 115
Otto, Rudolf, 138
Oue, Professor, 209
Oura Catholic church, Nagasaki, 234
Owen, Dr. Ray, 84
Oxford, 34, 162, 252
Oyama, Professor, 161
Oyodo river, 245

Pacific Ocean, 205, 206, 247, 262, 263
Paikche, 145
Pam-pam, 90
Panayia, 118
Parent-teachers' associations, 43
Paris, 26, 132
Past, the, 31, 46, 53
Paternalism, 202
Patmore, Coventry, 55
Patriotism (Mishima), 88
Pearl Island, 147, 151
Peasants, 29, 175, 194, 224
Peking, 105
P.E.N. Club, 252
Perception, 109

Permissiveness, 44
Perry, Commodore, 21, 261
Peru, 207
Peshawar, 207
Picard, Max, 105
Pilcher, Sir John, 251
Pillow Book (Sei Shonagon), 102, 120, 259
Pollution, 20, 26, 213, 218, 249
Polytheism, 165
Pontocho, 131, 132
Pop artists, 106
'Pop transcendentalism', 108
Pope, the, 87, 248
Pornography, 89
Portuguese, the, 207, 234, 260
Pottery, 172, 174, 210, 231
Printing, 136
Prostitutes, 75, 77, 78, 89, 90
Protection-rackets, 76
Pryce-Jones, Alan, 199
Pound, Ezra, 115
Psyche, 20, 22, 28, 46, 212, 213, 223
Psychological Clinic (Matsushita Electric Company), 203
Puritanism, 77

Radiation sickness, 212, 213, 214
Radioactivity, 20, 21
Reischauer, E. O., 19
Religion, 46, 47, 48, 49, 61, 109, 177, 191, 223, 241
Rengeoin (temple), 105
Restaurants, 36, 37, 38, 97, 106
Reverence for life, 46
Rice, 72, 108, 120, 154, 180, 185, 198, 223, 231
Richardson, Charles, 239
Ritchie, Donald, 245
Ritsurin Park (Takamatsu), 204
Ritual, 16, 73, 150, 200
Roben, 135
Robson, Professor William, 25
Roggendorf, Father, 245
Romanticism, 41
Ronin, 35, 245, 261
Roshana (*see* Vairocana), 134
Rundall, Sir Francis, 22, 255

Russo-Japanese War, 32, 262
Ryokan, 97, 141, 155, 161, 168, 182, 190, 229, 231
Ryotsu, 185

Sacred, the, 20, 47, 48, 117, 165, 192, 223
Sacred Heart University (Tokyo), 45, 171, 172
Sado Island, 177, 184–8, 200, 232
Saga, 231
Saigo Takamori, 169, 238, 239, 243, 244, 261
St. Alban's Church, 256
Saitobaru, 247
Sakamoto, Professor, 245
Sakata city, 179, 180, 182
Sake, 35, 37, 38, 79, 81, 106, 163, 173, 175, 181–2, 183, 187, 211, 223, 227, 239, 240, 246, 251, 253
Sakurajima, 238, 239
Sakya clan, 134
Sakyamuni (the Buddha), 110, 191
Samboin (temple), 112, 125, 126
Samisen, 205
Samurai, 59, 105, 158, 174, 186, 239, 261
Sanjusangendo, 104–6, 110, 125, 139
Sankaku Bay (Sado Island), 186
Sanskrit, 119, 121
Sapporo beer, 37
Saragaku, 142
Sato Eisaku, 46
Sato, Professor, 236, 237, 238, 242
Satori, 108, 109
Satsuma clan, 169, 225, 239, 243, 244
Scepticism, 110
School-children, 52
Scottish dancing, 39, 187
Sea, cultivation of, 27
Sebastian, St., 88
Second World War, 23, 31, 146, 207, 212, 216
Secular, the, 20, 49, 117, 192, 196, 223
Seine, the, 25
Seishin University (Okayama), 151
Sei Shonagon, 102, 110, 128, 259
Sekigahara, battle of, 260

O-sembe, 142
Sendai, 67
Sengakuji temple, 35
Sengu-no-gi ('spirit-moving ceremony'), 150
Senno-Rikyu, 124
Sense of guilt, 19
Sense of humour, 40
Sense of security, 28, 38, 48, 50
Sense of sin, 19
Seppuku (*hara-kiri*), 88, 239, 244, 261, 263
Sesshu, 166
Setsubun (bean-throwing festival), 48
Sex, 40, 41, 77, 89, 106, 119, 132
Shakespeare, 51, 200
Shakespeare Society of Japan, 161
Shamazu (*daimyo*), 243
Shanghai, 239
Shiba, 195
Shibuya, 63, 64, 74
Shichi-go-san (Asakusa), 78
Shichi-go-san festival, 189
Shigeto, Dr., 214
Shigi, 149
Shikoku, 174, 201–12, 225, 257
Shimabara peninsula, 236, 261
Shimai, 116
Shimane, 152, 158
Shimida, Professor, 207
Shimizu, Mr., 186
Shimizu, Professor, 197
Shimoda, 168
Shingeki, 224
Shingon sect, 110, 117, 119, 123, 205, 219
Shinji, Lake, 162
Shinjuku, 62, 63, 74, 77, 92
Shinto, 20, 47, 61, 92, 104, 109, 129, 139, 145, 146, 147, 149, 150, 151, 154, 157, 162, 164–5, 181, 193, 196, 218, 221, 223, 228, 239, 242, 247, 259
Shirayama peninsula, 166
Shirozake, 189
Shogun, 182, 186, 236, 241, 242, 261
Shoin Yoshida, 166
Shoji, 36, 80, 160
Shojin-ryori (vegetarian food), 107, 119

Shojuji (temple), 210
Shomu, Emperor, 134, 135
Shonai plain, 180
Short, David, 236
Shosoin (Nara), 135–6
Shoto-cho, 63, 91
Shotoku Taishi (Prince Umayado), 115, 136, 137, 259
Shrines, 48, 60, 194
Shugakuin Detached Palace, 112
Siberia, 189
Silence, 104, 105, 210
Silk, 114, 208
Silver Pavilion (*see* Ginkakuji), 112
Sims, Revd. Bennett, 256
Sinker, Sir Paul, 22, 107
Sitwell, Sacheverell, 137
Sizing up Tokyo (White Paper), 25
Smith, Revd. R. M., 256
Smriti, 119
Snow Country, 117, 188–91, 200
Snow Country (*see* Yukiguni)
Soami, 111, 112
Soba, 95
Society, 15, 29, 39, 46, 52
Sofukuji (temple), 234
Soga family, 114
Soka-Gakkai, 185
Soma-San, 54, 55, 57, 58, 59, 61, 63, 64, 65, 67, 69, 198, 255, 256
Song of Songs, 128
Sono Hyako, 45
Sophia University, 165
South America, 140
South-East Asia, 68, 82, 86, 206, 217, 257
Souto, Mr., 209
Soviet Russia, 32, 86, 152, 174, 214
Spaniards, the, 234
State education, 30, 31, 42, 43, 46, 192
Steel industry, 225–6
Stevenson, R. L., 166
Stone Garden (*see* Ryoanji)
Stopes, Marie, 48
Storks, 153
Strip-tease, 82
Student protest, 31, 32, 44
Students, 30, 31, 43, 52

Study of History, A (Toynbee), 253
Suicide, 88
Suizenji gardens, Kumamoto, 237
Sumida River, 79, 81
Sumo, 50, 90, 220
Sun Goddess (*see* Amaterasu)
Sun King, 103
Susa-no-o, 144, 164, 218
Sushi, 78, 79, 187
Sutras, 108, 116, 128, 130, 188
Suwa shrine, 234
Suzuki Daisetz, 105, 106, 199
Symbolism, 49, 223, 234

Taboo, 20, 170, 218, 221
Tada, Professor, 161
Tadakoro, Professor, 208
Taira clan (*see also* Heike clan), 135, 204, 260
Taisha, 162
Taito Ward, 85
Taiwan, 257
Takahashi Koretake, 34
Takamatsu, 204
Takamatsu, Mr., 168
Takamura, Dr., 72
Takanawa, 35
Takase, Professor, 197
Takasu, Professor, 245
Takasumi Primary School, 189
Takato, Mount, 226
Takeda, Mr., 191–2
Takesue, Professor, 234
Takeuchi shrine, 160
Tale of Genji, The (Lady Murasaki), 102, 120, 126, 127, 128, 259
Tamatsukuri, 160–1
Tanabe Moichi, 77
Tanaka, President, 232
Tange Kenzo, 27, 28, 84
Tankei, 105
Tanugui, 97
Taoism, 106, 110
Tatami, 36, 71, 95, 97, 108, 125, 130, 160, 179, 184, 186, 195, 208, 254
Tatoko, Mount, 166
Taxi-drivers, 66, 72, 73
Tea Ceremony (*Chanoyu*), 21, 50, 81,

105, 108, 116, 127, 133, 149, 156, 160, 188, 229, 260
Teachers, 177
Teiko-San, 54–69, 198, 215, 252, 255, 256, 257
Temple of the Azure Cloud (Peking), 105
Temple of the Golden Pavilion, 104
Temple of the Golden Pavilion (Mishima), 124
Temples, 48, 60, 61, 106, 111, 117, 180
Tempura, 207, 238
Tendai sect, 105, 110, 117, 119, 124, 125, 154, 229
Tennyson, 187
Tenri, 133, 136, 200
Tenrikyo, 47, 139–41
Terakoya schools, 29, 50
Terauchi, Field Marshal, 217
Thailand, 138, 257
Thames, the, 25
Theophany, 104
Things Japanese (Chamberlain), 21, 194
T'ien-t'ai (*see* Tendai sect)
Tino, 226
Tipping, 73
Toba, 151, 171
Tobata, 225, 226
Todaiji (temple), 134–6, 259
Tofu, 119
Togo, Admiral, 239
Tokaido highway, 104, 114, 172
Toki, 185
Tokiwa Park (Mito), 199
Tokonoma, 36, 80
Tokugawa family, 119, 154, 166, 169, 170, 234, 237, 261
Tokugawa Shogunate, 29, 30, 154, 156, 169, 260
Tokugawa Yoshitomo, 169
Tokushima, 205, 206
Tokyo, 18, 21, 23–9, 35, 52, 54, 63, 64, 66, 67, 69, 70–91, 104, 131, 148, 161, 178, 184, 186, 188, 203, 233, 234, 236, 238, 242, 243, 252–8, 261, 263
Tokyo Bay, 27
Tokyo, climate of, 28
Tokyo Essays (Tomlin), 251, 257

Tokyo, fire raids on, 20, 23, 212, 234, 242
Tokyo Metropolitan Government, 25, 27, 72, 84
Tokyo underground, 16, 98
Tokyo University, 30, 31, 32, 115, 129, 130, 177, 194, 259
Tokyo University of the Arts, 167
Tomb Culture, 148, 259
Tonomura, Mr., 173
Torigoe District, 85
Torii, 147, 149, 218, 239
Torrey Canyon, 226
Toshi centre, 256
Tottori, 152, 153–4
Toyama, 197
Toynbee, Arnold, 253–4
Toyooka, 153
Tradition, 17, 27, 29, 31, 49, 52, 61, 200
Traditional regalia, 144
Traffic, 26, 83
Traherne, 148
Travel, 48, 97
Trinity, the, 119
True Face of Japan, The (Nohara), 17
Tsuda College, 91
Tsurami, Mount, 248
Typhoons, 68, 179, 236

Ueno, 74
Uino, Professor, 207
Ukiyo, 42, 227, 261
Ukiyo-e, 42, 261
Umayado, Prince (*see* Shotoku Taishi)
United Nations, 263
United States, the, 21, 25, 26, 41, 42, 76, 77, 86, 87, 106, 155, 174, 192, 213, 216, 227, 237, 262, 263
Universities, 100
Unzen, 235–6
Urakami Catholic church, Nagasaki, 234

Vairocana (universal Buddha), 134, 135
van der Post, Laurens, 217
Vedanta, 110
Venus de Milo, 91
Vice, 76

Victoria, Queen, 121
Vietnam, 32, 257
Villages, 178, 179, 191
Volcanoes, 236, 237, 238, 239

Wa, 145
Waitresses, 37, 73, 79, 239, 246
Wakamatsu, 225, 226
Wakato Ohashi suspension bridge, 226
Wakayama, 208
Wakayama prefecture, 118
Waley, Arthur, 126
Waseda University, 32, 172
Weaving, 173
Webber, Father Peter, 256
Wei Chih, 145
Weil, Simone, 111
Wellings, Mr., 228
West, the, 20, 21, 22, 38, 39, 41, 86, 89, 102, 109, 115, 131, 138, 155, 156, 157, 174, 177, 189, 197, 200, 210, 213, 242, 243
Whitehead, A. N., 227
Willis, Dr. William, 242–4, 245
Witch, 221
Women, 28, 32, 33, 37, 40, 42, 45, 57, 65, 118, 126, 132, 171, 182, 183, 188, 215
Women's Lib., 41, 42
Wood-block prints (*see Ukiyo-e*)
Wordsworth, 109
World Federalism, 113
World of Dew, The (Enright), 78
World of Silence, The (Picard), 105
World of the Shining Prince, The (Morris), 103

Xavier, St. Francis, 48, 169, 239–42, 260

Yaegaki shrine, 159, 160, 165
Yahata, 225

Yamabushi, 92, 96, 195, 219, 220
Yamagata prefecture, 179
Yamaguchi, 168, 170
Yamakawa, Mr., 199
Yamatai, 145
Yamato, 142, 144, 145, 147, 148, 164, 259
Yango, 161
Yashima plateau, 204
Yasui Sokken, 248
Yawata Iron and Steel Works (Tobata), 225–6
Yayoi, 153
Yayoi culture, 165, 259
Yazuko, Princess, 132
Yeats, W. B., 115
Yin and *Yang*, 254
Yoga, 109
Yokohama, 253
Yomiuri Shimbun, 68
Yoshida, Professor, 153
Yoshida Shigeru, 53, 252
Yoshii, Mr., 172
Yoshino River, 206
Yoshitsune, 204
Yoshiwara district, 76
Yotsuya, 70
Young Samurai (Mishima), 87
Youth, 53, 74, 192, 224
Yoyogi, 84
Yuasa, Professor, 213, 218, 219, 220
Yukata, 97, 113, 152, 208, 239, 248
Yuki (Kirkbride), 42
Yukiguni (Kawabata), 189, 190

Zadankai, 100, 197, 290, 232, 247
Zazen, 108, 223
Zen, 105–10, 129, 130, 134, 135, 173, 223, 229, 234, 260
Zen in the Art of Archery (Herrigel), 105
Zenkoji (temple), 193
Zentsuji (temple), 205